Music Criticism and Music Critics
in Early Francoist Spain

Currents in Latin American & Iberian Music

WALTER CLARK, SERIES EDITOR

MUSIC CRITICISM AND MUSIC CRITICS IN EARLY FRANCOIST SPAIN

Eva Moreda Rodríguez

OXFORD
UNIVERSITY PRESS

OXFORD

UNIVERSITY PRESS

Oxford University Press is a department of the University of Oxford. It furthers
the University's objective of excellence in research, scholarship, and education
by publishing worldwide. Oxford is a registered trade mark of Oxford University
Press in the UK and certain other countries.

Published in the United States of America by Oxford University Press
198 Madison Avenue, New York, NY 10016, United States of America.

This volume is published with the generous support of the AMS 75 PAYS Endowment
of the American Musicological Society, funded in part by the National Endowment
for the Humanities and the Andrew W. Mellon Foundation.

Library of Congress Cataloging-in-Publication Data
Moreda Rodríguez, Eva, author.
Music criticism and music critics in early Francoist Spain / Eva Moreda Rodríguez.
pages cm
Includes bibliographical references.
ISBN 978-0-19-021586-6
1. Musical criticism—Spain—History—20th century.   2. Music critics—Spain.   I. Title.
ML3785.M67 2015
781.1'7—dc23
2014026406

9 8 7 6 5 4 3 2 1
Printed by Edwards Brothers Malloy, United States of America

CONTENTS

ACKNOWLEDGMENTS

When I first started research for this book in 2006, I considered the subject of my research to be a corpus of music criticism writings. At some point during the following years, while still interested in the writings, I became more interested in the men (and the few women) who penned them. I am grateful, first and foremost, to these men and women for many moments of stimulating, if sometimes challenging, reading, thinking, and writing over the past eight years. Other people and institutions crucially contributed to this process too. A work of this nature requires extensive archival work; I am grateful to the staff of the Archivo Histórico del Seminario de Loyola, Biblioteca Nacional de Catalunya, Biblioteca Nacional de España, British Library, Institut d'Estudis Vallencs, National Library of Scotland, Senate House Library, and Westminster Music Library for making me always look forward to my stints of archival research. Travel to archives was financially supported by Royal Holloway's Dame Margaret Duke Travel Bursary, two Carnegie Trust small research grants, and an award from the Open University's Associate Lecturers' Development Fund. I am also grateful to the School of Culture and Creative Arts at the University of Glasgow for hosting me and my research and providing logistical support as this manuscript was completed.

My thanks go as well to colleagues who have encouraged, inspired, and challenged my thinking, especially Erik Levi and Rachel Beckles-Willson during the first life of this book as a Ph.D. thesis, and, more recently, my colleagues at the University of Glasgow. Over the years, sections of this book were presented at various conferences and seminars. I am grateful for all the feedback I received on those occasions, and I would like to give special thanks to Teresa Cascudo and María Palacios for organizing the first meeting of the research group Música e Ideología in Logroño in 2008, which crucially shaped my thinking on music criticism and ideology in Spain. Thanks also to Suzanne Ryan, Adam Cohen, and Lisbeth Redfield at Oxford University Press, and to the anonymous reviewers for their valuable feedback. Through the last eight years, my family has been a source of constant support and encouragement; to them I would like to express my most heartfelt thanks.

ABBREVIATIONS

AHSL   Archivo Histórico del Seminario de Loyola
BNC   Biblioteca Nacional de Catalunya
BNE   Biblioteca Nacional de España
FJM   Fundación Juan March

Introduction

Spanish music of the 1940s has often been defined by opposition to either the period preceding or the period following that decade—and the verdict has often been that the 1940s were not as significant, interesting, or prosperous as the two other periods.[1] Preceding the 1940s, there stands the *Edad de Plata* (Silver Age) of Spanish culture, an era that many have described as one of almost unprecedented development in the arts and sciences, starting in the early twentieth century and reaching its peak under the Second Republic, fostered by the Republic's democratic and progressive ideals.[2] Musically, the *Edad de Plata* ideals are typically thought to be embodied by the Grupo de los Ocho (Group of Eight), an association of composers modeled on the French Les Six.[3] Under the influence of music critic Adolfo Salazar, the Grupo de los Ocho attempted to renovate Spanish music by absorbing some of the innovations of European modernism, namely, Stravinsky's neoclassicism, Debussy's impressionism, and Falla's cosmopolitan approach to Spanish nationalism.

The dissemination, from the 1980s onward, of the term Generación del 27 (Generation of '27) to refer to the Grupo de los Ocho and other composers and musicians in their periphery has further emphasized the perceived prestige and innovativeness of such generation. The term was indeed modeled on the literary Generación del 27, which included celebrated authors such as Rafael Alberti, Luis Cernuda, and most prominently Federico García Lorca.[4] In the last few years, however, Spanish musicology has started to point out some of the issues with this picture of music and musical life in the *Edad de Plata*: the Grupo de los Ocho itself was a loose association of composers who had come together mainly as a strategy to promote their music and not so much on the basis of shared aesthetic and artistic ideals[5];

the Grupo can hardly be regarded as a product of the progressive influences of the Second Republic, since most of their innovative work was composed under the dictatorship of Miguel Primo de Rivera, during the 1920s[6]; and Salazar did not really support the Grupo in its entirety, but he dedicated most of his attention and efforts to Ernesto Halffter instead.[7]

The period following the 1940s, by contrast, still remains a milestone in the historiography of Spanish music. It was in the 1950s, it has often been claimed, that the Generación del 51 (Generation of '51)[8] put an end to the alleged isolation of Spanish music during the 1940s and definitely integrated Spain into the post-Webernian international avant-garde.[9] The assumptions about the history of music as progress and historical inevitability that underpin narratives about the Generación del 51 have received less critical attention than the *Edad de Plata,* and are still to be examined in depth.[10]

With the 1940s invariably paling by comparison, it was only from the mid-1990s, and even more so in the 2000s, that Spanish scholars started to turn their attention to the music of this decade. Such studies have tended to focus on political control of music and musical life rather than on the music per se.[11] More specifically, in doing so, some studies have adopted a somewhat narrow perspective, focusing on very visible factions of early Francoism, such as the Falange (short for Falange Española y de las J.O.N.S., a fascist party founded in 1933 and the single party throughout the dictatorship) or, more generally, those aspects more closely related to Italian and German fascism. [12] With the precedent of studies of music under the Nazi regime[13] and, more generally, the scholarly interest or even fascination that authoritarian control of the arts tends to stimulate, this should hardly come as a surprise. Nevertheless, the starting point of this book is not the belief that we should focus more on the elusive category of the music per se[14] and less on the political, but rather that the categories of the political should be expanded. They should be expanded, for example, to include factions of the regime that may not have been as visible and obviously influential as the Falange but nevertheless had an impact on music and musical life. They should also be expanded to account for the fact that many of the debates that preoccupied Spanish musicians in the 1940s— perhaps most conspicuously, concerning Spanish nationalism—were of a political nature and had their roots well before the Francisco Franco regime started; therefore, many of the opinions and ideas expressed in the context of such debates, although not necessarily promoted by the government, reflect the multifarious political dimensions of the musical landscape of the 1940s. In order to expand and problematize the categories of the political in this way, this book proposes an examination of the musical press.

It cannot be denied that the Franco regime gave music political uses (although not to the same extent that Nazi Germany did). It cannot be denied either that music criticism, which, like any other journalistic practice, was subject to a considerable degree of control and direction, provided a space for disseminating government-sponsored musical events and policies, and for crafting the accompanying discourse. Several music critics, moreover, had administrative positions in government institutions, among them Joaquín Turina, Antonio de las Heras, Federico Sopeña, and Joaquín Rodrigo. It may be tempting to overrely on music criticism to tell us exactly what the regime's official line was on any issue related to music,[15] even though it has been repeatedly pointed out that it is dubious such a line existed.[16] Nor did an official line exist in the musical press: certainly, different approaches to the central issues, contradictions, and even dissent abound, and it is imperative that they be explained in order to gain a view of how political music criticism really was. Music critics did have political views; most of them felt ideologically at home under Francoism inasmuch as they identified with conservative and nationalist ideas, both politically and musically. But the terms *conservative* and *nationalist* tend not to be of much help when trying to make sense of the landscape of 1940s music criticism. Between the early twentieth century and 1939, musical and political conservatism and nationalism adopted diverse forms in Spain, and individual music critics in the 1940s typically drank from one or more such traditions. Similarly, many of the main topics they engaged with—new music, Spanish early music, traditional music—had, by 1939, been for decades at the center of debates that were political in nature, debates having to do with what Spanish music should be like, where it should be going, and what its role should be in the organization of the state. Of course, in the 1940s critics could not simply forget the decadelong history and how it had shaped their own opinions about music and its political role; such opinions sometimes happened to fit well with the regime's outlook, or the outlook of specific factions under the regime, but sometimes they needed to be adapted or at least expressed with caution.

In a way, the present study aims at complicating rather than simplifying or streamlining current understandings of the musical press and of the political uses of music under the early Franco regime, and it does so through adopting different foci. The first of them is examination of several music magazines that have received little scholarly attention so far. *Ritmo*, as the most widely circulated Spanish music magazine of the 1940s (and currently the longest-running), has been regularly used as a source in studies of the period, and *Vértice*, being a Falange publication, has been the object of a separate article for its unique position along the ideological spectrum[17]; but smaller, niche publications have received far less attention. Although the main concerns for musicians and music critics were often the same regardless of the focus or scope of the publication, less-well-known magazines illustrate the efforts, and sometimes the vicissitudes, of music journalists to adapt such concerns to particular readerships (for example, *Harmonía* and *Boletín del Colegio de Directores de Bandas de Música Civiles* addressing an audience of wind band conductors), or to particular niche genres (*Ritmo y melodía* focusing on jazz, *Tesoro sacro-musical* focusing on religious and liturgical music). Similarly, although it would be a herculean task to track down and research every nonmusic magazine that at any point published something on music during the 1940s, this book studies several of the most widely circulated nonmusic periodicals having regular sections on music, including academic periodicals published by the Consejo Superior de Investigaciones Científicas (*Arbor, Revista de ideas estéticas*) and a variety of Falange publications (*Radio Nacional, Escorial, El Español, La estafeta literaria*). Although it was commonplace for critics to complain that other arts and humanities had historically paid little attention to music, such publications illustrate the importance that various factions within the regime and the critics themselves gave to music in connection with other disciplines.

Second, this book relies on a close analysis of selected examples of music criticism. In some sections, of course, more breadth than depth has been necessary to reflect the multiplicity of views on a particular issue, but often, rather than offering a general overview of a particular publication or author, the choice has been to select a few significant and representative writings pertaining to such publication or author and analyze them in detail. This allows nuances and shades surrounding the main issues that preoccupied music critics in the 1940s to emerge. For the missing gaps, existing studies on specific music critics may provide a more overarching perspective on the writings of such individuals,[18] and hopefully more such studies will be published in the future, expanding at the margins or further complicating, rather than simplifying, the problems this study brings to light.

This preference for in-depth analysis of texts leads to the third focus of this book: its protagonists. Of course, it would be impossible to analyze to some level of detail, in a monograph of reasonable length, the writings of every music critic of 1940s Spain, or even of the twenty or thirty most widely published names in music magazines and music columns in newspapers. Instead, seven music critics were selected, as were four themes with which they and others engaged most prominently. The critics selected are, by order of appearance, Joaquín Turina, Regino Sáinz de la Maza, Federico Sopeña, Nemesio Otaño, Higinio Anglès, Julio Gómez, and

Joaquín Rodrigo; the themes are music performance, new music, Spanish early music, and Spanish traditional music. With regard to the selection of critics, I do not claim that these seven critics were the most widely read, the most influential, or the most prolific (although Sopeña is a likely contestant for the last one), but they were all reasonably visible as music critics and most of them had other prominent roles in the musical life of the early Franco regime as composers, performers, researchers, or administrators. Most importantly for the purposes of selection, they represent a relatively wide range of political ideologies (in some cases quite closely aligned with specific ideological factions within the early Franco regime, but also including decidedly anti-Franco ideological traits in the case of Gómez and Anglès) and also of approaches to music and to the four chosen themes.

The book discusses such ideologies and approaches not only in connection with these critics' writings in the press, but also, on one hand, through an examination of their correspondence and other personal writings, and on the other, through contextualization of the four themes in the intellectual history of Spain from the late nineteenth century onward, including the writings of their contemporaries. Indeed, although the above-mentioned selection may seem unsatisfactory to some, other critics also have a continuous, if secondary, presence in this book, among them (in alphabetical order) Luis Araque, Conrado del Campo, Antonio Fernández-Cid, José María Franco, Antonio de las Heras, Antonio Iglesias, Xavier Montsalvatge, Víctor Ruiz Albéniz, Rodrigo A. de Santiago, and still others who did not have a prominent career in music criticism or music more generally and about whom few records remain, but who nevertheless contributed to discussions and debate around the four themes.

Through this book, the term "early Francoism" refers to the period between 1939 and 1951. The initial date requires little explanation. On April 1, 1939, the Spanish Civil War officially ended with the entrance of Franco's troops into Madrid and the annihilation of the last Republican forces of resistance. Franco ruled, almost without limitations, all over Spain, with the aspiration of reconstructing the country, both materially and spiritually, after three years of conflict. It was also at the end of the Civil War that some of the critics discussed in this study (Rodrigo, Sopeña, Fernández-Cid, Montsalvatge) started their careers in music criticism, whose ranks had been decimated by war and exile. The reader will certainly find references to music criticism published on the nationalist side during the Civil War, as, in many cases, it was the war that saw the emergence of some ideas and approaches that were then developed and became prominent after the war. Some very significant publications of the early Franco regime (such as *Radio Nacional* and *Vértice*) were indeed launched by the national side before Franco's final victory, and survived beyond 1939 with little change in their editorial policy. Nevertheless, this book is not meant to be a study of the Spanish musical press in a time of war, which would require explaining a different set of contradictions and complications. To start with, there is the fact that music criticism, which is by definition intended to be published regularly, was actually not regular or systematic at all; disruption of concert life, scarcity of paper supplies, and the priorities of wartime publications resulted in opportunities to listen to music and to review it being few and far between.

The decision to end at the year 1951 is less self-explanatory. The early 1950s certainly were a turning point for the Franco regime: after friendly relations with the Axis during the Second World War and international isolation after 1945, the period saw integration of Spain into the Western Bloc. Indeed, after intense negotiations between the Franco regime and the United States, the two countries signed three bilateral agreements regarding trade and defense in 1953 (*convenios hispano-norteamericanos* or *Pacto de Madrid*), which in practice confirmed Spain and the United States as allies in the fight against communism.[19] Culturally and musically, things started to change as well: although the Generación del 51 did not actually became widely visible in 1951, but rather in the mid-to-late 1950s,[20] there had been hints of change since at least 1947 with the Círculo Manuel de Falla in Barcelona—the first time since the Grupo de los Ocho that a group of young composers came together with the specific aim of renovating Spanish music.[21]

The landscape of music criticism was changing as well, not necessarily out of a desire of renovation, but often simply because of the life circumstances of its protagonists. Turina died in 1949 and del Campo in 1953. Others simply left the profession or at least moved from writing daily to doing so only occasionally: Sáinz de la Maza left his position of staff music critic at *ABC* and Rodrigo ended his three-year stint at the sports newspaper *Marca* in 1949. As had happened in 1939, younger critics were stepping in to fill some of these vacancies: Enrique Franco started to write for *Arriba* in 1952, and he promptly became a supporter of the Spanish avant-garde. Some of the members of the Generación del 51 also started to write music criticism themselves, among them Luis de Pablo and Ramón Barce. Although setting 1950 or 1952 as the endpoint of this study would not make such a big difference to its main arguments, there is a particular reason 1951 has been chosen. Sopeña, whose meteoric career in the 1940s can be considered to embody the desire of reconstruction and regeneration on the part of the early regime, moved to Rome in 1949 and was called back to Spain in 1951 to head up the Conservatorio de Madrid. The appointment was, in a way, a reward to Sopeña's commitment to reconstruction of the country through music criticism, bestowing on him the ultimate honor of shaping the aesthetic ideals of future musicians through the directorship of the Conservatorio in a time of political change for the country.[22]

Although the period 1939–1951 is relatively short, it was also an era of almost constant change and adjustment for the regime, both internally and in response to events in the outside world. Internally, Francoism was supported by disparate factions, some of them with a significant pre–Civil War history. Such factions—or *familias* (families), as Armando de Miguel influentially named them[23]—came together mainly because they shared a desire to replace the Second Republic with a return to ultraconservatism, and as well the belief that ultraconservatism should be implemented by a dictatorial or authoritarian regime.[24] *Familias* under the early Franco regime included the Falange; the Asociación Católica de Propagandistas (or simply *propagandistas*), founded in 1900, which aimed at creating a Catholic elite to lead the masses politically and socially; the Opus Dei (a theologically conservative prelature of the Catholic Church founded by Spanish priest José María Escrivá de Balaguer in 1928; its members aimed at seeking sanctity in their everyday occupations, including, during the Franco regime, involvement in politics), also known as *tecnócratas* from the 1960s onward; the army; the monarchists, who supported Juan de Borbón, the designated heir to the Spanish throne, then in exile; the *Carlistas*, a strongly traditionalist political movement that sought to establish a separate line of the Bourbon family on the Spanish throne; and the Catholic church. The balance of power between the factions was often a complicated one, and the regime has often been periodized according to the dominating faction at various times; for example, the *desarrollismo* period is considered to start in 1957 when a number of Opus Dei *tecnócratas* were appointed as ministers.

Delineation of such factions and their rivalries, however, does not necessarily translate well to music or music criticism. It is true that a few critics belonged, more or less clearly, to any particular faction, most notably the Falange (of which Sopeña and Sáinz de la Maza were members). However, most of them cannot be so clearly ascribed to a single faction. Critics did not always chose their loyalties according to factions anyway; Sáinz de la Maza did not write for Falange but for a monarchist newspaper, and Rodrigo, who did not particularly agree with Falange ideals, wrote regularly for two Falange-controlled publications (*Pueblo* and *Radio Nacional*). Nevertheless, on a general level, the chronology of the rivalries and the balance of power between the factions in the years 1939–1951 had a significant impact on the press as a crucial—and attractive—part of the state apparatus.

During the Civil War, the Falange quickly established itself as the ruling faction on the nationalist side, and during the initial years of the regime it was hegemonic over other groups. Music criticism did not escape the Falange's hegemony; several Falange publications (most notably *Vértice* and *Radio Nacional*) gave music a significant role in their efforts to construct the *Nuevo Estado* (new state), and the falangist writer Ernesto Giménez Caballero was influential with several critics, as will be discussed in Chapter 2. Nevertheless, it should not be assumed that everything resembling music and cultural policies under German and Italian fascism was, by definition, fascist. Increased interest in early and traditional music provides an illustrative example; it is true that Nazi Germany and to a lesser extent fascist Italy are well known for their promotion of early and traditional music for nation-building purposes,[25] and more generally fascism is thought of as a reactionary ideology, so it should be no surprise that the music of the past was celebrated. Nevertheless, interest in and research into early and traditional music had a history of their own in Spain independent of fascist developments, with some well-known scholars (Jesús Bal y Gay, Eduardo Martínez Torner) being decidedly antifascist. Difidence toward or rejection of new music should not be written off as a fascist legacy either, although here the reasoning is slightly different: since at least the 1960s, scholars have questioned the interpretation of Nazi Germany as reactionary and emphasized its modernizing aspects instead,[26] and the similarly modernizing aspects of Italian fascism, such as futurism itself or more generally the appeal of Mussolini's regime for intellectuals committed to modernity, have also been the object of scholarly attention.[27] It must not be forgotten that most fascisms ultimately sought to articulate a solution to a perceived crisis of modern times, and as such the past was not simply regarded with nostalgia, but also seen as a tool to shape times to come[28]; similarly, with fascisms being by nature proteic movements drawing on a number of preexisting ideas, they could draw on modernism as well insofar as it could satisfactorily advance their aims.[29] Modernity, therefore, did have a place in fascism—and certainly it did in Spanish fascism, although again, not every critic who defended or engaged with new music was doing so on the basis of fascist ideas.

Falange influence on the Francoist government started to decline as early as 1942, with the regime detaching itself from Germany and Italy. The *propagandistas* finally became the major force in the government in 1945[30]; the Falange nevertheless remained the single party in Spain until the end of the regime and kept a substantial influence in a few areas, specially those connected with youth education and leisure.[31] Nevertheless, it was not straightforward for the Franco regime to integrate itself into the Western Bloc, partially abandoning its initial commitment to autarky (*autarquía*) in an attempt to guarantee its own survival.[32] In 1946, France closed its border with Spain and the United Nations issued a declaration, UN General Assembly Resolution 39(I) on the Spanish question, in which it recognized the Franco regime as a past ally of Germany and Italy and, on such basis, banned Spain from UN membership. However, as the Cold War started to take shape with the Greek Civil War and the uprising of communism in Czechoslovakia, the Western Bloc started to slowly change their attitude toward the Franco regime[33]; in particular, the United States partially abandoned its initial postwar commitment to internationalism and instead set out to look for allies against communism.[34] Franco himself seized the opportunity and spent most of 1947 trying to approach the United States.[35] In 1948, France reopened the border with Spain, and Franco received visits from American representatives trying to convince him to align with the Western Bloc.[36] At the same time, discussions about Spain in the UN were moving forward, albeit at a rather slow pace, and it was not until November 1950 that the 1946 resolution was revoked.[37] By then, the United States was well aware of the benefits of an alliance with Franco in its rivalry with communism, which made it adopt a compromise with the dictatorship. Spanish-American bilateral negotiations continued through 1952 and 1953 and concluded with the signing of the aforementioned agreements.

Since the political developments in Spain and the outside world had an impact on music and music criticism as well, the chronology of events is certainly reflected to some extent in every chapter of this book. Nevertheless, since I have chosen to put the focus on individual music critics, the reader will not find a strictly chronological narrative here; instead, each chapter has been conceived of as a window opening onto the life and writings of one, or two, or three critics, without losing sight of the broader landscape they worked and wrote in. The *dramatis personae* of this book should not be understood rigidly either; all seven critics I discuss in depth will make appearances outside their allocated chapter, since all of them wrote, to one extent or another, about the four themes discussed in this book and were active in Spanish musical life of the 1940s in other ways. Chapter 1 begins by focusing on Joaquín Turina, who in 1939 was a well-established, veteran composer and the newly appointed comisario de música (commissar for music), in order to discuss the expectations and restrictions the regime placed on music criticism through press laws and doctrinaire handbooks. Turina's use of humor as a strategy to respond to such expectations and restrictions is perhaps unique in the 1940s milieu, and is contextualized through discussion of other critics' reflections on their own work. The second half of the chapter looks more closely at one of these expectations, namely, the assumption that critics should frequently and positively review music performances in Spain to communicate to their readership the idea that musical life and the country itself were on their way to fully recovering after the war. The critic I have chosen here to focus on is Regino Sáinz de la Maza, who as a well-known performer himself was hailed by other critics as a crucial actor in the reconstruction of the country, and who, as a critic, repeatedly wrote on the action of performing as a reenactment of values of Spain's historical past and therefore a contribution to regeneration of the country, following Falange conceptions of *Hispanidad*.

Chapter 2 focuses on Federico Sopeña, one of the few critics active primarily in music criticism (as opposed to composition, performance, or administration) during the 1940s and also one of the few to systematically engage with contemporary music and discuss what path should Spanish contemporary music follow. Sopeña's writings on new music will be discussed with a particular focus on his two main influences: the music critic Adolfo Salazar, who had been similarly interested in new music in the period 1918–1936 and exiled at the beginning of the Civil War; and Giménez Caballero, who discussed the role art should have in a fascist state in the book *Arte y estado*. Giménez Caballero's influence on other critics will be discussed as well, with a view to articulating Sopeña's role as one of the few music critics who envisioned a new way of writing Spanish music with roots in the past, but at the same time conspicuously new—in line with the Falange's initial aims of renovation through looking back at Spain's past.

Chapter 3 focuses on defense and promotion of early music in the writings of three musicologists who also wrote music criticism. Nemesio Otaño and Higinio Anglès were both priests and held prominent administrative positions with the Franco regime, the former as comisario de música and then head of the Conservatorio de Madrid, and the latter as founding director of the Instituto Español de Musicología. Whereas Anglès and Otaño celebrated in their writings music from the Middle Ages to the seventeenth century as an incarnation of the true Spanish values that Francoism was now allegedly reviving, I will examine both their academic background and their personal relationships during the 1940s in order to bring to light the differences between them: Otaño heavily relied on *Hispanidad*, whereas Anglès's intellectual origins must be sought in Felipe Pedrell (1841–1922, composer and a founding figure of Spanish musicology) and his dislike of Italian opera. Julio Gómez, on the other hand, was not as visible as Otaño and Anglès, and he wrote mostly for a niche magazine, *Harmonía;* the last section of the chapter will examine how Gómez expressed his dissent with how research into early music was conducted and disseminated under the regime as dictated by Anglès and Otaño, contextualizing such dissent within Gómez's personal politics and unique approach to music nationalism.

Chapter 4 deals with Spanish traditional music; its first half does not focus on a particular critic, but rather on the multiplicity of writers and publications—many of them nonspecialized—that amplified and disseminated the work of the Sección Femenina's Coros y Danzas, through which the regime turned traditional music into a tool for national regeneration, national unity, and international prestige. The second half of the chapter considers discussions about how traditional music should inform Spanish art music; it will focus on Joaquín Rodrigo, a star composer in early Francoism in his own right who, while keeping within Francoist expectations of regeneration and national identity, also drew from a tradition that had its roots in Falla and the Grupo de los Ocho.

NOTES

1. See, for example, the first general accounts of Spanish music in the 1940s: Antonio Fernández-Cid, *La década musical de los cuarenta* (Madrid: Real Academia de Bellas Artes de San Fernando, 1980); Tomás Marco, "Los años cuarenta," in *España en la música de Occidente*, ed. Emilio Casares Rodicio, Ismael Fernández de la Cuesta, and José López Calo, vol. 2 (Madrid: Instituto Nacional de las Artes Escénicas y de la Música, 1987), 399–412.

2. Although already in use in literary and cultural historiography from the 1940s onward, the term *Edad de Plata* became widespread with José Carlos Mainer, *La Edad de Plata (1902–1931): ensayo de interpretación de un proceso cultural* (Barcelona: Asenet, 1975).

3. The composer members of the Grupo de los Ocho were Salvador Bacarisse, Julián Bautista, Rosa García Ascot, Ernesto Halffter, Rodolfo Halffter, Juan José Mantecón, Gustavo Pittaluga, and Fernando Remacha.

4. The term *Generación del 27* in reference to musicians was first used in the 1970s, still under Francoism; see Cristóbal L. García Gallardo, "La imposible inocencia del musicólogo: el proceso de construcción histórica de la Generación musical del 27 o de la República," in *Música y cultura en la Edad de Plata 1915–1939*, ed. María Nagore, Leticia Sánchez de Andrés and Elena Torres (Madrid: ICCMU, 2009), 40. It became more widespread after Emilio Casares Rodicio curated in 1986 an exhibition under the name *La música en la Generación del 27*; see also Emilio Casares Rodicio, "Música y músicos de la Generación del 27," in *La música en la Generación del 27. Homenaje a Lorca 1915–1939*, ed. Emilio Casares Rodicio (Madrid: Ministerio de Cultura/INAEM, 1986), 20.

5. María Palacios, *La renovación musical en Madrid durante la dictadura de Primo de Rivera. El Grupo de los Ocho (1923–1931)* (Madrid: Sociedad Española de Musicología, 2008), 7; García Gallardo, "La imposible inocencia del musicólogo," 43.

6. Palacios, *La renovación musical*, 11.

7. Ibid., 14; Javier Suárez-Pajares, "Adolfo Salazar: luz y sombras," in *Música y cultura en la Edad de Plata 1915–1939*, ed. María Nagore, Leticia Sánchez de Andrés and Elena Torres (Madrid: ICCMU, 2009), 211. For the testimony of a member of the Grupo de los Ocho, see Rodolfo Halffter, "Julián Bautista," *Música*, no. 1 (1938), 9.

8. The term *Generación del 51* was coined by composer Cristóbal Halffter, himself a member of the generation. Unlike the Grupo de los Ocho, the Generation of '51 was never an association of composers, but rather a historiographic label; other composers normally regarded as members of the Generation of '51 are Carmelo Bernaola, Ramón Barce, Luis de Pablo, Antón García Abril, Ángel González Acilu, and Juan Hidalgo.

9. Manuel Valls, *La música española después de Manuel de Falla* (Madrid: Revista de Occidente, 1962), 22–24; Tomás Marco, *Música española de vanguardia* (Madrid: Guadarrama, 1970), 17–23; Marco, *La música de la España contemporánea* (Madrid: Publicaciones Españolas, 1970), 14–21; Marco, *Spanish Music in the Twentieth Century* (Cambridge and London: Harvard University Press, 1993), 155–156.

10. Understandings of history of music (and particularly of the avant-garde) as progress are hardly limited to the historiography of Spanish music; see, for example, Leo Treitler, "What Kind of Story Is History?" *19th-Century Music*, vol. 7, no. 3 (1984), 363–373; Susan McClary, "Terminal Prestige: The Case of Avant-Garde Music Composition," *Cultural Critique*, no. 12 (1989), 57–81; Richard Taruskin, "Revising Revision," *Journal of the American Musicological Society*, no. 46 (1993), 114–138; Taruskin, "A Myth of the Twentieth Century: The Rite of Spring, the Tradition of the New, and 'The Music Itself'," *Modernism/Modernity*, vol. 2, no. 1 (1995), 1–26. The most recent history of Spanish music, although it flags lesser studied aspects of the Spanish avant-garde for further research and emphasizes some continuities with the previous period, does not engage in a full-fledged critique examining long-held historiographical assumptions; see Germán Gan Quesada, "A la altura de las circunstancias . . . Continuidad y pautas de renovación en la música española," in *Historia de la música en España e Hispanoamérica, vol. 7, La música en España en el siglo XX*, ed. Alberto González Lapuente (Ciudad de México: Fondo de Cultura Económica, 2012), 169–231.

11. A pioneering study in this regard was Gemma Pérez Zalduondo's 1995 Ph.D. thesis, published as Gemma Pérez Zalduondo, *La música en España durante el franquismo a través de la legislación (1936–1951)* (Granada: Universidad de Granada, 2002).

12. See, for example, Gemma Pérez Zalduondo, "El imperio de la propaganda: la música en los fastos conmemorativos del primer Franquismo," in *Discursos y prácticas musicales nacionalistas (1900–1970)*, ed. Pilar Ramos López (Logroño: Universidad de La Rioja, 2012), 339.

13. Such as Pamela Potter, *Most German of the Arts* (New Haven: Yale University Press, 1998); Erik Levi, *Music in the Third Reich* (London: Palgrave Macmillan, 1994).

14. Taruskin, "A Myth of the Twentieth Century," 4–5.

15. See, for example, Iván Iglesias, "(Re)construyendo la identidad musical española: el jazz y el discurso cultural del Franquismo durante la Segunda Guerra Mundial," *Historia Actual Online*, no. 23 (2010), 124–127; Gemma Pérez Zalduondo, "De la tradición a la vanguardia: música, discursos e instituciones desde la Guerra Civil hasta 1956," in *Historia de la música en España e Hispanoamérica, vol. 7: La música en España en el siglo XX*, ed. Alberto González Lapuente (Ciudad de México: Fondo de Cultura Económica, 2012), 106–107.

16. Iglesias, "(Re)construyendo la identidad musical española," 119–120; Javier Suárez-Pajares, "Joaquín Rodrigo en la vida musical y la cultura española de los años cuarenta. Ficciones, realidades, verdades y mentiras de un tiempo extraño," in *Joaquín Rodrigo y la música española de los años cuarenta*, ed. Javier Suárez-Pajares (Valladolid: Glares, 2003), 15–17.

17. Gemma Pérez Zalduondo, "La música en la revista *Vértice* (1937–1946)," *Nassarre*, no. 11 (1995), 407–426.

18. For example, José Antonio Gutiérrez, "La labor crítica de Joaquín Rodrigo en el diario *Pueblo* (1940–1946)," in *Joaquín Rodrigo y la música española de los años cuarenta*, ed. Javier Suárez-Pajares (Valladolid: Glares, 1995), 403–430; Leopoldo Neri de Caso, "Regino Sainz de la Maza: crítico musical en ABC (1939–1952)," in *Joaquín Rodrigo y la música española de los años cuarenta*, ed. Javier Suárez-Pajares (Valladolid: Glares, 2005), 371–401; Beatriz Martínez del Fresno, *Julio Gómez. Una época de la música española* (Madrid: ICCMU, 1999), 217–234; Germán Gan Quesada, "*De musica in verbis*. Notas sobre la literatura musical de Xavier Montsalvatge en un momento de transición (1948–1953)," in *Música, Ciencia y Pensamiento en España e Iberoamérica durante el siglo XX* (Madrid: Universidad Autónoma de Madrid, 2013), 87–105.

19. María del Rocío Piñeiro Álvarez, "Los convenios hispano-norteamericanos de 1953," *Historia Actual Online*, no. 11 (2006), 175–181; Jill Edwards, *Anglo-American Relations and the Franco Question 1945–1955* (Oxford: Clarendon Press, 1999), 263; Benny Pollack and Graham Hunter, *The Paradox of Spanish Foreign Policy: Spain's International Relations from Franco to Democracy* (London: Pinter, 1987), 151–152.

20. Ángel Medina, "Primeras oleadas vanguardistas en el área de Madrid," in *España en la música de Occidente*, ed. José López-Calo, Ismael Fernández de la Cuesta, and Emilio Casares Rodicio, vol. 2 (Madrid: Instituto Nacional de las Artes Escénicas y de la Música, 1987), 375–377.

21. Luis Gásser, "El "círculo Manuel de Falla" de Barcelona (1947–c. 1956)," in *Manuel de Falla: Latinité et universalité*, ed. Louis Jambou (Paris: Presses de l'université de Paris-Sorbonne, 1999), 496–507.

22. Igor Contreras, "El 'empeño apostólico-literario de Federico Sopeña," in *Los señores de la crítica. Periodismo musical e ideología del modernismo en Madrid (1900–1950)*, ed. Teresa Cascudo and María Palacios (Sevilla: Doble J, 2011), 331–334.

23. Armando de Miguel, *Sociología del franquismo. Análisis ideológico de los ministros del Régimen* (Barcelona: Euros, 1975). Linz similarly spoke of "limited pluralism" as one of the traits of Francoism as an authoritarian (as opposed to totalitarian) regime; see reprinted in Juan J. Linz, "An Authoritarian Regime: The Case of Spain," in *Mass Politics: Studies in Political Sociology*, ed. Erik Allardt and Stein Rokkan (New York: Free Press, 1970), 255.

24. Glicerio Sánchez Recio, "Familias políticas, estructuras de poder, instituciones del régimen," in *Las culturas políticas del fascismo en la España de Franco (1936–1975)*, ed. Miguel Ángel Ruiz Carnicer (Zaragoza: Institución Fernando el Católico, 2013), 217–218.

25. See for example Potter, *Most German of the Arts*; Dietrich Kamper, "Nationale und international Aspekte in der Italienischen Musik des Frühen 20. Jahrhunderts," *Revista de Musicología*, no. 16 (1993), 637–638; Fiamma Nicolodi, "Nationalistische Aspekte im Mythos von der 'alten Musik' in Italien und Frankreich," in *Nationale Stil und Europäische Dimension von der Musik der Jahrhundertwende*, ed. Helga de la Motte-Haber (Darmstadt: Wissenschaftliche Buchgesellschaft, 1991), 102–121; Michael Meyer, "The Nazi Musicologist as Myth Maker in the Third Reich,"

Journal of Contemporary History, vol. 10, no. 4 (1975), 649–665; Pamela Potter, "Did Himmler Really Like Gregorian Chant? The SS and Musicology," *Modernism/Modernity*, vol. 2, no. 3 (1995), 45–68.

26. Paul Betts, "The New Fascination with Fascism: The Case of Nazi Modernism," *Journal of Contemporary History*, vol. 37, no. 4 (2002), 541 and 549.

27. Andrew Hewitt, "Fascist Modernism, Futurism, and Post-modernity," in *Fascism, Aesthetics, and Culture*, ed. Richard J. Golsan (Hanover and London: University Press of New England, 1992), 38; Ruth Ben-Ghiat, "Italian Fascism and the Aesthetics of the 'Third Way'," *Journal of Contemporary History*, vol. 31, no. 2 (1996), 293–294.

28. Roger Griffin, "Fascism," in *The Blackwell Dictionary of Twentieth-Century Social Thought*, ed. William Outhwaite and T. B. Bottomore (Oxford: Blackwell, 1993), 223.

29. Roger Griffin, "Staging the Nation's Rebirth: The Politics and Aesthetics of Performance in the Context of Fascist Studies," in *Fascism and Theatre: Comparative Studies on the Aesthetics and Politics of Performance in Europe, 1925–45*, ed. Gunter Berghaus (Providence; Oxford: Berghahn, 1996), 12; Mark Antliff, "Fascism, Modernism, and Modernity," *Art Bulletin*, vol. 84, no. 1 (2002), 148–149.

30. Sánchez Recio, "Familias políticas," 219.

31. Stanley G. Payne, *The Franco Regime. 1936–1975* (Madison: University of Wisconsin Press, 1987), 286–293.

32. José Luis Neila Hernández, "The Foreign Policy Administration in Franco's Spain: From Isolation to International Realignment," in *Spain in an International Context, 1936–1959*, ed. Christian Leitz and David J. Dunthorn (New York: Berghahn, 1999), 277.

33. Qasim Ahmad, *Britain, Franco Spain, and the Cold War, 1945–1950* (New York: Garland, 1992), 46–73.

34. Edwards, *Anglo-American Relations*, 90.

35. Qasim Ahmad, "Britain and the Isolation of Franco, 1945–1950." In *Spain in an International Context, 1936–1959*, ed. Christian Leitz and David J. Dunthorn (New York: Berghahn Books, 1999), 239.

36. Ibid., 240.

37. Ahmad, *Britain, Franco Spain*, 271–290.

CHAPTER 1

How to Be a Music Critic in 1940s Spain

Expectations and Restrictions

If a tally had been conducted at the end of the Civil War of Spanish musicians still active in Spain, as suggested by the composer and newly appointed comisario de música, Joaquín Turina, its results would surely have been less than encouraging.[1] Many of the younger composers born at the turn of the century who had made a name for themselves in 1920s and 1930s Madrid and Barcelona for their attempts at renovating Spanish music were now in exile, notably Julián Bautista, Salvador Bacarisse, Rodolfo Halffter, Gustavo Pittaluga, Enrique Casal Chapí, Gustavo Durán, and Roberto Gerhard. Another young composer, Antonio José, had been executed by a Falange firing squad in 1936, whereas a few older, more established composers such as Óscar Esplá and Jaume Pahissa had chosen to leave Spain as well. With many of these composers employed in teaching positions at the Conservatorio de Madrid or the Escola Municipal de Mùsica de Barcelona, it seemed as if the training of young musicians was also at risk of being compromised under the new regime.

Other spheres of musical life seemed similarly decimated: prominent performers such as Pau Casals, Andrés Segovia, and Conxita Badia were now living abroad, as were musicologists and critics such as Adolfo Salazar, Jesús Bal y Gay, Eduardo Martínez Torner, and Otto Mayer-Serra. Although not fleeing Francoist repression, Manuel de Falla—who was at the time the best-known Spanish composer internationally—left Spain in September 1939 to conduct a series of concerts in Argentina and remained there until his death in November 1946, not showing much interest in the attempts of the Franco regime to attract him back to Spain.[2] Falla's student Ernesto Halffter, who had been one of the most visible young composers of the 1920s and 1930s, detached himself from Spanish musical life and was now spending most of his time in Lisbon, only occasionally visiting Madrid with conducting engagements during the 1940s.[3] The list of remaining active musicians was further narrowed down by the deaths of music critics Rogelio Villar (1937) and Ángel María Castell (1938), and of conductor Enrique Fernández Arbós (1939) for causes unrelated to the war or the subsequent repression; and by the purges that temporarily affected musicians suspected of having supported the Second Republic, such as composers Julio Gómez and Pablo Sorozábal, conductor Bartolomé Pérez Casas, and musicologist José Subirá.[4]

Although Turina lamented that his figurative tally had resulted in "an empty space, a void" in Spanish musical life,[5] he was also confident that this was simply the product of a necessary, if painful, process. The three years of war, according to Turina, were also three years of debunking "postulates which many took for granted," namely, the "dehumanization" of art that gave rise to "all those styles gathered around the vulgar denomination of 'avant-garde'."[6] Turina did not blame anyone in particular for that situation, which was not at all unusual; indeed, it was only on very rare occasions that specific musicians who opposed the Franco regime were openly and explicitly criticized by music critics writing under Francoism. The critic Antonio de las Heras congratulated himself that the Orquesta Filarmónica of Madrid lost most of its members after the Civil War "because its hordes were so unashamedly left-wing,"[7] and composer Antonio Torres Climent claimed in 1945 that Spanish audiences had very few good memories left of the works of Bacarisse, Bautista, and Pittaluga and instead remembered them mostly "with revulsion."[8] These instances of open, politically motivated criticism were, however, the exception rather than the rule. Nevertheless, those who had known Turina as the music critic of the Catholic newspaper *El Debate* before the Civil War would be sufficiently familiar with his likes and dislikes to understand whom he was referring to. During his term at *El Debate*, Turina repeatedly abhorred the dehumanization of art as understood by the philosopher José Ortega y Gasset, who claimed that the main characteristic of modern music from Debussy onward was the emotional distance it placed between the composer and the audience[9]; more generally, such an emotional distance allegedly made art suitable for the elites only and thus deprived it of the significance, transcendence, and appeal to the broader public that it held in the nineteenth century.[10] Dehumanization had been embraced, at least partially, by Adolfo

Salazar and the Grupo de los Ocho as a reaction against Romanticism and as a way to avoid sentimentalism and, in the words of Rodolfo Halffter, overreliance on "primary feelings."[11] Turina, on the other hand, considered dehumanization a "mockery,"[12] and even if he acknowledged that some of the members of the Grupo were talented musicians, he warned them that they would ultimately amount to nothing if they let themselves be influenced by the international avant-garde.[13] Turina, who had studied in Paris under D'Indy and Moszkowski and had since strived to write music with a clear Spanish touch but an appeal to international audiences, regarded the "polytonal acrobatics" that he thought ubiquitous in Spanish music after the First World War, especially in the works of Ernesto Halffter, Salazar, Juan José Mantecón, and Durán, as an expression of selfishness that went against the internationalization of music.[14]

Turina understood excision of the avant-garde and dehumanization from Spanish music as a process of purification and cleansing in a bluntly physical, even medical way ("The victory of our soldiers has swept away, at least in the realm of music, all this mess").[15] These words resonated well with the context in which they were written; indeed, Marxism, separatism, and everything else deemed to be contrary to Spanish identity and values were frequently depicted during early Francoism as an impurity or illness, with the Civil War and subsequent repression being the cleansing or the medical treatment that would take care of it. It was not uncommon for Republican prisoners to be subjected to punishments directly referring to purification, such as ingesting castor oil or having one's head completely shaven.[16] Just as Spain was being purified of non-Spanish elements through Francoist repression, Spanish music had been, in Turina's eyes, purified from dehumanization, avant-garde, and selfishness through military victories.

Turina's own life, in a way, had too been purified, or at least significantly improved, by Franco's victory; when the Francoist troops entered Madrid on March 28, 1939, he succinctly recorded the event in his journal as a "new stage."[17] The following day, he visited the headquarters of El Debate— whose last issue was published on July 19, 1936, after which its office was confiscated by the Republican government—with the intention of taking up again his post as staff music critic. Turina recorded his visit to El Debate with an equally significant commentary: "We start to live again."[18] His thirty-two months in Madrid during the Civil War had been anything but easy; his conservative ideals, including work as a music critic for a Catholic newspaper, made him suspicious in a city under Republican control,[19] but he finally managed to secure a steady income and protection through John Milanés, who was at the time the British consul in Madrid and an amateur composer; Milanés gave Turina an administrative job in the Evacuation

Office of the British Embassy.[20] Turina's health also suffered during the war, and he temporarily abandoned composition.[21] Nevertheless, as soon as the Francoist army took control of Madrid, Turina quickly applied himself to collaborating with the newly established regime in the task of filling the void he himself had identified in the landscape of Spanish music. On June 27, 1939, he was made a member of the committee for the reorganization of the conservatoire of Madrid,[22] and he spent most of the summer working at the Ministry of National Education—first under the general director of fine arts, Eugenio D'Ors, and then under his successor, the Marquis of Lozoya—to launch the Comisaría de Música (Commission for Music) and its flagship project, the Orquesta Nacional (Spanish National Orchestra). Turina soon started to write music criticism again too, which he also regarded as a crucial part of his contribution to reconstruction of the country. He duly recorded in his diary his first published article after the end of the war—not in *El Debate*, whose publication was never resumed, but in *Ya*, which, like *El Debate*, was owned by Editorial Católica.[23] Turina regularly wrote for *Ya* during summer 1939, but did not eventually become its staff music critic; the job went to the composer and conductor José María Franco instead. In February 1940, however, Turina took up another music criticism post, at a newly founded magazine by the title of *Dígame*.

Both *Dígame* and Turina's music criticism column in the magazine may strike the reader as extravagant in a time when the consequences of a three-year civil war, including starvation, repression, and international isolation, were still deeply felt in most sectors of Spanish society. *Dígame* did pay some lighthearted attention to current affairs, but its main focuses were the performing arts, humor, and caricature. Similarly, along these lines of thought, Turina's style was conspicuously facetious through his nine-year tenure at the magazine: he referred to the violinist Henryk Szeryng as "the chap (*pollo*) with his hand on his chest" (after El Greco's *The Nobleman with His Hand on His Chest*) for having placed his hand to his chest when taking a bow after a recital,[24] and he labeled a Wagner and Beethoven concert of the Orquesta Sinfónica as a "symphonic Asturian stew (*fabada*)," for its ambition and popularity among audiences; the concert was conducted by composer Conrado del Campo, who "has grown a morning coat"[25]—referring to the increasing number of conducting engagements that del Campo had been accepting since the end of the war.

Humor, however, was sometimes a way for Turina to covertly express some of the contradictory feelings he experienced toward Spanish musical life after the war—on which, as comisario de música, he had a certain amount of responsibility. Turina's readiness to accept an appointment at the Comisaría and to resume his career as a music critic certainly speaks of commitment to rebuilding Spanish musical life. Nevertheless, he was also an aging composer whose newly acquired responsibilities did not leave him much time for composition. Moreover, even though many of the composers and critics Turina abhorred during the Second Republic were no longer active in Spain, he still had significant rivalries with some of the men who collaborated with him in the task of reconstructing Spanish musical life. He initially shared the directorship of the Comisaría with pianist José Cubiles and writer (and occasional music critic) Gerardo Diego, both of whom had actively taken part in the musical life of the National side during the Civil War and with whom Turina got along well. Diego, however, was replaced in March 1940 by musicologist and priest Nemesio Otaño, also a very substantial contributor to music on the Francoist side during the war whom Turina regarded with less sympathy.[26] Otaño eventually left the Comisaría, with Turina remaining as sole comisario, in April 1941,[27] but some of the new recruits proved similarly problematic; Federico Sopeña, a young administrator and music critic with whom Turina soon developed a close relationship, left the Comisaría in 1943 after three years as secretary to train as a priest at the Vitoria Seminary.[28] Sopeña's replacement, Antonio de las Heras (also staff music critic at the newspaper *Informaciones*), was initially well received by Turina, but disagreements between the two men, together with the fact that the Comisaría's responsibilities were virtually limited to managing the Orquesta and the Agrupación Nacional de Música de Cámara (National Chamber Music Ensemble), eventually led Turina to resign from his office; the Marquis of Lozoya, however, did not accept Turina's resignation.[29] Turina then remained comisario de música until his death on January 14, 1949.

Turina's reviews for *Dígame* are often illustrative of the fact that the composer was split between his personal sympathies and antipathies on one hand, and his commitment to reconstructing Spanish musical life from a position of power on the other. This is already noticeable in Turina's first-ever review for *Dígame*, in which he addressed the alleged scarcity of solid orchestral conductors in post–Civil War Spain. Turina was not alone in addressing this issue; in the few years following the end of the war, it became a widespread concern in both music criticism and private correspondence among musicians, and was sometimes dealt with in rather dramatic terms. The main pillars of orchestral music in Madrid before 1939 were the Orquesta Filarmónica, under Pérez Casas, and the Orquesta Sinfónica, under Fernández Arbós. Now, with Pérez Casas and Fernández Arbós absent from Spanish musical life—albeit the former only temporarily—and the imminent launch of the Orquesta Nacional under the auspices of the Comisaría, the need for reliable, solid conductors seemed more pressing than ever. Otaño reported in a letter to Falla in

1939 in a disapproving tone that several musicians ("the ambitious ones"), including José María Franco, Cubiles, and composer Francisco Calés, were hopelessly trying to establish themselves as leading conductors in spite of their poor grasp of conducting technique and the orchestral repertoire, "and all they will achieve with all of this is what always happens in a divided kingdom: devastation."[30] Julio Gómez, in a letter to his friend José Subirá, spoke of a veritable "struggle" to occupy Fernández Arbós's place at the Orquesta Sinfónica—a struggle in which the participants were, according to Gómez, José María Franco, Cubiles, del Campo, wind band conductor Emilio Vega, and others.[31] Turina, however, instead of presenting the issue in dramatic terms, chose to humorously compare the Orquesta Sinfónica concerts at the Teatro Monumental to a state examination (*oposiciones*) in which a desirable, secure position as principal conductor was at stake and which music lovers attended "to check who is winning."[32] In Turina's opinion, Cubiles was clearly one of the winners: "His pianophilia extends to every aspect of life," he wrote in his review. "Cubiles believes that humankind can be split up in black keys and white keys." Turina—unlike Otaño—ultimately thought that Cubiles was good at conducting because "the piano is a synthesis of the orchestra, and pianists are usually skilled at penetrating the complex forest which is a concert orchestra."

But Turina used humor not just to express his preferences and sympathies without betraying the equanimity that was expected of him as comisario de música; sometimes, his humor disguised what otherwise could have been read as a blunt personal attack. On the occasion of Ernesto Halffter's visit to Madrid to conduct Falla's *El retablo de maese Pedro* in October 1941 under the auspices of the Comisaría de Música, Turina, in his review of the event, addressed Halffter in the diminutive, as "Ernestito," and warned him that "you are going bald."[33] This seemingly harmless, humorous remark becomes somewhat crude when taking into account that Halffter, born in 1905 and therefore in his midthirties at the time, had first risen to prominence at only twenty years of age after he won the Premio Nacional de Música with his *Sinfonietta*; his precociousness was duly noted by his protector, Adolfo Salazar, in his 1930 book *La música contemporánea en España*, in which Halffter was portrayed as the heir of Falla and the most significant composer of the Spanish younger generation.[34] With Salazar now in exile and unable to further support Halffter's career, and Halffter himself increasingly being replaced by Rodrigo as the leading young composer in Francoist Spain, Turina's remark may thus be read as an attack on an aging child prodigy who had not quite become a leading figure in his mature years—an attack that, with Turina himself organizing the event, could have been less acceptable if not presented through the guise of humor.[35]

Nevertheless, Turina's reviews normally made use of humor in a more straightforward, positive way; even his mild criticism of the music of Mahler, Bruckner, and Reger[36] seemed rather a humorous quarrel with his protégé Sopeña—a pioneer in Spain in his defense the music of these three composers, especially Mahler—than anything else. Turina was usually benevolent when reviewing new Spanish music, and in April 1940 he was already confident that the void perceived in Spanish musical composition just a few months before had been filled thanks to three young composers: Joaquín Rodrigo, José Moreno Gans, and José Moreno Bascuñana, and especially Rodrigo, whose "personality and rhythmic force I believe will become stronger in the future, as he becomes more and more rooted in the homeland."[37] Turina's tone when giving balanced reviews of performances ranged from approving to openly enthusiastic—the latter applying mostly to the small group of musicians whom he called his "nephews" and "goddaughters," among them singers Carmen Pérez Durías and Lola Rodríguez Aragón, conductor Eduardo Toldrà, pianist Antonio Lucas Moreno, violinist Enrique Iniesta, and two junior members of the Comisaría, Sopeña and de las Heras.[38]

That Turina's reviews were mostly positive and that he did not hesitate to review the events organized by the Comisaría itself may make his writings for *Dígame* seem unreliable and scarcely illustrative of what was happening in Madrid concert life at the time—whether music actually started to recover right after the end of the war under the auspices of the Comisaría, with the absence of the exiles and other supporters of the Republic having little impact. To be sure, one could harbor some reasonable doubt as to whether the overwhelming majority of the concerts taking part in Madrid at that time were of the high standard described by Turina. But, even if we accept that his—and other critics'—appraisals should not be taken at face value, such writings are helpful in understanding the role of music criticism in such reconstruction, what music criticism was about after three years of war, what expectations were placed on music critics by the regime, how the critics themselves understood their role, and who was writing music criticism in early Francoism (and for what reasons).

MUSIC CRITICISM IN EARLY FRANCOIST SPAIN: WHO AND HOW?

Despite Federico Sopeña's claim in 1943 that music criticism in Spain was mostly in the hands of professionals,[39] very few critics—Sopeña himself being one of the few exceptions—managed to make a living solely or mainly from writing concert reviews and newspaper articles on music. Moreover, unlike in countries such as Germany, there was no established academic or career path for aspiring music critics; nor was there any union or professional association to protect their interests. Critic-composers who also taught, conducted, or were engaged in some form of arts administration on the side, such as Turina, were the norm; further examples are Julio Gómez and Eduardo López-Chavarri, both of whom had considerable experience in writing music criticism before the Civil War. Other composers were now doing so for the first time after war and exile made it necessary for newspapers and magazines to recruit new contributors; among them were del Campo, Rodrigo, Xavier Montsalvatge, and Ángel Martín Pompey. Regino Sáinz de la Maza was one of the few performers who also wrote music criticism, whereas musicologists such as Nemesio Otaño, Higinio Anglès, and Norberto Almandoz also regularly wrote about music for nonacademic publications.

Coming from different generations and backgrounds, these and other music critics brought with them a rich landscape of influences borne out of the complex Spanish intellectual and philosophical landscape of the 1898–1936 period. Indeed, as the older critics such as Turina, del Campo, and Gómez were starting their careers in the early twentieth century, a number of Spanish writers and intellectuals who then came to be grouped under the label Generación del 98 (Generation of '98) were simultaneously articulating their concerns about the regeneration of Spain. Their proposed solutions ranged from imitating industrialized, civilized Western European nations to preserving and promoting the spiritual values germane to Spain, which were allegedly to be found mostly in the region of Castile.[40] The so-called Generación del 14 (Generation of '14) further elaborated such concerns for the regeneration of Spain, proposing European intellectual and philosophical trends (Krausism, rationalism) as the solution to reinvigorate Spain. A further intellectual contribution of the Generation of '14 was Ortega y Gasset's concept of the dehumanization of art, which still caused negative reactions among some Spanish critics, including Turina, in the 1940s. Finally, many of the concerns that had preoccupied Spanish musicians during the 1920s and 1930s were still current among critics writing under Francoism, for example, the desire to renovate Spanish music consonantly with the perceived identity of the country; the role of Manuel de Falla in the process of musical renovation; collecting, editing, and promoting Spanish traditional and early music; and the role the state should have in all of these processes.[41] It is indeed highly illustrative of this continuity that the flagship project of the Junta Nacional de Música y Teatros Líricos (National Junta of Music and Lyric Theatres) under the

Second Republic—the launch of a national, state-sponsored symphonic orchestra—was taken over by the Francoist side during the Civil War, and then finally materialized in record time under the auspices of the Comisaría de Música; the Orquesta Nacional gave its first public performance in July 1940, just over fifteen months after the end of the war.[42]

Francoist music critics, however, did not write under the conditions of the 1920s and 1930s; they were, indeed, workers in an industry the new regime had quickly identified as a key pillar in controlling public opinion following military conquest and achieving legitimacy in the international context by counterbalancing the propaganda efforts of the Republican side.[43] The first Gabinete de Prensa (Press Cabinet) on the Francoist side was in fact founded a mere two weeks after the coup, on August 5, 1936. It was replaced in January 1937 by the Delegación para Prensa y Propaganda (Delegation for Press and Propaganda), which was in turn transformed, in February 1938, into the Delegación Nacional de Prensa y Propaganda (National Delegation for Press and Propaganda), a department of the Ministerio del Interior (Ministry of Interior). The Delegación Nacional de Prensa y Propaganda thus effectively fell under the control of the Falange— and so it remained after the Civil War, through the first six years of the dictatorship.[44] In 1945, General Franco restructured his government. The new organization reflected the progressive loss of power by the Falange within the regime; press and propaganda competencies were now passed over to the Ministry for National Education, whose minister, José Ibáñez Martín, was a member of the Catholic *propagandista* faction rather than of the Falange.[45]

These shifts in control certainly exerted some impact on music criticism, the most conspicuous example being perhaps Federico Sopeña's career, which will be discussed in Chapter Two. But the conditions under which music critics did their job did in fact not change much; until 1966, the press remained subject to the 1938 Ley de Prensa (press law). Established in a time of war, the law was based on the belief that journalism was a powerful tool that could be abused by the enemies of the state and therefore needed to be closely controlled. During the Civil War, the new state apparatus, mainly through the Falange, founded its own newspapers (*Arriba, Pueblo*) and magazines (*Radio Nacional, Escorial*). Privately owned media certainly existed, and they were still subject to the control of the state to a remarkable extent. The Delegación de la Prensa (Press Directorate) decided and dictated which information was to be published in the press and under what form, mainly through the mechanisms of previous censorship and detailed instructions about content and form (*consignas*).[46] Such *consignas* were concerned with all aspects of public and private life under Francoism, and sometimes they were even directed against individuals or factions that, although theoretically supportive of the regime, were perceived as a challenge to the interests of the state.[47] Moreover, the Delegación de la Prensa placed observers in the editorial office of every newspaper, and censors carefully read every issue before publication (*censura previa*), returning it with changes to be made or announcement of financial penalties to be paid. Newspaper editors were appointed (and dismissed) by the Ministerio del Interior (Ministry of Home Affairs). Journalists were controlled by means of compulsory membership in the Registro Oficial de Periodistas (Official Registry for Journalists), and every act of noncompliance with the norms established by the Delegación was punished. Paper supplies were scarce during the 1940s, with the state allocating a fixed amount of paper for printing to the various publications, which gave the state a further opportunity to control and shape the media landscape; in the realm of the musical press, *Boletín del Colegio de Directores de Bandas de Música Civiles*, which ceased publication in 1936, could not be published again until 1945, allegedly owing to the scarcity of paper.[48] The same year, *Revista Literaria Musical* changed its periodicity from monthly to quarterly, for the same reason.[49]

The state's close control over the press was understood as a necessary solution to rectify the alleged liberalism and frivolity of the majority of the Spanish press in the years before 1936, in which the formative qualities of journalism had been put aside or misused, as described by the journalist Manuel Prados y López in his influential doctrinaire handbook *Ética y estética del periodismo español*.[50] Instead, Prados y López advocated that Spanish journalists should work in close collaboration with the Nuevo Estado, thus fulfilling a patriotic duty: a journalist was "a Spaniard on duty"[51] with the responsibility of "recording facts for History."[52] In a time of rapid changes being implemented by the Franco government with the aim of reconstructing the country, the mission of journalism was "to explain, to teach, and to persuade',"[53] so the Spanish population could comprehend the historical importance of the events that were taking place before their eyes.

Arts criticism, according to Prados y López, also had a role to play in this process. He believed that a critic's duty to his country was to help the general public cultivate "deeply Spanish" aesthetic inclinations. Prados y López did not explain what qualified as "deeply Spanish," but he did discuss in some detail how arts critics should help the population develop such inclinations: critics, he argued, should adopt an objective perspective, moderate their language, and avoid rhetorical excess. Criticism should always be "positive and constructive" because "in this new Spain in which it is of vital interest to seize all talents available, negative criticism not only expresses bad taste, but is intolerable and dangerous for the mission of the State."[54]

Prados y López's guidelines were not just lip service to the regime's plans for state-guided reconstruction; the censorship apparatus of the newly established regime very much regarded negative criticism as a potential obstacle to the government's efforts. Shortly after Joaquín Rodrigo started to work as staff music critic at *Pueblo* in 1940, the Dirección General de Prensa sent a complaint to the newspaper's editor, arguing that Rodrigo was too harsh in his judgment of musical events, and especially of those organized by the state under one form or another. The Dirección General de Prensa warned Rodrigo that the critics should approach "official" concerts—that is, those organized by the Comisaría or any other government institution—in a mild and benevolent way, in order not to hinder the State's efforts to promote "the musical recovery of Spain."[55] Similarly, the efforts of critics to address the lack of organization and diversity of musical life in Madrid, while at the same time sparing the Comisaría de Música and other government institutions from any criticism and laying the blame only on privately organized concerts, border sometimes on the comical. For example, when pointing out the organizational problems affecting the Orquesta Nacional in 1944, Antonio Fernández-Cid enthusiastically praised "the regime who freed Spain from chaos and catastrophe, [and] in its protection of music has reached thus far unknown standards in our homeland," and blamed instead the musicians of the Orquesta Nacional for accepting other jobs and not always being available for rehearsals.[56] Requests to the government to further support the musical life of Spain, sometimes with protectionist measures, were usually expressed cautiously and accompanied by passionate praise and gratitude for what the government had done for music thus far.[57]

Prados y López's guidelines also explain why Miguel Delibes's characterization of the press landscape in early Francoism as "monotonous and boring uniformity"[58] seems to be appropriate, at least superficially, for music criticism in early Francoism. Indeed, praise was the norm not just in Turina's reviews; negative remarks are also difficult to find in other critics' writings, even in cases where they did not hesitate to express their reserves privately. On the occasion of the first concert of the Orquesta Sinfónica 1939—a short-lived project put together by José María Franco aimed at reviving symphonic music in Madrid as soon as possible after the end of the war—Turina described Franco's conducting as "bland and cold."[59] His concert review for *Ya*, however, was far more benevolent and appreciative of Franco's efforts.[60] Remarkably, while enthusiastically praising the speedy recovery of Madrid's musical life under Francoism,[61] in private

Turina complained to a former student, pianist Paquita Velerda, that "perhaps we are having too much music."[62]

Such attempts at combining a generally enthusiastic overview of musical life with cautiously expressed reservations, so as to avoid presenting obstacles to the reconstruction of Spain, can be found in the critics' own appraisal of the state of music criticism and of whether it was indeed fulfilling the task it had been assigned. No music critic wrote a doctrinaire handbook comparable to *Ética y estética del periodismo español*, which absence illustrates how music critics perceived and responded to the expectations placed on journalists by the regime's apparatus; critics, however, occasionally interspersed their thoughts about their professional practice in their concert reviews and articles. Especially in the early 1940s, such thoughts were well in line with Prados y López's claims about arts criticism: in its first issue after the Civil War, the music magazine *Ritmo* announced in its opening manifesto the intention to "put together and arrange the various expressions of concert life and Spanish art"—thus doing honor to its very title and mirroring Franco's efforts in bringing back "the normal rhythm of all activities."[63] *Ritmo* was founded in 1929 by Rogelio Villar and ceased publication after the beginning of the Civil War; its relaunch, under the auspices of the Comisaría de Música and Nemesio Otaño, his newly appointed editor, was presented in the opening article as "a pressing need," given that no other music magazines for the general public were being published in Spain at the time.[64] As in Prados y López's handbook, *Ritmo* claimed that an "impartial and objective examination of the musical events" was crucial for the future success of the magazine, as was "exemplary austerity, free from stylistic prejudices, from fanatic partisanship and, of course, from passionate personal preferences, which are not at all appropriate for a public platform."[65] Again, the author of the opening article did not target any particular critics, newspapers, or magazines from the past. But it is not difficult to imagine that his mention would have heavily reminded readers of Adolfo Salazar and his various interlocutors; indeed, Salazar's passionate defense of the Junta Nacional de Música and of new music, and his open attacks on certain factions of Spanish musicology and criticism—which were then met with equally enthusiastic replies from right- and left-wing writers alike, including Turina, Castell, Julio Gómez, and Subirá[66]—would be inconceivable in 1940s Spanish music criticism, subject as it was to constant expectations of optimism and constructive commentary.

Nevertheless, in spite of *Ritmo*'s expectations and of Eugenio D'Ors's triumphant claim in 1945 that "how much I wish visual arts criticism had by now reached the same standards as music criticism,"[67] music critics sometimes appeared fully aware of their material and intellectual limitations to fulfilling the expectations placed on them. Some critics were worried that there were not enough opportunities for training and professionalization. In 1946, *Música* partially reiterated *Ritmo*'s ideals about what Spanish music criticism should be: to inform the general public and help them develop specific aesthetic ideals in them, and to support performers in their development and improvement. Nevertheless, all of this, according to the anonymous author, required in-depth knowledge of various music instruments, the repertoire, and cultural history, as well as strong writing skills; in his opinion, there was no critic in Spain who met all of these specifications.[68] At the end of the 1940s, ten years after Franco's rise to power, some critics seemed perplexed and slightly disappointed that music criticism was not thriving yet in Spain; the Catalan critic Arturo Menéndez Aleyxandre expressed his disappointment that music criticism was not still regarded as an intellectual activity, but rather as entertainment.[69] Fernández-Cid, while acknowledging the efforts of the government and highlighting that his colleagues possessed a solid music background and good writing skills, lamented that neither *Ritmo* nor any other magazine had risen to the challenge of becoming the high-quality music magazine of Spanish criticism[70]; and Gerardo Diego optimistically described the standard of music criticism in Spanish newspapers as appropriate or even exceptional, but again complained that "the great music magazine we have always dreamt of" failed to materialize in the years since Franco's victory.[71]

Conflicts of interest were another area some critics perceived as a problem. Sopeña was concerned that Spanish music criticism had been unable to attain the standards of "strict impartiality" the regime expected, given that most critics were also active as composers, performers, teachers, or administrators, which led to conflicts of interest.[72] Sáinz de la Maza admitted that, with staff music critics in newspapers being forced to attend several concerts a week and review them, there was little space for "serious critical judgment" and thus for truly educating the public, although he ultimately thought that Spanish music criticism was generally impartial and generous to performers.[73] Funnily enough, both Sopeña and Sáinz de la Maza repeatedly incurred conflicts of interest—the former regularly reviewed the concerts of the Orquesta Nacional and the Comisaría de Música during his tenure as secretary, and the latter did occasionally review his own concerts[74]—as did others such as Turina and Otaño. In a context in which music criticism was, as a result of the war, in the hands of a very small number of individuals who had other jobs elsewhere, priority was given to contributing to the reconstruction of Spain by means of regular, positive reviews of musical events to the audiences, rather than to fulfilling ethical standards (although this is not to say that critics were completely oblivious to such standards, with Sopeña and Sáinz de la Maza pointing them out).

MUSIC CRITICISM AND PERFORMANCE IN EARLY FRANCOISM: REGINO SÁINZ DE LA MAZA

The strategy of prioritizing positive reviews over conflicts of interest and avoiding open attack and controversy certainly fits well within contemporary regimes of a similar nature; in Nazi Germany, Goebbels banned arts criticism in 1936 on account of polemics being detrimental to the role of the critic as an informer.[75] Nevertheless, it was not that Francoist music criticism was entirely dictated by and subjected to the needs of the state apparatus, with Turina, as comisario de música, or another critic, deciding what officially sanctioned music criticism should be like: there were some spaces left for critics to express their dissent with the regime's musical policies (as in the case of Gómez, which will be discussed in Chapter Three). And even those who supported and held offices within the Franco regime (Turina, Otaño, Anglès, Sopeña) brought different backgrounds, interests, and approaches to the table—all of which could, theoretically, fit within the Franco regime, but which sometimes manifested themselves as not easily reconcilable, as will be discussed in subsequent chapters. It is with the tension between the regime's expectations and the music critics' reality in mind that Spanish music criticism of the 1940s should be read—as was the case with Turina and his way of using humor to encourage developments he was skeptic about in private, or to mask criticisms that would have hardly been acceptable in the climate of optimism and enthusiasm the press was supposed to foster.

In the case of other critics, however, such tensions are much less evident, to the point that they seemed to accommodate themselves almost perfectly to the requirements of the new regime. This is the case with Regino Sáinz de la Maza, whose work as a critic and a performer seems to fully mirror two key components of early Francoism: on one hand, *Hispanidad,* or the idea that the Franco regime was bringing on national rebirth; on the other, and specific to the domain of music, performance as the staging of such national regeneration. Born in Burgos in 1896, Sáinz de la Maza had already built a solid international career as a guitarist by 1936; he was on tour in America when the Civil War started. Although the Francoist press often reported that he immediately returned to Spain to offer his services to Franco and the national cause,[76] Sáinz de la Maza actually went on to finish his American tour and did not return to his native country until September

1937, as initially planned, although he kept in touch with prominent supporters of the Francoist side, such as his own brother-in-law, Víctor de la Serna, the editor of the newspaper *Informaciones*.[77] On his return, however, Sáinz de la Maza was immediately made into an exemplary artist and musician by the Francoist press. This was an example of not only "patriotic" but also specifically "falangist" behavior,[78] someone who had given up an international career for the sake of Spain,[79] and a paragon of modesty, of effort in the front line of propaganda who did not ask for any luxuries or privileges in return for his support, as well as a model of Castilian austerity.[80] Besides his public performances, Sáinz de la Maza's expressed his commitment to the newly established regime as a music critic, a job he did not have significant experience at before the war. As early as April 1939, he was offered a position as staff music critic by the Marquis of Luca de Tena, who had recently regained control of the conservative newspaper *ABC*.[81] Sáinz de la Maza was also a regular contributor to *Vértice* and *Radio Nacional*, which, being published by the Falange, were more in touch with Sáinz de la Maza's political affiliation than the privately owned *ABC*, whose conservatism was rather of the Catholic-monarchist persuasion.

As was the case with other staff music critics employed by daily or weekly newspapers, most of Sáinz de la Maza's writings for *ABC* focused on reviewing music performance. Negative remarks were, again, scarce—and carefully phrased to avoid openly attacking governmental policies. Sáinz de la Maza normally chose instead to turn his criticisms into a call for collaboration and joint efforts for the sake of the homeland; when Cubiles conducted the Orquesta Sinfónica in February 1940 with Beethoven's *Eroica* on the program, Sáinz de la Maza claimed that performing such a "truthful" work required "a constant effort to make it possible for the orchestra to identify with its conductor, with both of them inspired by the same desire of perfection." However, explained Sáinz de la Maza, the Orquesta Sinfónica still suffered from the consequences of the Civil War and had still not appointed a permanent conductor; this prevented making an effort that truly guaranteed perfection. Nevertheless, Sáinz de la Maza thought the performance ultimately turned out all right because of "Cubiles' well-earned authority."[82] Sáinz de la Maza seemed thus to establish a parallel between the Orquesta Sinfónica and its organizational problems with Spain in its entirety, working together toward a newly established goal under Franco's allegedly well-earned authority, but still suffering from the problems caused by having to restructure the musical life of a country just out of a civil war. In other reviews, Sáinz de la Maza was more explicit about the crucial role performance could and should have in the new regime: he thought that Fernández Arbós's death was particularly untimely "now that his egregious figure could be so beneficial in the new landscape of Spain,"[83] and he wrote about the importance of getting all Spanish children involved in performance through singing traditional music to foster among them love of both music and the fatherland.[84]

Sáinz de la Maza's notion that solid, well-conducted music performance was inextricably linked to the health and well-being of the country was not an exception among music critics in early Francoism; in post-civil war Spain music performance was not regarded as a mere artistic pursuit, but rather as a measure of the vigor and strength of the regime itself and its ability to reconstruct the musical and artistic life of the country in a way fully consonant with the newly arising understandings of national identity. This made it especially important, for national regeneration, to have critics provide constantly positive, even enthusiastic opinions, on music performances happening under the new regime. A further sign of the significance awarded to performance was the fact that Comisaría de Música's flagship project was, from its very foundation, to launch and manage performing ensembles—the Orquesta Nacional and the Agrupación Nacional de Música de Cámara. Composition did not seem as relevant; the Comisaría did not, for example, commission new works or award grants to composers, although it did organize annual composition contests with various levels of success.[85] During the Civil War, it was performers such as Sáinz de la Maza and others who were repeatedly portrayed by the nationalist press as examples of patriotic commitment. The Republican side, by contrast, tended to put considerably stronger emphasis on musical composition as part of the war effort; the Consejo Central de la Música was formed mostly by composers (Bacarisse, Rodolfo Halffter, Bautista, Gerhard) who regularly published their own and others' works as part of the war effort under the auspices of the Consejo itself.[86]

Cubiles was another conspicuous example of performed-turned-national-hero; during the Civil War, he toured the National zone playing Falla's *Noches en los jardines de España*, and also visited Nazi Germany in a propaganda effort for the newly established regime.[87] The tenor Miguel Fleta, who had enjoyed an international career during the 1920s, followed the Francoist army to A Coruña, in northwestern Spain, and it was in this city that he died in May 1938—not as a consequence of armed conflict, but rather of kidney failure. As was the case with Sáinz de la Maza, it was in music criticism written during the Civil War and immediately afterward—sometimes by nonspecialists—that the link between performance and the war effort seems stronger and clearer: on the occasion of the third anniversary of Fleta's death, Rafael Salazar wrote that Fleta "fought in the ranks of the national army," which must be understood figuratively, given that Fleta was thirty-eight when the war started and never fought at the front. Tropes about self-sacrifice are to be found in Fleta's portrayal as well, with Rafael Salazar stating that Fleta, in joining the National side, canceled a tour to America "to better serve Franco's Spain," with the highlight of Fleta's contribution being "having improvised a *jota* in the presence of Franco" in Seville.[88] The sextet of Radio Nacional were praised for their "commitment to Spain" ever since the Francoist government invited them to Salamanca in 1937 to support the war effort, and for always including at least one Spanish work in their programs.[89] Anonymous performers in choirs and wind bands were celebrated as soldiers too; the Orfeón Pamplonés was described as the second wave of soldiers who, hailing from the region of Navarre, filled the inhabitants of Castile during the war with "faith, courage and optimism."[90]

Such views on performance were sometimes extended to deceased performers as well. Still during the Civil War, Alberto Huerta wrote that if violinist Pablo Sarasate—who died in 1908—were still alive, "his joy would be impossible to describe" at Franco's victories; Huerta claimed that Sarasate would not only have supported Franco, but would have also become a soldier and an ambassador of National Spain abroad.[91] After a visit to Sarasate's grave in Pamplona, Federico García Sánchez noted that the grave was surrounded by other tombs of "heroes of the war for God and for Spain," referring to those who had fallen supporting Franco and national Spain.[92] Other writers also claimed that tenor Julián Gayarre would similarly be a Franco supporter were he alive.[93]

The extensive press coverage of the visits of German performers to Spain from 1940 to 1944—notably Herbert von Karajan guest conducting the Orquesta Filarmónica de Madrid, four Spanish tours of the Berliner Philharmoniker, appearances by the Hitler Youth choral and folk groups, and three Hispanic-German art music festivals in Bad Elster, Bilbao, and Madrid[94]—similarly reveals that Spanish music critics of the time closely associated public performance of music with expressing and reconstructing national identity. Concerts by German performers were enthusiastically celebrated and perceived as crucial in revitalizing Madrid's concert life: on the occasion of von Karajan's visit in May 1940, Otaño claimed that musical life in Spain had made an incredibly speedy recovery and was now even livelier than was the case before 1936[95]—which did not stop him from admitting, in a letter to Falla, that although von Karajan's performance was indeed "formidable," musical life in Madrid more generally was simply "mediocre."[96]

It was definitely German performance rather than composition that Spanish music critics were interested in—meaning not just performance *by* German musicians, but performance according to allegedly German standards. When tenor Alf Rauch and conductor Franz Konwitschny visited Madrid in 1941, Sáinz de la Maza himself wrote that what made such visits interesting was not the possibility that conductors would offer a "personal, so-far-unknown interpretation" of standard repertoire, but rather the opportunity to observe firsthand "performance criteria which follow from the good German tradition."[97] On the occasion of the second Hispanic-German festival held in Madrid and Bilbao in January 1942, Joaquín Rodrigo stated that one of the main goals of such international festivals was to have first-rate performers produce "model versions" of the standard repertoire, particularly the German one; examples of such model versions were, according to Rodrigo, Herbert Albert's performance of Strauss's *Till Eulenspiegel* and of Brahms's first symphony.[98] The successes of Spanish musicians when performing German music for German audiences were also enthusiastically reviewed in the Spanish press; Conrado del Campo was reported to having been selected by the Reich's government itself to conduct the Berliner Philharmoniker in January 1942 for his knowledge of and affinity with the German repertoire,[99] and he was allegedly so convincing in his rendition that "the intelligent German public had to bow to the evidence."[100] Cubiles received similar praise after he performed Schumann's piano concerto as part of the third Hispanic-German Festival in Bad Elster.[101] German contemporary composition, though, did not elicit the same kind of interest from Spanish critics[102]: after works by Max Trapp, Ottmar Gerster, "Berger," and "Ingenbrandt" were performed in the second Hispanic-German festival, Rodrigo described Gerster and Ingenbrandt as "of little interest," especially the latter, whose *Bolero* "justifies any kind of suspicions about his talent." He described Trapp, in contrast, as mildly interesting, although he did not approve of Trapp's use of modality, "which is bound to be a passing fancy and will probably not bear any fruit."[103] Rodrigo's review for *Radio Nacional* was more benevolent, but his praise amounted to describing Gerster's compositions as "healthy provincial music."[104] Other critics reviewing the same festival made only brief references to contemporary German music and focused instead on the performances of the German repertoire.[105]

Sáinz de la Maza and other Spanish performers highly active in early Francoism—among them Cubiles, Rodríguez Aragón, Gaspar Cassadó, and the young Ataúlfo Argenta, as well as the Orquesta Nacional and the Quinteto Nacional—in turn visited Germany in 1941 and 1942 on the occasion of the Hispanic-German music festivals in Bad Elster to present the Spanish canon there. This ranged from the sixteenth century *vihuelistas*, performed in guitar transcription by Sáinz de la Maza himself, to Rodrigo.[106]

But the music of the *vihuelistas* was not only suitable to be played abroad to promote Spanish music; it had to be disseminated in Spain as well, and Sáinz de la Maza—practically the only high-profile guitarist active in Spain at the time, since Andrés Segovia was living in America, and Narciso Yepes did not start his Madrid career until 1947—seemed to be the person for the job, through his recitals, lectures, and writings on the topic. Under Francoism, the guitar did acquire a special significance that Sáinz de la Maza helped develop; it was appreciated not so much for the connection to tradi- tional music, or the music of "the people," as was the case during the 1920s and 1930s, but rather because of its connection to Spain's imperial past as a derivation of the *vihuela*. Sáinz de la Maza regularly included transcriptions of the music of the Spanish *vihuelistas*, including Luis de Narváez and Luis de Millán, in his recitals, and in his talks and writings he repeatedly spoke of the guitar as the twentieth-century incarnation of the *vihuela*[107]; several other critics echoed this connection between the *vihuela* and the guitar in their own reviews, implying that, in the same way Francoism was bringing Spain's imperial past back to life, Sáinz de la Maza was reviving the music of imperial Spain.[108]

Sáinz de la Maza himself was well aware of the connection between his own practice and the advent of the Franco regime, and frequently cel- ebrated it in his writings. Unlike Turina, who welcomed the new regime because it had swept away the avant-garde trends brought over by the dehumanization of art, Sáinz de la Maza went further back in time and regarded the new regime as a comeback of imperial Spain to which he was contributing as a performer and critic. In one of his first articles for *ABC*, he wrote that "now, mysticism, epic poetry and traditional song bloom in Spanish ardently and amorously"[109]; in this new climate, he argued, it was every Spaniard's right and duty to listen and enjoy music instead of feed- ing the "childish fear of not understanding music"—again, a likely refer- ence to the perceived intellectualism and elitism of the Grupo de los Ocho and their self-confessed disdain for Spanish audiences.[110] Sáinz de la Maza praised the projects the Ministerio de Educación Nacional carried out for Spanish music, not only because he thought they would be beneficial for postwar musical life, but because they would also help Spanish music "accomplish its universal destiny"[111]—thus presenting history as destiny, consonant with falangist notions.[112] Veiled criticism of the Second Republic can be detected in a comment he made: "Today is not like yesterday used to be. Now, the words of those who have in their hands the future of the Nation are not void or mere clichés to escape problems." This, according to Sáinz de la Maza, was further proof that Francoism was a comeback of imperial Spain, since imperial rulers, from Isabella the Catholic onward, had given the utmost importance to music. He was also aware of the significance music performance enjoyed in Spain's imperial past, which he believed would be mirrored under the new regime; he discussed Antonio de Cabezón not just as a composer but also as an organist whose "utterly Castilian art" had caused a deep impression in all Europe during Cabezón's travels accompanying Philip II.[113]

Sáinz de la Maza's views on the Franco regime as the restoration of imperial Spain were fully consonant with the concept of *Hispanidad*, so prevalent in the rhetoric of the earlier regime, and particularly within the Falange. The concept, however, was by no means an invention of the Franco regime; it must be understood as one of the products of the long-lasting debates about Spanish national identity and regeneration that occupied Spanish intellectuals from the late nineteenth century onward. The loss of the last colonies in 1898 caused a national identity crisis that was still deeply felt in the 1930s, and this is the context in which the two conceptualizations of *Hispanidad* that were most influential on the Franco regime were developed: those of Ramiro de Maeztu and Giménez Caballero. Maeztu was part of the Generation of '98 in his youth; he subsequently evolved toward far-right positions and took part in the political organization Acción Española (modeled after Action Française) during the 1930s.[114] Maeztu described *Hispanidad* as an objective spirit that expresses itself in the art and culture produced by Spain; it is eternal, unchangeable, and intrinsically linked to Roman Catholicism, but it needs the right economic and geographical circumstances to fully materialize.[115] Giménez Caballero, on the other hand, traced the origins of what he called *genio de España* (genius or spirit of Spain) to Roman times; the *genio* allegedly crystallized for the first time with political unification of the Peninsula under the Visigoth monarchy and subsequently achieved its peak with the Catholic monarchs in 1492, the year in which the *genio de España* achieved not only the political but also the racial and religious unity of Spain and, additionally, the foundations for the expansion of the *genio* into America were established. This providentially turned 1492 into the moment for which "Saint Isidore, El Cid, Fernán González, Alfonso X the Wise, Don Juan Manuel, had been longing for centuries."[116] The *genio de España* was allegedly so strong that it had managed to produce remarkable personalities even in the adverse context of the Muslim domination, figures such as Maimonides and Averroes, and produced its most illustrious glories "whenever it remained faithful to its origins"[117]—by which Giménez Caballero meant Catholicism and imperial expansion.

During the Civil War and the first years of the regime, the concept of *Hispanidad* was further developed and adapted to provide justification for the very existence of the Franco regime. In a speech in Barcelona on February 21, 1939, shortly after Catalonia was occupied and the government of the Second Republic was forced out of Spain, Franco claimed, "I do not think I am mistaken to say that Spain will soon come to life again, in a manner unprecedented since our Golden Century." Moreover, it was not by chance, he argued, that the "moral foundations of our future Empire" were established in a physical space built during the times of the other empire: the *alcázar* of Toledo, which had been under siege by the Republican troops for several months at the beginning of the Civil War and was then occupied by the Francoist army, quickly becoming a milestone in the imaginary of the new regime.

Writing in 1938, Manuel García Morente echoed Giménez Caballero's and Maeztu's belief that *Hispanidad* was a timeless concept existing well before Spain materialized as a political unity; the inhabitants of Roman Hispania allegedly showed already "some of the virtues which, through the centuries, they developed further in a magnificent way," and they already exhibited their strength and commitment to *Hispanidad* by fiercely resisting the Romans, which marked, in García Morente's opinion, the first crucial moment in the history of Spain.[118] The second and third such moments were the war against the Muslims during the Middle Ages ("a continuous struggle against an alien, contrary, exotic and impossible religious conviction"[119]) and the building of the Spanish Empire, throughout which *Hispanidad*, after having accomplished the task of unifying Spain, further extended its potential by expanding to the exterior and ensuring Spain's political, religious, and moral leadership.[120] García Morente added something new to Maeztu's and Giménez Caballero's accounts, though: he considered the advent of the Franco regime to be the fourth and last important moment in the history of Spain. The nation was, again, fulfilling its destiny and putting itself in the forefront of the world because Franco, in defeating communism, had demonstrated that national values such as *Hispanidad* should prevail over "'transnational' ideologies"[121]—the Franco regime, in other words, was a providential inevitability. *Hispanidad* was also absorbed into the regime's rituals and policies. During the war and the first years of the regime, Franco was repeatedly presented as a crusader for Spain and the successor of Charles V and Philip II,[122] and *Hispanidad* was also used to further ostracize those political and intellectual trends contrary to the Franco regime (liberalism, socialism, communism, feminism) as contrary to the Spanish soul itself and therefore unacceptable.[123]

With *Hispanidad* at the very foundation of the Franco regime, and with music performance being an important component of such restoration, it may be easy to regard Sáinz de la Maza as a sort of spokesperson of official music criticism, making the central ideas that sustained the regime's very existence come alive in his own practice as a performer and in his writings. Nevertheless, this figure is a little more difficult to accommodate into narrow political categories. Even though his music criticism fully supports the idea that Francoism had rightly replaced the avant-garde by a return to Spanish traditional values, he was friends with several crucial names of said avant-garde: Federico García Lorca himself dedicated "Seis caprichos" from *Poema del Cante Jondo* to Sáinz de la Maza, and Rosa García Ascot and her husband, Jesús Bal y Gay, now in exile, both wrote works for the guitarist during the 1930s. During the first years of the Franco regime, Sáinz de la Maza temporarily cut off his ties with his former friends—during the 1940s, Salazar repeatedly complained that he had not heard from him anymore after the war[124]—but eventually reunited with some of them; it was thanks to Salazar, Bal y Gay, and Rodolfo Halffter that Sáinz de la Maza was invited by Carlos Chávez to perform Rodrigo's *Concierto de Aranjuez* with the Orquesta Sinfónica Nacional of Mexico in 1952.[125] Sáinz de la Maza was also one of the first prominent performers under Francoism to include works of the exiles in his recitals, as the regime slowly started to advance toward a more liberal stance. As early as 1949, his programs included Gustavo Pittaluga and Jaume Pahissa.[126]

It must not be forgotten, however, that there were other sides to the regime, and even to the Falange, apart from *Hispanidad*. Some music critics represent some of these facets better than Sáinz de la Maza did. For example, a section of the Falange, which later came to be known under the name of Falange Liberal, was more interested in building a true *Nuevo Estado* than in simply glossing nostalgically over the past. This conspicuous desire for renovation—even at the risk of enraging other more conservative, less change-enthusiastic factions of the Franco regime—left its footprint in music criticism as well. And it was not Sáinz de la Maza—who rarely engaged with contemporary music in his articles, except for the few occasions where a work by Stravinsky or a contemporary Spanish composer was performed by one of the Madrid orchestras—who is best suited to exemplify this renovating, almost revolutionary streak within the early Franco regime, but rather a young music critic by the name of Federico Sopeña.

NOTES

1. Joaquín Turina, "La nueva España musical," *Radio Nacional*, no. 50 (1939), 13.
2. For a discussion of Falla's attitude toward the Franco regime, his decision to leave Spain, and the attempts of the Franco regime to attract him back to Spain for

reasons of cultural prestige, see Carol A. Hess, *Sacred Passions: The Life and Music of Manuel de Falla* (Oxford: Oxford University Press, 2005), 232–246; Raanan Rein, "La lucha por los restos de Manuel de Falla," *Journal of Iberian and Latin American Studies*, no. 2 (1996), 22–39; Eva Moreda Rodríguez, "A Catholic, a Patriot, a Good Modernist: Manuel de Falla and the Francoist Musical Press," *Hispanic Research Journal*, vol. 14, no. 3 (2013), 212–226.

3. See Yolanda Acker, "Ernesto Halffter: A Study of the Years 1905–1946," *Revista de Musicología*, vol. 17, no. 1–2 (1994), 143–154.

4. For examples of the purges affecting the staff of the Conservatorio de Madrid, see Igor Contreras, "Un ejemplo del reajuste del ámbito musical bajo el Franquismo: la depuración de los profesores del Conservatorio Superior de Música de Madrid," *Revista de musicología*, vol. 32, no. 1 (2009), 569–583.

5. Turina, "La nueva España musical," 13.

6. Ibid.

7. Antonio de las Heras, "Música," *Informaciones*, June 8, 1939, 7. De las Heras did not specifically name any musician involved with the orchestra—not even its conductor, Pérez Casas, who was at the time being investigated for having collaborated with the Republican government during the war.

8. Antonio Torres Climent, "La música de esta posguerra," *Música. Revista quincenal*, no. 19 (1945), 9.

9. José Ortega y Gasset, "Musicalia," *El Espectador*, no. 25 (1921).

10. José Ortega y Gasset, *The Dehumanization of Art*, trans. by Helene Weyl (Princeton: Princeton University Press, 1968).

11. Rodolfo Halffter, "Manuel de Falla y los compositores del Grupo de Madrid de la Generación del 27," in *Rodolfo Halffter. Tema, nueve décadas y final*, ed. Antonio Iglesias (Madrid: Fundación Banco Exterior, 1991), 412. See also Emilio Casares Rodicio, "Música y músicos de la Generación del 27," 25.

12. Joaquín Turina, "Música," Jan. 18, 1933, 7.

13. Turina, "El año musical," Jan. 1, 1932, 6.

14. Turina, "Musique espagnole moderne," *Le Courier Musical*, no. 4 (1926).

15. Turina, "La nueva España musical," 13.

16. Michael Richards, *A Time of Silence: Civil War and the Culture of Repression in Franco's Spain, 1936–1945* (Cambridge: Cambridge University Press, 1998), 55–58.

17. Turina, unpublished diary, Jan. 1–Dec. 31, 1939, Mar. 28 [FJM, LJT-M-Per-9].

18. Ibid., Mar. 29.

19. Beatriz Martínez del Fresno, *Julio Gómez. Una época de la música española* (Madrid: ICCMU, 1999), 381.

20. Turina, unpublished diary, Jan. 1–Dec. 31, 1937, Nov. 19 [FJM, LJT-M-Per-9].

21. Letter from Turina to Eduardo López-Chavarri, Oct. 7, 1939, unpublished [FJM, LJT-Cor-Tur-14].

22. Turina, unpublished diary, Jan. 1–Dec. 31, 1939, June 27.

23. Ibid., June 7.

24. Turina, "El pollo de la mano al pecho," *Dígame*, May 14, 1940, 7.

25. Turina, "En el yunque," *Dígame*, Apr. 30, 1940, 6.

26. Turina, unpublished diary, Jan. 1–Dec. 31, 1940, Mar. 2 [FJM, LJT-M-Per-9]; Turina, unpublished diary, Jan. 1–Dec. 31, 1941, May 12 [FJM, LJT-M-Per-9].

27. Turina, unpublished diary, Jan. 1–Dec. 31, 1941, Apr. 5.

28. Turina, unpublished diary, Jan. 1–Dec. 31, 1940, Apr. 13 and Nov. 12; Turina, "Y va de cuento," *Dígame*, Feb. 15, 1944, 6.

29. Letter from Turina to the Marquis of Lozoya, Oct. 2, 1945, unpublished [FJM, LJT-Cor-Tur-15]; letter from the Marquis of Lozoya to Turina, Oct. 16, 1945, unpublished [FJM, LJT-Cor-81]; letter from Turina to Eduardo López-Chavarri, Oct. 25, 1945, unpublished [FJM, LJT-Cor-Tur-14].

30. Letter from Nemesio Otaño to Manuel de Falla, July 20, 1939, unpublished [AHSL, 004/010.012].

31. Letter from Julio Gómez to José Subirá, Apr. 9, 1940, unpublished [BNE, M.SUBIRÁ/1/105].

32. Turina, "Disonancias musicales," *Dígame*, Feb. 27, 1940, 7.

33. Turina, "Homenaje a Falla," *Dígame*, Oct. 21, 1941, 9.

34. Adolfo Salazar, *La música contemporánea en España* (Madrid: Ediciones La Nave, 1930), 247–255.

35. Turina also complained, in his diaries, about Halffter's "hypocrisy," "scheming," and "shamelessness" in the rehearsals leading up to the performance, which may have been another reason for the sarcastic comment. See Turina, unpublished diary, Jan. 1–Dec. 31, 1941, Oct. 11 and Nov. 7.

36. Turina, "Crónica pianística'," *Dígame*, Jan. 15, 1944, 7; Turina, "Música, clarines y voces," *Dígame*, Apr. 2, 1946, 7; Turina, "Las divagaciones de un oyente," *Dígame*, Oct. 15, 1946, 6.

37. Turina, "Ya somos tres," *Dígame*, Apr. 23, 1940, 7.

38. Letter from Turina to Pilar Mendicuti, Mar. 2, 1946, unpublished [FJM, LJT-Cor-Tur-18]; Turina, "In memoriam," *Dígame*, Feb. 1, 1944, 7; Turina, "Y va de cuento," 6.

39. Federico Sopeña, "Cuatro estados de la crítica musical madrileña. En torno a Peña y Goñi," *El Español*, Mar. 27, 1943, 9.

40. Alan Hoyle, "Introduction: The Intellectual Debate," in *Spain's 1898 Crisis: Regenerationism, Modernism, Postcolonialism*, ed. Joseph Harrison and Alan Hoyle (Manchester: Manchester University Press, 2000), 26–32.

41. María Palacios, *La renovación musical en Madrid durante la dictadura de Primo de Rivera. El Grupo de los Ocho (1923–1931)*. Madrid: Sociedad Española de Musicología, 2008, 11–13; Casares, "Música y músicos," 20.

42. For other continuities between the Second Republic and the Franco regime, see also Gemma Pérez Zalduondo, "Continuidades y rupturas en la música española durante el primer franquismo," in *Joaquín Rodrigo y la música española de los años cuarenta*, ed Javier Suárez-Pajares (Valladolid: Glares, 2005), 55–78; Germán Gan Quesada, "*Músicas para después de una guerra* ... Compromisos, retiradas y resistencias," in *Discursos y prácticas musicales nacionalistas (1900–1970)*, ed. Pilar Ramos López (Logroño: Universidad de La Rioja, 2012), 278–279.

43. Florence Belmonte, "Los periodistas de la prensa del Movimiento (1937–1945): entre la ética y el realismo," in *Del gacetero al profesional del periodismo. Evolución histórica de los actores humanos del cuarto poder*, ed. Carlos Barrera (Madrid: Fragua, 1999), 145–146; Concha Langa Nuño, "El periodista-combatiente. La imagen de la prensa desde la prensa 'nacional' (1936–1939)," in *Del gacetero al profesional del periodismo. Evolución histórica de los actores humanos del cuarto poder*, ed. Carlos Barrera (Madrid: Fragua, 1999), 128–129.

44. Belmonte, "Los periodistas de la prensa del Movimiento," 145–154; Javier Terrón, *La prensa de España durante el regimen de Franco. Un intento de análisis politico* (Madrid: Centro de Investigaciones, 1991), 46–86.

45. Terrón, *La prensa de España*, 106; Rosa Cal, "Apuntes sobre la actividad de la Dirección General de Propaganda del Franquismo (1945–1951)," *Historia y Comunicación Social*, no. 4 (1999), 19–20.

46. José Javier Sánchez Aranda and Carlos Barrera del Barrio, *Historia del periodismo español desde sus orígenes hasta 1975* (Pamplona: Eunsa, 1992), 454–503.

47. For a first-person account on *consignas*, see Miguel Delibes, *La censura de prensa en los años 40 (y otros ensayos)* (Madrid: Ámbito, 1995), 9.

48. Anonymous, "Editorial," *Boletín del Colegio de Directores de Bandas de Música Civiles*, no. 23 (1945), 3.

49. Anonymous, "Editorial," *Revista Literaria Musical*, no. 28 (1945), 3.

50. Manuel Prados y López, *Ética y estética del periodismo español* (Madrid: Espasa Calpe, 1943), 19.

51. Ibid., 31.

52. Ibid., 41.

53. Ibid., 31.

54. Ibid., 72.

55. José Antonio Gutiérrez, "La labor crítica de Joaquín Rodrigo en el diario *Pueblo* (1940–1946)," in *Joaquín Rodrigo y la música española de los años cuarenta*, ed. Javier Suárez-Pajares (Valladolid: Glares, 1995), 404–405.

56. Antonio Fernández-Cid, "La orquesta nacional y sus problemas," *La estafeta literaria*, no. 17 (1944), 8. See also Tomás Andrade de Silva, "El año musical," *Música. Revista quincenal*, no. 2 (1945), 3; and Joaquín Rodrigo, "Necesidad de una estrecha colaboración musical," *Radio Nacional*, no. 117 (1941), 10.

57. See, for example, Rodrigo A. de Santiago, "Los concursos nacionales de música," *Boletín del Colegio de Directores de Bandas de Música Civiles*, no. 36 (1946), 12, requesting the launch of state-funded orchestras to perform prize-winning works in the Spanish provinces; and Nemesio Otaño, "La temporada musical en Madrid," *Ritmo*, no. 139 (1940), 3, asking the government to take charge of musical life in Madrid to avoid miscoordination and to build an adequate concert hall.

58. Delibes, *La censura de prensa*, 9.

59. Turina, unpublished diary, Jan. 1–Dec. 31, 1939, July 16.

60. Turina, "La Orquesta Sinfónica 1939," *Ya*, July 19, 1939, 7.

61. Turina, "En el yunque," 6; Turina, "¡Bien por ese sindicato!" *Dígame*, Nov. 29, 1942, 6.

62. Letter from Turina to Paquita Velerda, Apr. 12, 1941, unpublished [FJM—LJT-Cor-Tur-28].

63. Anonymous, "Propósitos," *Ritmo*, no. 133 (1940), 3. Although the article is not credited to an author, it is highly likely that the author was Otaño himself.

64. Ibid., 3. See also, on the issue of the relaunch of *Ritmo*, Joaquín Rodrigo, "Reaparición de la revista *Ritmo*," *Radio Nacional*, no. 88 (1940), 15.

65. Anonymous, "Propósitos," 3.

66. Francisco Parralejo Masa, "Jóvenes y selectos: Salazar y Ortega en el entorno europeo de su generación," in *Los señores de la crítica. Periodismo musical e ideología del modernismo en Madrid (1900–1950)*, ed. Teresa Cascudo and María Palacios (Sevilla: Doble J, 2011), 71–72; Parralejo, "Crítica musical y radicalización política durante la II República: el caso de *ABC*," *Revista de musicología*, vol. 20, no. 1 (2009), 537–552.

67. Eugenio D'Ors, "Glosas para abrir una revista nueva," *Música. Revista quincenal*, no. 1 (1944), 3.

68. Anonymous, "Editorial," *Música. Revista Quincenal*, no. 22 (1946), 3.

69. Arturo Menéndez Aleyxandre, "Cultura Musical," *Ritmo*, no. 223 (1949), 4.

70. Antonio Fernández-Cid, *Panorama de la música en España* (Madrid: Espasa-Calpe, 1949), 267–268.

71. Gerardo Diego, Joaquín Rodrigo, and Federico Sopeña, *Diez años de música en España* (Madrid: Espasa Calpe, 1949), 70. Although the book was jointly credited to Diego, Rodrigo, and Sopeña, differences in the writing style and approach suggest that Sopeña wrote the chapter on composition and Rodrigo the chapter on performance, with Diego in charge of music criticism and musicology. This distribution also avoided the potential conflict of interest posed by having Rodrigo write on composition, or Sopeña on music criticism.

72. Sopeña, "Cuatro estados," 9.

73. Antonio Fernández-Cid, "Entrevista con Regino Sainz de la Maza," *El Español*, no. 20 (1945), 12. Fernández-Cid raised a similar point in arguing that most music critics held other jobs and as a result musical circles in Madrid were quite small, which, in his view, was a source of "moral problems"; see Fernández-Cid, *Panorama*, 267.

74. Regino Sáinz de la Maza, "Informaciones musicales," *ABC*, June 12, 1942, 13.

75. Karen Painter, *Symphonic Aspirations: German Music and Politics 1900–1945* (Cambridge, MA: Harvard University Press, 2009), 209.

76. For example in Anonymous, "Peregrino de la Falange por los senderos de España," *Vértice*, no. 7–8 (1937–38), 22; Antonio de las Heras, "Música," *Informaciones*, Nov. 16, 1939, 7.

77. Leopoldo Neri de Caso, "La guitarra como símbolo nacional: de la música a la ideología en la España franquista" (2006), http://secc.es/media/docs/22_3_NERI_DE_CASO.pdf (accessed April 2014); Neri de Caso, "Regino Sainz de la Maza: crítico musical," 372–373.

78. Anonymous, "Peregrino de la Falange."

79. Antonio de las Heras, "Éxito de Sainz de la Maza en el Español," *Informaciones*, Nov. 28, 1944, 1 and 3.

80. Anonymous, "Peregrino de la Falange."

81. Neri de Caso, "La guitarra como símbolo nacional."

82. Regino Sáinz de la Maza, "Informaciones teatrales. Orquesta Sinfónica," *ABC*, Feb. 27, 1940, 14.

83. Sáinz de la Maza, "Acorde en la ausencia del maestro Arbós," *Vértice*, no. 23 (1939), 7.

84. Sáinz de la Maza, "Acción educadora de la música," *Radio Nacional*, no. 135 (1941), 16.

85. Gemma Pérez Zalduondo, "La música en el contexto del pensamiento artístico durante el franquismo," in *Dos décadas de cultura artística en el Franquismo (1936–1956)*, ed. Ignacio Henares Cuéllar, Cabrera García, María Isabel, Gemma Pérez Zalduondo and José Castillo Ruiz (Granada: Universidad de Granada, 2001), 94. One of these contests has been analyzed in Christiane Heine, "El cuarteto de cuerda en el Concurso Nacional de Música de 1949," in *Joaquín Rodrigo y la música española de los añs cuarenta*, ed. Javier Suárez-Pajares (Valladolid: Universidad de Valladolid, 2005), 149–172.

86. Examples of musical works published by Ediciones del Consejo Central de la Música are Enrique Casal Chapí, *El caballero de Olmedo*; Eduardo Martínez Torner, *Canciones populares españolas*; Salvador Bacarisse, *Nana del niño muerto* and *Tres movimientos concertantes*; Evaristo Fernández Blanco, *Trío en do mayor*.

87. See, for example, José María Franco, "Informaciones musicales," *Ya*, July 11, 1939, 7; Anonymous, "Informaciones y noticias musicales," *ABC*, July 6, 1939, 19; Anonymous, "Los nuevos académicos de Bellas Artes," *Ritmo*, no. 134 (1940), 3.

88. Rafael Salazar, "Miguel Fleta," *Radio Nacional*, no. 73 (1941), 5.

89. Anonymous, "El sexteto de Radio Nacional," *Radio Nacional*, no. 39 (1939), 5.

90. Anonymous, "Bodas de oro del Orfeón Pamplonés," *Tesoro sacro-musical*, no. 12 (1942).

91. Alberto Huerta, "Sarasate," *Arriba España*, Sep. 21, 1937, 4.

92. Federico García Sánchez, "Por los siglos de los siglos. Navarra en el centenario de Sarasate y Gayarre," *ABC*, June 30, 1944, 17. See also, on Sarasate, Ángel Sagardía, "El españolismo de Pablo Sarasate a través de sus actos, frases y labor de compositor," *El Español*, Aug. 5, 1944, 6.

93. Anonymous, "Música," *Arriba España*, Jan. 19, 1937, 4. See also, on Gayarre, Gabriel de Ybarra, "Gayarre y su Roncal. Memorias en la tierra que le oía cantar," *El Español*, Aug. 5, 1944, 7.

94. On Hispanic-German music exchanges, see Eva Moreda Rodríguez, "Hispanic-German Music Festivals During the Second World War," in *The Impact of Nazism on Twentieth-Century Music*, ed. Erik Levi (Vienna: Böhlau Verlag, 2014), 309–322; Javier Suárez-Pajares, "Festivals and Orchestras: Nazi Musical Propaganda in Spain During the Early 1940s," in *Music and Francoism*, ed. Gemma Pérez Zalduondo and Germán Gan Quesada (Turnhout, Belgium: Brepols, 2013), 59–98. Music exchanges with Italy were also significant, with reviewers focusing heavily on the Latin or Mediterranean character that allegedly united Spain and Italy. See Eva Moreda Rodríguez, "Italian Musicians in Francoist Spain, 1939–1945: The Perspective of Music Critics," *Music and Politics*, 2 (2008), http://quod.lib. umich.edu/m/mp/9460447.0002.105/--italian-musicians-in-francoist-spain-1939–1945?rgn=main;view=fulltext [last access: June 2016].

95. Nemesio Otaño, "El eminente director de orquesta alemán Herbert von Karajan, en Madrid," *ABC*, May 21, 1940, 16.

96. Letter from Nemesio Otaño to Manuel de Falla, July 1, 1940, unpublished [AHSL, 004/010.019].

97. Regino Sáinz de la Maza, "El director Franz Kowitschny y el tenor Alf Rauch, en el círculo de Bellas Artes," *ABC*, Feb. 12, 1941, 12.

98. Joaquín Rodrigo, "Al margen del festival de música hispanoalemán," *Escorial*, no. 17 (1942), 423.

99. Anonymous, "Conrado del Campo dirige en Berlín dos conciertos," *El Alcázar*, Jan. 10, 1942, 6.

100. Anonymous, "Ha regresado de Berlín el maestro Conrado del Campo," *El Alcázar*, Jan. 23, 1942, 7.

101. Anonymous, "La semana musical hispano-alemana a través de la prensa del Reich," *Ritmo*, no. 159 (1942), 7.

102. Lydia Goehr, "In the Shadow of the Canon," *Musical Quarterly*, vol. 86, no. 2 (2002), 314. According to Goehr, with the musical canon taking shape throughout the nineteenth century, "having at least found its history, Germany was no longer living or making one"; this indeed seems to have been the approach Spanish critics took to German music, being interested in the German canon only up to Richard Strauss.

103. Rodrigo, "Al margen del festival," 423.

104. Rodrigo, "Los festivales de música hispano-alemanes," *Radio Nacional*, no. 170 (1942), 12.

105. For example, Conrado del Campo, "Primer festival hispano-alemán," *El Alcázar*, Jan. 27, 1942, 7.

106. See Moreda Rodríguez, "Hispanic-German Music Festivals," 318–321.

107. For example, in Regino Sáinz de la Maza, "Don Luis Millán y la música cifrada para vihuela," *Vértice*, no. 30–31 (1940), 8, reprinted in *Radio Nacional*, no. 151 (1941), 4;

Sáinz de la Maza, "Variaciones sobre la guitarra," *Música. Revista Quincenal*, no. 4 (1945), 8–9; also Antonio Fernández-Cid, "Entrevista a Regino Sáinz de la Maza," 12.

108. For example, Federico Sopeña, "Música, ausencias y homenaje," *Arriba*, Oct. 17, 1939, 7; Manuel Ruiz Aguirre, "La guitarra," *El Español*, Nov. 11, 1944, 8; Sopeña, "Informaciones musicales," *ABC*, Nov. 11, 1943, 19; Joaquín Turina, "Recital de Sainz de la Maza," *Ya*, Nov. 18, 1939, 6; José María Arozamena, "Español: Recital de guitarra Sainz de la Maza," *ABC*, June 7, 1939, 20.

109. Regino Sáinz de la Maza, "Si no escucháis la música, amigos . . ." *ABC*, Aug. 6, 1939, 3.

110. See, for example, Julio Gómez and Rodolfo Halffter on Bacarisse's disdain for the audience: Julio Gómez, "Sociedad Filarmónica Cuarteto Rafael," *El liberal*, Mar. 28, 1933; Rodolfo Halffter, "Tres movimientos concertantes para violin, violonchelo y orquesta, op. 18, de Salvador Bacarisse," *La Voz*, May 15, 1935. See also Parralejo Masa, "Jóvenes y selectos," 67–68.

111. Regino Sáinz de la Maza, "Revuelo y júbilo en la grey musical," *ABC*, Oct. 7, 1939, 3.

112. See Primo de Rivera's speech on the occasion of the founding of Falange in 1933, reprinted in José Antonio Primo de Rivera, *Discurso fundacional de Falange Española* (Madrid: Consejo Nacional del Movimiento, 1970).

113. Regino Sáinz de la Maza, "Artistas imperiales. Antonio de Cabezón, músico y organista," *Vértice*, no. 14 (1938), 8.

114. See Alistair Hennessy, "Ramiro de Maeztu: *Hispanidad* and the Search for a Surrogate Imperialism," in *Spain's 1898 Crisis: Regenerationism, Modernism, Postcolonialism*, ed. Joseph Harrison and Alan Hoyle (Manchester: Manchester University Press, 2000), 105–120.

115. Ramiro de Maeztu, *Defensa de la Hispanidad* (Madrid: Acción Española, 1934).

116. Ernesto Giménez Caballero, *Genio de España* (Madrid: Ediciones de La Gaceta Literaria, 1932), 29–30.

117. Ibid., 176.

118. Manuel García Morente, *Idea de la Hispanidad* (Buenos Aires: Espasa Calpe, 1938), 9.

119. Ibid., 13.

120. Ibid., 14.

121. Ibid., 14.

122. Giuliana di Febo, *Ritos de guerra y de victoria en la España Franquista* (Bilbao: Desclée de Brouwer, 2002), 83–87.

123. Richards, *A Time of Silence*, 16.

124. Letter from Adolfo Salazar to Ernesto Halffter, Aug. 26, 1943, reprinted in Consuelo Carredano (ed.), *Adolfo Salazar. Epistolario. 1912–1958* (Madrid: Fundación Scherzo/Publicaciones de la Residencia de Estudiantes, 2008), 588; and letter from Adolfo Salazar to Ernesto Halffter, Dec. 3, 1945, reprinted in ibid., 638.

125. Letter from Adolfo Salazar, Rodolfo Halffter, and Jesús Bal y Gay to Carlos Chávez, Nov. 27, 1951, reprinted in ibid., 801–802.

126. Antonio de las Heras, "Regino Sainz de la Maza en el María Guerrero," *Informaciones*, Feb. 25, 1949, 5.

CHAPTER 2

Reviewing Contemporary Music

With Turina and Sáinz de la Maza having a prominent role in recon-structing Spanish musical life, it is not surprising that both of them were involved in two of the most widely reviewed and influential concerts to take place in the aftermath of the Civil War. The first was the Madrid perfor-mance of Joaquín Rodrigo's *Concierto de Aranjuez*, with Sáinz de la Maza as the soloist and the Orquesta Nacional conducted by Jesús Arámbarri under the sponsorship of Turina's Comisaría on December 11, 1940.[1] The second was a concert-homage to Manuel de Falla on October 14, 1941, organized again by the Comisaría at the Teatro Nacional, with Ernesto Halffter con-ducting the Orquesta Nacional in *Noches en los jardines de España,* dances from *El amor brujo* and *El sombrero de tres picos*, and a semistaged perfor-mance of *El retablo de maese Pedro* (in its first performance in Madrid since 1933). Federico Sopeña, then at the beginning of his four-decade career as a critic and arts administrator, attended and reviewed both events for *Arriba*. This in itself was not at all remarkable, since prominent events organized by the Comisaría were bound to be attended, and enthusiastically reviewed, by the major Madrid newspapers and magazines. Unlike with other review-ers, however, Sopeña's assessment of these two events came to be consid-erably influential in the historiography and criticism of twentieth-century Spanish music—in the same way that Adolfo Salazar's opinions on new music during the 1920s and 1930s survived beyond his time.

In the early 1940s, however, Sopeña was an unlikely candidate to become such an influential figure. Born in 1917, he was still a teenager and a student of the Conservatorio de Madrid during the years in which the Grupo de los Ocho were active in Madrid, but he attended new music concerts with a keen interest[2] and had a fascination with the writings of

Salazar[3]; unlike most other music critics in early Francoism, however, he never developed a career as a practical musician before or after the war. According to Sopeña's own narrative, he was forced to spend the Civil War in Republican Madrid.[4] After the war ended, with a law degree under his belt but not interested in practicing law professionally, he learned in September 1939 that Manuel de Falla had left for Buenos Aires. This encouraged him to write an article on Falla, which he sent to *Arriba* "as a spontaneous contributor."[5] Without any other effort on his part, or so the narrative goes, he was then hired ("The article was published, and then someone phoned me and offered me the post of music critic"),[6] in time for him to review in full the first concert season in Madrid after the Civil War, which promptly started in October. A year later, in November 1940, without any significant experience of arts administration, he was appointed secretary of the Comisaría de Música. It would be disingenuous, however, to think that Sopeña's trajectory was the product of sheer luck; his networking skills also seem to have played a very significant role. Before his appointment at *Arriba*, he was already acquainted with Antonio Tovar,[7] a falangist intellectual who had been put in charge of Radio Nacional during the Civil War. Similarly, Sopeña soon became part of the circle of close friends of Joaquín Turina's[8] and a member of the *tertulia* (a social gathering for discussing literary or artistic matters) held at the Lyon d'Or café,[9] which included Turina and such other well-known musicians as Cubiles, Rodrigo, and Sáinz de la Maza, as well as falangist intellectuals such as Pedro Laín Entralgo.

Sopeña's meteoric rise in the aftermath of the Civil War makes him a product of the early Franco regime in a very particular way. Turina, Sáinz de la Maza, and others already had careers in criticism or other areas of music before the Civil War, and it is with this in mind that their writings should be read; they adapted to the newly established regime by capitalizing on ways of thinking about music that they had been following for years, but that acquired new meanings or new relevance under Francoism. Sopeña's early and subsequent career, in contrast, would never had happened—or at least, not as it did—outside the Franco regime, specifically outside the Falange intellectual environment that came to be known as Falange Liberal.

Some of the most prominent members of the Falange Liberal, or liberal falangists, such as Dionisio Ridruejo, Tovar, and Laín Entralgo, started their political careers during the Civil War working for the press and propaganda services of the Franco regime; most of them were in their late twenties or early thirties at the time and had a university education. Concerned with intellectual and artistic engagement as a way of reshaping all facets of the *Nuevo Estado* under fascist principles after the Civil War, under the auspices of the Dirección de Prensa y Propaganda of Falange and of the minister for foreign affairs, Ramón Serrano Suñer (a falangist himself and also Franco's brother-in-law), a number of them founded the periodical *Escorial* in 1940, all the while keeping control of the state's press and propaganda apparatus.

The Falange Liberal's romance with the Franco regime was short-lived, though. Serrano Suñer was forced to resign as early as 1940, and by 1945 control over the press and propaganda had been transferred to the Opus Dei Catholic faction, with fascist ceremony and rhetoric being preserved by the regime only as lip service to the ideals of José Antonio Primo de Rivera. Some liberal falangists then progressively detached themselves from Francoism, becoming more critical of the regime, among them Emiliano Aguado, José Luis Aranguren, and most conspicuously Dionisio Ridruejo, who famously ended up leaving Spain. This detachment involved reinterpreting and reshaping the relationship between the Falange and the Franco regime between the Civil War and 1945 so as to present the Falange Liberal under a new light. The Falange (thus argued the newly self-described liberal falangists) had never shared with early Franco governments the desire to annihilate and send the enemies of Francoism and their intellectual contributions into oblivion; rather, in the turmoil and confusion of the early 1940s, they had always attempted to make sure that the diverse points of view and strands of Spanish intellectual life, including liberalism, were well represented and heard, at least in publications such as *Escorial*.[10] As early as 1952, Ridruejo included himself and other members of the Falange on the side of the *comprensivos* (the comprehensive), as opposed to the *excluyentes* (the exclusive), by which Ridruejo referred to the Catholic–Opus Dei faction led by Rafael Calvo Serer; the latter group, according to Ridruejo, worked to "exclude" other Spaniards, and the former tried to "convert, convince, integrate, and redeem other Spaniards," including those who had differing political opinions, such as the exiles.[11] Ridruejo's words themselves, however, leave little doubt that a focus on inclusion was not informed by true liberal concerns, but rather by fascist ideals of "stripping one's adversary of any valid points he might have or have had by appropriating such points for oneself," in Ridruejo's own words.[12] Nevertheless, with the Catholic *excluyentes* now in control of press and propaganda and with memories of the Francoist repression of the early 1940s still fresh, Ridruejo succeeded in portraying the *comprensivos* as a sort of internal dissidence throughout the regime, from its very beginnings during the Civil War—a portrayal that greatly informed perceptions of the Falange Liberal in late Francoism and beyond.[13]

Sopeña seemed happy to describe himself as a member of the Falange Liberal and claimed that he was the "baby brother" of Laín Entralgo, Tovar,

Ridruejo, and other falangist intellectuals.[14] Indeed, unlike most other liberal falangists, Sopeña did not start his career during the Civil War, but had to wait until the Franco regime was established, not only because he was seven to ten years younger than the others, but because he perceived his own intellectual training as somewhat lacking in comparison with the rest; the others

> had already graduated from university when the war started, they were in the prime of life, they knew Europe, while I was a frustrated musician and pianist, and still a student . . ., and still a bit of an adolescent, because I was a bookworm, because my family was very modest . . ., because I was too much of a romantic.[15]

There are other significant components that merit attention in Sopeña's self-portrait as a member of the Falange Liberal. The most crucial is perhaps his admiration of Salazar and other musicians ostracized in early Francoism, such as Bartolomé Pérez Casas, which he cited as proof that he shared the Falange Liberal's concern to make sure that prominent intellectuals who did not support the Franco regime but were nevertheless of excellent caliber were not excluded from construction of the *Nuevo Estado*.[16] Sopeña himself repeatedly named Salazar as a model and an inspiration both for himself and for Spanish music critics more generally.[17] It is true that he did so mostly from the 1950s onward and that he made very few references to Salazar during the 1940s, a time in which memories of the Second Republic Civil War were still fresh and exiles were rarely mentioned by name, whether to criticize or to praise them. Nevertheless, Sopeña's similarities with Salazar did not go unnoticed even in the early years of the regime: on the subject of Sopeña's and Salazar's preference for French over German music, Julio Gómez tellingly complained in a letter to his friend, José Subirá: "You already know by heart all the commonplaces of the little Parisian musical games: everything German, or related to Germany, is a bore. . . . Alas! We have not moved on yet—but those who have remained with us are even worse than those who have left."[18]

Consonant with Sopeña's self-identification with the Falange Liberal, in his memoirs he drew on his admiration for Salazar and other exiles to portray himself and the other liberal falangists as internal dissidents even during the very first years of the Franco regime. Indeed, Sopeña claimed that, throughout the Franco regime, his career had been fraught with difficulties because he was "too liberal" and because he had always strived to "defend the intellectuals."[19] He portrayed the Falange Liberal, led by Serrano Suñer, as single-handedly trying to keep the Spanish intellectual tradition alive during the first years of the regime, driven by "the pleasure of fighting against the most stubborn *propagandistas*" and, more generally, against the "fastidious cultural indigence of the powers-that-be,"[20] without describing precisely what kind of difficulties he and his Falange Liberal colleagues had faced.

Sopeña's portrayal of his early career, and of the Falange Liberal more generally, as a struggle against a regime stubbornly set on intellectual mediocrity is difficult to reconcile, not only with the Falange Liberal's hegemony on press and propaganda during the years 1938–1945, but also with Sopeña's meteoric rise during these years. Indeed, apart from his appointments at *Arriba* and the Comisaría de Música, which gave him the opportunity to take part in a number of high-profile international events with propaganda and diplomatic aims,[21] shortly after the start of his career he was writing for some of the most visible and prestigious music and arts periodicals, and published several single-authored books, including biographies of Turina and Rodrigo. It becomes even more puzzling if we consider that, unlike Ridruejo, Aranguren, and other liberal falangists, Sopeña was never ostracized in the later stages of the Franco regime. Having been one of the few music critics to repeatedly argue that music should have a place at Spanish universities, or that Spanish conservatoires should at the least provide universitylike training in music,[22] and having taught extracurricular courses in music at the universities of Salamanca and Madrid,[23] he was appointed director of the Conservatorio de Madrid from 1951 to 1956. Additionally, he was elected as a member of the Academia de Bellas Artes de San Fernando in 1958, he was comisario de música from 1971 and 1972, and after the Franco regime came to an end he was director of the Museo del Prado from 1981 to 1983—all the while advancing his career as a music critic and a very prolific writer of books on music.

There is a crucial difference, however, with Ridruejo and others: Sopeña detached itself from the Falange Liberal at a relatively early stage and was probably not too affected by its later demise. Crucially, he left Madrid and his appointment at the Comisaría de Música in October 1943 to train as a priest at the Vitoria seminary, in the Basque Country, just as the Falange Liberal was starting to decline.[24] He also left his staff post as music critic at *Arriba*, although he still contributed occasionally to it and other publications. Thus, when ordained as a priest in 1946, he was able go back to Madrid and take on again a more active role in Spanish musical life with his prestige intact.

Considering Sopeña as a member of the Falange Liberal, and one who identified as such even after the Falange Liberal was dismantled, crucially helps understand several aspects of his career as a music critic during the

1940s. Clearly, he was interested not only in reviving the past, but also in shaping the future of the *Nuevo Estado*. Among music critics writing in the 1940s, he was the only one who engaged with contemporary music (from Stravinsky to Messiaen, and from Falla to Rodrigo) systematically, beyond the opportunities for doing so provided by his staff music critic routine. He was also the only one to constantly ask himself how Spanish and foreign models could be successfully applied in order to create music that was truly Spanish but also *new*; that is, Sopeña did not simply long for the avant-garde to be swept away and for the new order to be restored, as Turina did, but instead sought to adapt some of the elements brought over by the avant-garde to Spanish music, so long as they could be suitably national.

In this regard, whereas other critics, particularly those writing daily for newspapers, sometimes appeared overwhelmed by the task of giving unrelentingly positive reviews to whatever was happening in Madrid and as a consequence often did not reflect on where it was that such developments were taking Spanish music, Sopeña never quite lost sight of the big picture and did not hesitate to turn some of those events into milestones of the rebirth of Spanish music under Franco. He clearly thought that he was not *just* writing music criticism, but writing music history. Indeed, in writing in his memoir that "When I see our 'official' musicologists who are unable to write true history from the archives, I am almost glad that I did not fall into the Roman nets of Anglès,"[25] he seemed to imply that he was writing *true* history by recording contemporary events for posterity. Sopeña's disdain for Spanish musicology, which had typically focused on Spanish music mostly from the Middle Ages to the Baroque Era and totally neglected contemporary music, was another trait he shared with Salazar, who, during the 1920s and 1930s, had expressed similar reservations about Spanish musicology and those he had scornfully labeled as "the wise men of the archives."[26]

REWRITING RODRIGO AND FALLA

A prominent example of Sopeña writing history as it unfolded before his eyes—or rather, transforming an event into music history shortly after it happened—was the first Madrid performance of the *Concierto de Aranjuez*. It is true that the concert was touted as a significant event by several of the reviewing critics it was, after all, a premiere by a relatively unknown, young composer who could fill the gap that the Grupo de los Ocho had left, and it was also one of the first public performances of the Orquesta Nacional and an appearance by its star performer, Regino Sáinz de la Maza, playing one of the first concertos ever written for the guitar.[27] Nevertheless, few of critics articulated why exactly they thought the performance would be a milestone in post–Civil War Spanish music. Most reviews emphasized that the concerto was not only very solid technically, but also a truthful expression of Spanishness, borrowing from both low-brow popular Spanish culture (of which the guitar was a powerful symbol) and high art traditions such as Domenico Scarlatti. Nevertheless, they were less specific in articulating why they thought the concerto was significant for the present and future of Spanish music.[28] Moreover, not everyone regarded the first performance of the concerto with the same enthusiasm; Otaño himself, in a letter to Falla, expressed his horror that the work had been compared to Falla's *Noches en los jardines de España* and he felt obliged to argue against these opinions in a radio broadcast because Rodrigo "is subtle and well-intentioned, but his talent is limited."[29] Julio Gómez was also highly critical of the concerto's success and wrote to José Subirá, "The main event [in Madrid musical life] has been the first performance of *Concierto de Aranjuez*, by Joaquín Rodrigo, who has been the object of a pre-concert promotion and a post-concert success which has never been seen in Spain—not even in the best days of the Salazar-Halffter duo."[30]

However, the first performance of the *Concierto de Aranjuez* quickly stuck as one of the most significant musical events in post–Civil War Spain,[31] with music critics naming it as a milestone. The *Concierto* was repeatedly selected as one of the canonic works of Spanish contemporary music, to be performed in high-profile music exchanges between Francoist Spain and other countries: it was included in the program of the third Hispanic-German music festival in August 1942 and on the visit of the Orquesta Nacional and the Comisaría de Música to Lisbon in April 1943. Even in contemporary scholarship, the first performance of the *Concierto* is frequently named as the first significant milestone in musical life under the Franco regime.[32] Sopeña's input as a critic, writer, and member of the Comisaría was crucial in elevating the *Concierto de Aranjuez* to the status of turning point; after the work was performed in Madrid, Sopeña strived to portray it not only as an excellent work worth being part of the Spanish canon, but also as the exact work that both Spanish and international audiences were awaiting following the end of the Civil War.

An important part of this process was to make Rodrigo and the *Concierto* part of an illustrious, well-established genealogy in Spanish music; in this, Sopeña followed Salazar, whose narrative of Spanish music focused on a few quasi-heroic figures (Pedrell, Falla, and finally Ernesto Halffter) almost single-handedly leading Spanish music.[33] Sopeña's historiographic premises (history of music as a succession of hero figures) were almost identical to Salazar's, although the names were not exactly the same. For example, in a talk about Spanish music during the visit of the Comisaría to Lisbon, Sopeña chose to focus on Falla, Turina, and Rodrigo, crucially placing Rodrigo beside the two living Spanish composers having the most significant international reputations. What Falla, Turina, and Rodrigo shared, in Sopeña's opinion, was that their music was intrinsically Spanish, but never picturesque or provincial; it had a universal appeal because it was based on feeling and emotion.[34] Later that same year, in a retrospective account of how Spanish music had evolved and progressed in the first four years of the Franco regime, he portrayed the "generation of musicians ... led by Turina," who had gathered successes for Spanish music in Europe before the war, as the direct predecessors of Rodrigo and the *Concierto de Aranjuez* in 1940.[35] Sopeña thus entirely skipped the Grupo de los Ocho and the other young composers active during the Second Republic, with the exception of a passing mention of Ernesto Halffter, who thus lost the "hero" status he had held in Salazar's writings.

Nevertheless, Sopeña did not portray Rodrigo simply as a new reincarnation of Turina's and Falla's ideals, but as a reincarnation that perfectly befitted modern times. This is the main argument underpinning Sopeña's 1946 biography of Rodrigo[36]—in itself an exceptional book for many reasons. Indeed, rather than a proper academic biography complete with a scholarly apparatus, the book consists of a few biographical chapters profoundly and self-admittedly informed by Sopeña's friendship with Rodrigo, followed by commentaries of Rodrigo's works in a language accessible to a nonspecialist reader, focusing on the aesthetic values on the music rather than on detailed analytical work. It was also one of the first books to be published on a living and still relatively young Spanish composer, as acknowledged by Sopeña himself[37]; biographies of Falla were published by Pahissa and Sagardía in 1945 and 1946 respectively, shortly before the composer's death, but Falla was by then internationally known and had a long career behind him. Not surprisingly, in line with Sopeña's focus on hero figures, his book on Rodrigo was preceded by a similar book on Turina[38] and followed, in 1950, by a selection and edition of Falla's writings.[39]

A further work in which Sopeña developed at length the notion of Rodrigo as the composer who had best responded to the needs and wants of contemporary audiences was his chapter on music composition for *Diez años de música en España*. In despite of Sopeña's self-confessed aversion to music historiography, the chapter certainly comes quite close to being an attempt at writing a proper history of musical composition in the ten years following the Franco regime. No histories of Spanish music, contemporary or otherwise, had been published in Spain since Salazar's 1930 *La música contemporánea en España*[40]; it is therefore not difficult to imagine that, after his biographies of Turina and Rodrigo, Sopeña would have intended to transform his reflections on what he witnessed during the years 1939–1949 into proper music history. His narrative of Spanish music after the Civil War in these two works is crucially articulated around a need—thus presenting the events he narrated as inevitable rather than merely contingent on the historical circumstances[41]—to find a central figure for Spanish music after Falla left the country following the Civil War.[42] Sopeña argued that Falla's absence meant Spanish music had now no clear reference, and that the situation was perceived by other composers and audiences as "provisory" and unstable.[43]

Furthermore, Sopeña argued, neither international nor Spanish music seemed to have any valid models to offer to make up for Falla's absence. Contemporary music seemed to be increasingly alienated from its audiences and even from performers themselves ("I remember," he wrote, "the impression of strangeness after listening to [Stravinsky's] *Jeux de Cartes* or his violin concerto"),[44] and the only option left to audiences if they wanted to reconcile themselves with music was to look back at Brahms's symphonies and Beethoven's quartets.[45] Sopeña acknowledged that some had hoped that Ernesto Halffter, being Falla's student and the most prominent young composer during the 1920s and 1930s, could fill the void left by Falla in post–Civil War music. Nevertheless, although he admitted that Halffter was a fine composer and conductor, Sopeña argued that he had ultimately not quite risen to the challenge of becoming "the musician of *these* years"[46]; that honor went to Rodrigo instead.[47] In the same way Salazar had named Ernesto Halffter as *the* leading composer of the young generation, with members of the Grupo de los Ocho and others occupying a secondary position with respect to Halffter,[48] Sopeña did not hesitate to name Rodrigo as the lone leader ("the spotlight towards the new generation")[49] among the Spanish composers, young or not, active during the 1940s.[50] Perhaps even more crucially, Sopeña regarded Rodrigo's fate as closely interlinked with his own as a critic, not only because the two men developed a close friendship from 1940 onward,[51] but because Sopeña regarded his own career as a critic as dependent on discovering and elevating a new composer suitable for the new era he was living in ("There is no significant criticism without a 'new man' to be discovered, I told myself since autumn 1939").[52]

What had allowed Rodrigo and the *Concierto de Aranjuez* to inevitably prevail among other Spanish (and international) composers was, according to Sopeña, the fact that Rodrigo had dared to "move away from artificialness, from weirdness" and to fully bring feeling and emotion back to music,[53] thus giving Spanish audiences "a message suitable to things they had just sensed,"[54] and ensuring an unprecedented success.[55] As with Turina's articles, it is not difficult to imagine that Sopeña was directing his criticism toward the Grupo de los Ocho, some of whose members were particularly drawn to neoclassicism and specifically its ironic, antisentimental aspects.[56] For Sopeña, however, it was also of paramount importance to underline that Rodrigo did not simply represent a return to musical nationalism or to Spanish tradition; Sopeña was adamant that there was no way back and that the "new worlds of sound conquered in the twentieth century" should be absolutely preserved, though this should be necessarily accompanied by "tenderness" and by "a compulsory and personal Spanish accent."[57]

Sopeña's focus on feeling, emotion, and sincerity (as opposed to dehumanization) did not apply to the *Concierto de Aranjuez* only; Sopeña made use of similar categories to turn the 1941 homage to Falla, and more specifically the semistaged performance of the *Retablo*, into a milestone in Spanish music history post Civil War. As with the first performance of the *Concierto de Aranjuez*, the concert-homage to Falla quickly earned its place in the narrative of recovery of Spanish music following the war.[58] As was the case with the *Concierto*, enthusiasm was not uniform originally among reviewers, though; Rodrigo, for example, thanked the Comisaría for having organized the concert, but admitted that it would be "foolish" to regard the concert as proof that Spanish concert life had totally recovered, although he admitted that "we are certainly on our way to do so, and we can now see the possibilities and the ways to achieve this."[59] Again, Sopeña's contribution was not limited to praising the event and thanking the Comisaría; he also seized the opportunity to emphasize the values of feeling and emotion he saw in the *Retablo*. With this, he again framed the Franco regime as a new era for Spanish music in which the postulates of the Grupo de los Ocho were replaced by humanity.

In the 1920s the *Retablo*, together with Falla's harpsichord concerto, was the object of much admiration among Salazar, the Grupo de los Ocho, and other composers because Falla, in turning from Andalusia to Castille for musical inspiration, had proved that he could indeed be the model for a truly Spanish model for their music without sentimentality and clichés.[60] Rodrigo himself seemed to be close to the Grupo de los Ocho in his review of the Falla concert; he focused on the Castilian nature of the *Retablo* and considered Falla's neoclassical *castellanismo* as superior to his *andalucismo*, complaining even that *El sombrero de tres picos* (a conspicuously *andalucista* work) had been included in the program, because "it is perfectly useless and even harmful, even though it was a good performance."[61] Rodrigo's discussion of *castellanismo* was also deeply indebted to the thesis of Spanish musical mysticism first developed by the French Hispanist Henri Collet in 1913,[62] which further allowed Rodrigo to establish a connection between Falla and other Spanish composers allegedly influenced by mysticism, such as Tomás Luis de Victoria.

Sopeña agreed with Rodrigo—and with the Grupo de los Ocho—in preferring *castellanismo* to *andalucismo*. Nevertheless, Sopeña was not drawn to the neoclassical austerity of *castellanismo,* as the Grupo de los Ocho had been. Nor was he interested in *castellanismo* as a way of simply embracing the Spanish past, but rather of embracing it with a particular purpose: to drive away dehumanization of art and music and bring back feeling and emotion, thus inaugurating a new stage of Spanish modern music. In a way, what Sopeña was doing was reclaiming Falla from the Grupo de los Ocho. Or, as Sopeña put it in his commentary of the genesis and initial impact of the *Retablo:*

> In the years of *El retablo de maese Pedro,* the idea of music as sentimental projection was at death's door. It seemed as if divine grace had fled the world, and no one was thinking of combining skill with inspiration, of giving themselves ecstatically to a force coming from no one knows where [. . .]. A genius musician, Stravinsky, seemed to represent the only plausible approach: objectivity, order, rigorous formalism, plasticity, rejection of tenderness, a grandiose understanding of music as architecture.[63]

This was certainly not the last time Sopeña compared Stravinsky to Falla, with the former composer being the embodiment of coolness, detachment, dehumanization, and intellectualism, and the second bringing in emotion, feeling, sincerity, and inspiration with a distinctly Spanish-Castilian flavor to modernism. In his talk on Spanish music during his visit to Lisbon in April 1943, Sopeña argued: "For Falla, music is, above all, emotion, feeling, and when it is not feeling, it is only an artifice. Stravinsky, on the other hand, refuses the idea that music can express any kind of feeling and says it is useless to express emotions or passions."[64] Nevertheless, it is not that Sopeña disliked or despised Stravinsky, as other Spanish critics did; actually, he thought that Stravinsky and Falla were together "the two poles of genius of contemporary music."[65] He also wrote three articles on Stravinsky for *Radio Nacional* in 1941 in which he ultimately decided that Stravinsky was not a suitable model for new music because a composer "must not compose out of purely musical intuition, but rather must take an emotional state as his starting point."[66] Nevertheless, the articles show Sopeña's efforts to engage with Stravinsky's musical and aesthetic approaches rather than simply dismiss them. And it was not simply technical skill that Sopeña appreciated in Stravinsky; whereas, Sopeña argued, the years before the Civil War had seen an increasing popularity of atonality owing to "left-wing politics," Stravinsky nevertheless remained a point of reference for all musicians because of his sense of "order and hierarchy."[67] Sopeña also gave a positive review to Alexandre Tansman's "controversial" biography of Stravinsky, because it presented Stravinsky as "an orderly musician and the composer who brought over the restoration of tradition."[68]

THE FASCIST CONNECTION: GIMÉNEZ CABALLERO'S
ARTE Y ESTADO

In the context of an authoritarian regime, and with Sopeña being involved in a fascist party, at least initially, it may be easy to see his positive comments on Stravinsky's sense of order and hierarchy as the influence of political ideology on his music criticism. Nevertheless, the focus on feeling and emotion as the characteristics that brought Rodrigo and Falla to the forefront not only of Spanish but also of universal music has conspicuous fascist roots as well; in 1935, Ernesto Giménez Caballero claimed that contemporary art was in dire need of feeling and emotion in his book *Arte y estado*, and his ideas on the matter proved highly influential on Sopeña and other music critics, which will be discussed later, and also on other aspects of the arts and humanities under the Franco regime.[69]

Born in 1899 and initially an admirer of Ortega y Gasset, Giménez Caballero started his writing career in 1923 with a memoir of his years as a soldier in the Morocco campaigns (*Notas marruecas de un soldado*), which reflected his early thinking about Spain's *genio*[70]; later on, he tried his hand at avant-garde poetry and in 1927 founded a literary journal with the title *La Gaceta Literaria*. His experiments with the avant-garde stem, in a way, from his disillusionment with Ortega y Gasset during the 1920s; Giménez Caballero, by then already a staunch cultural nationalist, had come to despise Ortega y Gasset's cosmopolitanism. Although he still agreed with Ortega y Gasset in considering that contemporary art had alienated the masses, he argued that the avant-garde was not to be blamed for it; on the contrary, he believed that the avant-garde could help artists reconnect with the people of their own nation.[71] Avant-garde, however, did not help Giménez Caballero's standing as a writer; his poetry collection, *Yo, inspector de alcantarillas* (1928), was a commercial failure. However, he soon found a new way to channel his political activism, after a visit to Italy in 1928 during which he met Curzio Malaparte, Filippo Marinetti, and other prominent fascist intellectuals and artists. Giménez Caballero became fascinated with Mussolini's corporations of writers and artists, which, in his opinion, guaranteed that art was not a mere individualistic pursuit but rather served the interests of the nation; shortly thereafter, in February 1929, he developed in the pages of *La Gaceta* the notion of a Spanish fascism.[72]

Giménez Caballero's efforts to develop a specifically national fascism continued in his 1933 with his book *La nueva Catolicidad*. He described fascism as a movement toward universalism; it was crucial, however, that such universalism take its roots in regeneration of each country's own genius, otherwise it could become mere internationalism or cosmopolitanism.[73] In the same year, he was invited by José Antonio Primo de Rivera to become one of the founding members of Falange. Giménez Caballero's career within the party was not free from difficulties, though; whereas he insisted that the Falange should be a Spanish version of Italian, and secondarily German, fascism, other falangists, including Primo de Rivera himself, were wary of foreign influence. Such disagreements even resulted in Giménez Caballero being temporarily suspended from membership in the Falange shortly before the Civil War.[74]

In *La nueva Catolicidad*, Giménez Caballero gave art a prominent role in bringing over the regenerative political solutions that, in his view, Spain was in need of ("The Poet is the male of politics. And the political activist is his passive, maternal counterpart, the one who is fertilized and gives birth"[75]). Two years later, he published *Arte y estado*, which focused exclusively on the role of art in the fascist state.[76] With art and the world allegedly being "unbalanced,"[77] Giménez Caballero dedicated an extensive portion of the book to diagnosing the current problems of art and suggesting solutions. He argued that contemporary art was plagued by two opposed, but equally pervasive and detrimental, trends: liberal art and communist art. The art of nineteenth-century "liberal Europe" was "individualistic," and this clashed with his desire to appeal to the masses.[78] In the twentieth century, according to Giménez Caballero, liberal had evolved, under the influence of Judaism and capitalism, into "immediate, surrealist and materialist art"— the avant-garde.[79] He was, nevertheless, equally hostile to those art forms generated by communism ("oriental, Bolshevik" art[80]), which he considered "internationalist"—and, as such, not suited to reflect each nation's unique genius[81]—and the ultimate dehumanizing art.[82]

Giménez Caballero argued that both types of art were affected, to different extents, by the same three main problems that rendered them unable to be truly national and, as such, to be filled with feeling and emotion. The first was mechanization and the increasing importance of the machine over human intervention (in music, for example, player pianos, saxophones, radios, gramophones).[83] This fit well with his mistrust of technological progress more generally: in *Genio de España,* he had already warned about how technology rendered traditional social units and the individual himself more uniform, thus eroding the sense of national genius or national identity that had to be rekindled in order for national regeneration and rebirth to happen ("They wanted to substitute the Medieval guilds with the Machine. And they wanted . . . to provide the surprised masses with a humanist, liberal culture with no scope other than to make them believe in their own indefinite and hypothetical perfection").[84]

Elitism and pure art was the second main problem affecting contemporary art, in the East and the West[85]; this happened, allegedly, because artists had abandoned the excesses of romanticism and eliminated all traces of feeling and emotion from their art.[86] It is not difficult to see that Giménez Caballero was following his former mentor, Ortega y Gasset, here. But the focus on feeling and emotion has parallels in other fascist movements, with Italian, and especially German, fascism reacting against rationality as well—as the legacy of the Enlightenment and the French revolution—and emphasizing irrationality and sheer emotion instead.[87] The third problem named by Giménez Caballero was the absence of a market for such dehumanized artistic products, which forced the various national governments to subsidize art that was not able to connect with their people anymore.[88]

Giménez Caballero's solutions for the problems of art were fully consonant with his understanding of fascism as a movement toward universalism solidly rooted in regeneration of a country's own genius.[89] Art itself, he argued, necessarily had to transcend the boundaries of the individual; it had to push the person toward abandoning his individuality, "becoming fatherland," and ultimately achieving "the highest eternal state: the peace and contemplation of God."[90] In music, he further maintained, this would involve abandoning mechanization and technology, going back to "the most elementary: the singer of folk songs." This would make it possible for Spain to achieve the ultimate aim of art: contemplation of God.[91]

DEVELOPING A THEORY OF MODERNIST MUSIC

Focus on feeling and emotion as the way to redeem art was already a prominent element in Sopeña's reviews of *Concierto de Aranjuez* and *El retablo de maese Pedro,* as has been discussed earlier in this chapter. Nevertheless, it was only after he came back from the Vitoria Seminary that we find him consistently applying Giménez Caballero's ideals to his criticism of contemporary music, and more specifically his discussion of how authentically Spanish modern music should be; he did so in a series of articles published in *Arbor* starting 1947.[92] The *Arbor* articles synthesized and systematized some of the ideas on modern music he had developed in previous years as staff music critic for *Arriba* and as a writer for other publications; they are also a prelude to his undertaking, in the 1950s, of roles that allowed him a more active and influential contribution to shaping Spanish contemporary music, particularly the directorship of the Conservatorio de Madrid and the role of coordinator of the section for contemporary music within the Instituto Español de Musicología, both from 1951 onward.[93]

That Sopeña, a former liberal falangist, chose to publish some of his major articles in *Arbor* may raise some questions. Indeed, *Arbor*, which included articles in various humanities, arts, and sciences for an academic but not necessarily specialist audience, was published under the auspices of the Consejo Superior de Investigaciones Científicas. The CSIC, in turn, was founded by the Franco regime in 1939 to promote scientific research—with a distinctly Spanish and Catholic flavor—in all areas. From its origins, the CSIC was under the control of the *propagandistas* and the Opus Dei, who did not necessarily get along well with the Falange; the struggle between both factions was indeed rather intense around the years in which Sopeña published his three articles.[94] There are several explanations, however, for why Sopeña chose to go to a *propagandista* rather than Falange publication. The reasons may in part have been eminently practical: by 1947, some the Falange-controlled periodicals and magazines that could have been suitable outlets for his articles were no longer operative. *Vértice* ceased publication in 1944, *Radio Nacional* in 1945; *Arriba*, being a daily newspaper, and with Antonio Fernández-Cid having replaced Sopeña as staff music critic, was probably more apt for concert reviews than for extended articles, and Sopeña himself believed that musical life in Madrid was too monotonous to "build an entire doctrinal body upon it."[95] Publishing in *Arbor* therefore made sense professionally, besides helping him reestablish his career away from the Falange: one of Sopeña's long-term ambitions was to bring music into the current intellectual debate of early Francoist Spain by sharing a space with experts in other humanities disciplines.[96] *Arbor*, being a multidisciplinary periodical, gave him the opportunity to do this.

Nevertheless, the Falange still had outlets where Sopeña could have published his work; for example, *Escorial*, the Falange Liberal's flagship journal, did not cease publication until 1950, and Sopeña had published two articles there in 1941.[97] But it is likely that, by the time he came back from the Vitoria seminary, he wished to detach himself from a declining Falange and thus chose to write for *Arbor* instead. Nevertheless, although still heavily reminiscent of Giménez Caballero's *Arte y estado*, other elements praised by Sopeña, such as the return to the past and the focus on traditional music, could be welcomed by a generally conservative, pro-Franco audience without necessarily raising suspicions of falangism.

Indeed, it is worth noting that, despite the strong similarities between his thinking and Giménez Caballero's, Sopeña did not once name Giménez Caballero in his *Arbor* article series. With many former liberal falangists becoming ostracized in the late 1940s, this was probably to be expected; Giménez Caballero's career was itself in decline by the mid-to-late 1940s.[98] It may also seem rather surprising at first sight that, in the first of the three *Arbor* articles, Sopeña chose to present himself as a follower and successor of Salazar, at a time in which the exiles were still practically absent from musical life in Spain and were hardly ever named in the press—although Sopeña's mention of Salazar was lukewarm enough that it could hardly be mistaken for a defense of the exiles or a claim to bring them back into Spain. Salazar, claimed Sopeña, had experienced the Second World War and its consequences for art and music from far away; Salazar could therefore not understand contemporary music.[99] Sopeña thus acknowledged that Salazar had been the only Spanish critic to address new music systematically before the Civil War, but at the same time he was implicitly stripping Salazar—and, by definition, all of the Second Republic musical establishment—of his old, supposedly well-earned legitimacy to comment on contemporary music and to attract attention to himself as Salazar's successor in providing a well-informed, thorough assessment of contemporary music and its impact on Spain.

Nevertheless, even if Sopeña is comparable to Salazar in that both consistently addressed and judged new music and their direction in Spain, the content of Sopeña's articles is more reminiscent of the views of Giménez Caballero than of Salazar. Sopeña claimed that, by the mid-1930s, mechanization and technological progress in music ("angry, determined, dominating techniques, shaped in the course of years of morbid fascination with novelty") had reached the point of saturation; composers started to look for "an authentic channel for sincerity" instead.[100] In doing so, some young composers had mistakenly gone back to "a frank and often blunt neo-romanticism" that Sopeña considered too clichéd and stereotyped to be able to express true feeling.[101] Stravinsky and Schoenberg, although acknowledged by Sopeña as the two most significant innovators following the First World War, were similarly unsuitable as models for new music because both of them had purposefully avoided emotion.[102] Instead, Sopeña suggested that nationalism could be just what music needed to solve its most pressing problem—in the same way that Giménez Caballero thought art should go back to its national essence in order to be reinvigorated with emotion and feeling, and become universal. In this respect, Sopeña named Bartók along with Falla, whose *Retablo* Sopeña described as "boldness subjected to the dimensions of incandescent and pure humanity."[103] Sopeña warned that no younger composer had yet become the model others needed; nevertheless he saw some rays of hope, particularly in France: the "collective spirit" of French composers, which had allowed them to get away from pure music (again, reminiscent of Giménez Caballero's admiration for Italian corporations of writers and artists), and Messiaen's focus on "singing for God" as a way to bring back humanity.[104]

The second of Sopeña's articles focused on musical nationalism as the way forward for contemporary music. Following Giménez Caballero's reservations about nineteenth-century art, he was careful to make a distinction between "Romantic nationalism" (Smetana, Dvořák, Liszt, Grieg, some of Sibelius), which audiences liked not because of "racial criteria" but rather because they were based on easily recognizable "romantic patterns," and "essential" nationalism (exemplified by Bartók and Falla). According to Sopeña, it was only the latter, which derived from "folklore laboratory work," that could bring sincerity back into music and thus help composers attract an audience.[105] He again named Falla's *Retablo* as the work that had brought emotion back to Spanish music in the late 1920s, a time when Spanish audiences were starting to become disappointed with dehumanization and were already "receptive to the quest for universality, open to a brand of Spanish music sincerely made to the measure of man." After the Civil War, the *Retablo*, according to Sopeña, had definitely brought emotion back into Spanish music, not only influencing Rodrigo but also redeeming Ernesto Halffter, whose work had "matured . . . thanks to a joyful, carefree and heart-felt nationalism"[106]—once more, a likely reference to Halffter's initial forays into the avant-garde, from which he had then reportedly been redeemed by embracing feeling and emotion again. Sopeña's third article again explored the issue of feeling and emotion in the international landscape, concluding that postromanticism, which relied on trite formulae that did not allow achievement of sincerity, had been even worse than neoclassicism, which was elitist and did not have a "foundation in the community, roots in a complete universe."[107] Sopeña again suggested Messiaen and folklore as potential inspirations to compose music that was a reflection of the community while elevating the individual toward God.[108]

OTHER CRITICS ON MODERNIST MUSIC

Sopeña's steady commitment to discussing and reviewing contemporary music certainly singles him out from the other critics writing in early

Francoism. The 1940s in Spanish music have often been portrayed as a reaction against modernism and the avant-garde,[109] and in general terms there was a return to more traditional ways of understanding music. The 1940s saw a new golden age for composers of the older generation who practiced various brands of nationalism (Turina, Gómez, del Campo, Benito García de la Parra) and for younger composers who were, again, closer to Rodrigo or *andalucista* Falla then they were to Stravinsky, Schoenberg, or the Grupo de los Ocho (among that younger set, José Moreno Gans, Jesús García Leoz, Ángel Martín Pompey, José Muñoz Molleda). Similarly, a majority of critics were much less interested in, and much more critical of, modernist styles of music than Sopeña was.

Nevertheless, music critics other than Sopeña writing under Francoism did not share a uniformly negative attitude toward modernism, or to what 1940s critics and music historians usually labeled *música moderna* (modern) or *contemporánea* (contemporary),[110] which, broadly speaking, included Debussy, Richard Strauss, Schoenberg, Falla, Stravinsky, Ravel, and Dukas.[111] Most of the critics, coming from differing backgrounds and generations, found themselves sympathizing with some of these composers more than with others, which makes it difficult to uniformly characterize the attitude of Spanish music critics of early Francoism toward modernism. A further issue is that critics were not always knowledgeable of the music they were writing about. This was true especially of the early 1940s, with the Second World War and Franco's *autarquía* making it difficult for scores to be circulated and for new works to be performed in Spain. But in some cases it extended beyond these early years; Shostakovich was mentioned several times in the Spanish press between 1946 and 1948 as an example of the Soviet Union's rigid control of music, thus providing an opportunity to implicitly make the Franco regime appear more liberal by comparison, though most critics openly admitted they did not know Shostakovich's works.[112] This, however, did not prevent some of them from passing negative judgment on the Russian's music[113] or his submissive attitude and reluctance to defend his artistic autonomy.[114]

In other respects, however, as time moved on critics became familiar with a wider range of music and sometimes their opinions changed as a result; they also changed as a result of having moved on to a climate in which *autarquía* and self-sufficiency were no longer a badge of national pride and in which some of the most conspicuous traits of Civil War and early Francoism discourse (open racism and anti-Semitism, and a focus on physical annihilation of Spain's enemies) were slowly becoming anachronistic. An illustrative example was, from 1943 onward, a certain surge of interest in British contemporary music, as Spain tried to detach itself from the Axis and, later on, join the Western Bloc. British orchestral contemporary music was indeed a rarity in Madrid programs before 1945,[115] but from 1946 on several works by Britten were performed in Madrid for the first time (*Variations on a Theme by Frank Bridge, Simple Symphony, Sarabande, Passacaglia*), with music critics reacting positively and even enthusiastically.[116]

Giménez Caballero's ideas on art were certainly an important, although not the only, influence on a number of critics, particularly in writings published during the Civil War or shortly thereafter—although, unlike in Sopeña, such influences were not absorbed consistently so as to formulate a cohesive approach to modernist music. For example, at the beginning of the Civil War, Manuel Quesada agreed with Giménez Caballero in considering the avant-garde as the product of both an elitist approach brought over by the capitalist economy ("the divorce between producers and consumers . . . , the cause of which is primarily the materialistic politics of the years after the First World War") and the influence of Marxism "and its desire to destroy everything which means spirituality and culture, faith and devotion to the splendor of the Fatherland." The ultimate cause of both capitalism and Marxism was, in Quesada's opinion, Judaism.[117] Interestingly, among those composers who had managed to escape the avant-garde and were instead contributing to the momentum of Spanish music, Quesada named Falla, Turina, Jesús Guridi, and del Campo—but also Ernesto Halffter, who was closer to the elitist, avant-garde approach Quesada so despised.

Rodrigo's reservations about the radio and its harmful role in the development and dissemination of the avant-garde before the Civil War show a similar anticapitalistic, anti-industrial focus. He argued that the radio "falsified harmonic function, adulterated melodic progression and produced moody and meaningless music," in international modernism "and its sequel in Spain."[118] This, however, should not be read as proof that Francoist music critics, or even Rodrigo himself, were staunch luddites: Rodrigo acknowledged the important role radio could play in disseminating Spanish music,[119] which is fully consonant with the importance paid to radio as a propaganda tool in early Francoism.[120] However, this being a mere months after the end of the war and with some of the members of the Grupo de los Ocho having been actively involved in radio programming (Bacarisse, Fernando Remacha), it makes sense to read Rodrigo's remark as a rebuttal against those who were highly visible when he was starting his career rather than as a full-fledged antitechnological stance.

But it was perhaps Giménez Caballero's focus on emotion, feeling, and even the irrational that was his most influential legacy on Spanish critics reviewing modernist works. Conrado del Campo claimed in an interview that no one should feel ashamed "to feel emotion under the charm of a pure melody dressed with simple clothes" and confessed that he could not understand "those who think that music should not be a reflection of the most intimate feelings of the artist who writes it," by which he was likely referring to the self-confessed attempts at avoiding sentimentalism of the Grupo de los Ocho (some of whom, interestingly enough, had studied under del Campo at the Conservatorio de Madrid). Del Campo instead advocated going back to a "more sincere, emotional and disinterested way of thinking about musical problems."[121] In a similar attack on the Grupo's and Salazar's influence on music policies during the Second Republic, P. Yáñez wrote shortly after the war that "Because of those members of society who should direct and educate the audiences' taste, the audiences seem to increasingly veer towards easy and burlesque music." He then went on to deplore how feeling and humanity were nowhere to be found in modern art, and that "some prove a certain kind of silly pride when they abstain themselves from the great human emotions contained by works such as Franck's or Beethoven's."[122]

This did not mean, however, that emotion, feeling, sincerity, or lyricism could not be injected into works that otherwise exhibited the usual stylistic features of modernism, thus rendering it more acceptable and even desirable; many critics did not have an issue with specific musical techniques such as dissonance, polytonality, or atonality, but rather with the use of such elements to (it was feared) alienate audiences and avoid expressing any kind of emotional content. On the occasion of the first performance of the Portuguese composer Fernando Lopes-Graça's piano concerto in Madrid, de las Heras could not hide his bewilderment in writing that the work's construction was "bizarre, polytonal," but it was ultimately redeemed by its "sincerity" and its "hunger for truth," which Lopes-Graça had supposedly achieved by taking inspiration from two masterpieces of Spanish modernism: the asceticism and synthetic language of Falla's *Retablo* and the popular cheerfulness of Ernesto Halffter's *Rapsodia portuguesa*.[123] Similarly, Sáinz de la Maza enthusiastically wrote about a number of contemporary Chilean works performed in 1947 in Madrid[124] because, "in spite of the advanced language in which they are written, they are filled with a rough and ardent lyricism."[125]

It is no coincidence, however, that both de las Heras and Sáinz de la Maza were referring to Iberian and Ibero-American music respectively, since feeling and emotion were often understood as intrinsically Iberian, Mediterranean, or Latin characteristics. This made the avant-garde trends of the 1920s and 1930s even more harmful; they were not only negative for music itself, but also profoundly anti-Spanish and contrary to perceived national values. Antonio de las Heras described Stravinsky's neoclassicism as "glittering fireworks" that had attracted the attention of Spanish composers and thus destroyed the "racial elements" that, in de las Heras's opinion, should be the foundation of Spanish music. This negative influence had disappeared, it was said, only after the Civil War.[126] Composer José Forns, who also taught aesthetics of music at the Conservatorio de Madrid, praised the Italian composers of the Generazione dell'Ottanta (Casella, Respighi, Pizzetti) because they were respectful in their revisiting of the old Italian masters, injecting "vitality and human passion" in every rendition and fully following "ethnic characteristics" such as *chiaroscuro* and contrast in the musical phrases to avoid "intellectualism," which Forns regarded as a negative trait in music.[127]

Concerns about feeling and emotion also informed responses to Schoenberg and Stravinsky, possibly the two most contested and controversial modernist composers in early Francoism. Before the Civil War, the music of Schoenberg was certainly not universally embraced by music critics, not even those most firmly committed to modernism; it is true that Roberto Gerhard brought the music of the Second Viennese School, and even some of its members, to Barcelona, but responses there were mixed,[128] and Salazar never took Schoenberg, or his students such as Gerhard, too seriously.[129] But at least some publications, even if not fully enthusiastic about Schoenberg's ideas, discussed his project as the continuation of the Austro-Germanic tradition and hypothesized that, in the future, his work could become orthodoxy, in the same way Beethoven's and Wagner's had.[130] Salazar, as co-editor of *Nuestra Música*, which he founded in Mexico together with other Republican exiles, did commission and print an article by Schoenberg as part of a series in which composers wrote about their own aesthetics.[131] In Francoist Spain, by contrast, the music of Schoenberg had all but disappeared from concert programs, mentions in music criticism were scarce and dismissive,[132] and even the few critics who showed some familiarity with Schoenberg's techniques and approach to music, such as Monsalvatge and Forns, acknowledged his merit in sketching and developing new channels for expression but were severe in judging the outcomes. Montsalvatge admitted that Schoenberg could be deemed "a genius" due to his perseverance, but when it came to the music, he judged it as "intellectual, cold, deprived of emotion"[133]; Forns highlighted the "seriousness" of his musical constructions but doubted that Schoenberg's theories could be a fruitful influence on younger composers.[134]

Unlike Schoenberg, Stravinsky was generally considered a composer at least worth engaging with, and he was indeed the living non-Spanish composer who appeared most frequently in Spanish concert programs: *Jeux de Cartes, Petrouchka, The Firebird,* the Violin Concerto, and *L'Histoire du Soldat* were all performed by Madrid orchestras during the 1940s, and certainly Spanish critics knew Stravinsky's works better than they knew Schoenberg's or Shostakovich's. He enjoyed, at least on some level, the sympathy of the regime; at the beginning of the Civil War, he joined a group of French intellectuals in signing a manifesto in support of Franco,[135] and the Spanish government reciprocated by naming him an honorary member of the Academia de Bellas Artes de San Fernando. The criticism he received from the Soviet Union also earned him some praise, and he certainly had passionate supporters among Spanish music critics. Turina, in his inaugural speech at the Academia in 1940, praised Stravinsky because, like Bach and Beethoven, he had never totally abandoned tonality and at the same time introduced important innovations in musical form; Schoenberg, in contrast, had abandoned tonality, thus dehumanizing his music, but kept traditional musical forms as "old skeletons."[136] Montsalvatge appreciated Stravinsky's connection to "the milestones of Western civilization," with his music being intrinsically anti-communist and Christian.[137]

For other critics, however, Stravinsky still represented the main pillar in dehumanization of music, or, as put by Sáinz de la Maza in his review of *L'Histoire du soldat,* the "caricature-like, brutal way of expression which debases musical language with the most insolent nonchalance and the most premeditated aggressiveness."[138] Sáinz de la Maza argued that Stravinsky was to be blamed for introducing such ways of understanding music in Spain and leading Spanish composers to write "nonsense" during the 1920s and 1930s.[139] Sopeña likely played a significant role in disseminating the notion of Stravinsky as a symbol of dehumanization, and his comparison of Falla and Stravinsky as to their different approaches to emotion and feeling was repeatedly reused by several writers on music; for del Campo, Stravinsky was intrinsically "sad," which Falla, with his focus on feeling and emotion, was not.[140] Rafael Sánchez Mazas, a well-known falangist writer who occasionally wrote on music as well, found "elements of destruction, revolution and even of fury and cruelty" in Stravinsky's music; these elements, he stated, were nowhere to be found in Falla.[141]

SOPEÑA: THE MUSIC CRITIC OF EARLY FRANCOISM?

Sopeña's influence in shaping understandings of Spanish music did go beyond the Stravinsky-Falla dichotomy some of his contemporaries reproduced, or beyond his portrayal of Rodrigo as the composer Spanish audiences were waiting for after the Civil War. Indeed, as one of the few writers on Spanish contemporary music during the 1940s and through the remainder of the Franco regime, Sopeña has been and still is extensively quoted as a secondary source in bibliographies of Spanish music of the twentieth century and even the nineteenth century.[142] He can therefore be considered successful in his attempt at becoming Salazar's successor and acting not only as a reviewer of musical life under Francoism, but also as a historian who selected, recorded, and filled with meaning for posterity those composers, works, and events he considered worthy of being part of the Spanish canon.

It is more doubtful, however, that he was successful in promoting his specific brand of Spanish modernism among young composers and other critics; for example, when Messiaen visited Madrid and Barcelona for the first time in 1949, Sopeña was highly enthusiastic of his music as a potential model for Spanish composers, but other critics were far more skeptic, and it cannot be said that Messiaen exerted a transforming influence on Spanish composers.[143] And although Sopeña, during his tenure as director of the Conservatorio de Madrid, befriended and mentored a number of young composers who would then go on to become some of the main names of the Spanish avant-garde from the late 1950s, such as Cristóbal Halffter, these young composers did not draw mainly on nationalism and religious inspiration but rather on the European post-1945 avant-garde, and ultimately on Webern's legacy, which Sopeña would probably have regarded as dehumanized. [144] In contrast, the Spanish avant-garde, despite its aspirations to universalism, had a very clear commitment to renovating Spanish music *qua* Spanish music, in the same way as Sopeña had; much importance was placed by avant-garde composers on absorbing the various international avant-garde trends as a way of helping Spanish music evolve and develop, and reach a standard worthy of a civilized country.[145] And although the historiography of Spanish twentieth-century music—some of it written by avant-garde composers themselves—has tended to regard the avant-garde as ubiquitous from the late 1950s onward,[146] it cannot be forgotten that Sopeña's protégé, Joaquín Rodrigo, did manage to sustain a successful career during the later decades of Francoism while essentially remaining loyal to the style and postulates of the *Concierto de Aranjuez*, which Sopeña so praised in his writings. It can be argued that the not-always-straightforward success and influence of Sopeña's legacy under Francoism mirrors, in a way, the Falange's. Sopeña was not able to lead renovation of Spanish music according to his own postulates, in the same way as the Falange's hopes of national rebirth were shattered by the mid-1940s[147]; nevertheless, both the Falange and Sopeña managed to adapt and survive through the remaining decades of the Franco regime, and to reshape some of their discourse so that it became a significant milestone of the regime.

One reason Sopeña was able to remain influential was the broader appeal some elements of his theory of modernist music could have for other factions of the regime that were not necessarily fascist. Indeed, how Sopeña integrated traditional music and Spanish church music into his discourse on modernist music—and the fact that such a discourse was, in the first place, directed toward creating something specifically new *and* Spanish—is heavily reminiscent of Giménez Caballero, but, at the same time, it could easily be absorbed by various critics from different political backgrounds, writing under the Franco regime: interest in traditional and early music, which Sopeña had named as the milestones of the rebirth of Spanish music, had been commonplace in Spanish musical life at least since the late nineteenth century, with Felipe Pedrell. In other words, this does not mean that all mentions—and there are many—of Spanish traditional or early music in music criticism in the early Franco era must be understood as an influence of Sopeña, of Giménez Caballero, or of fascism more generally; very often, music critics who, coming from very diverse backgrounds, had become interested in traditional or early music found themselves adapting their writings on such subjects to the new circumstances. It was not always easy to do so, and Sopeña, for all of his enthusiasm, called folklore and early music "the two most rebellious fields" in Spanish musical life.[148] The vicissitudes of some of the critics in overcoming these difficulties will be the focus of the next two chapters.

NOTES

1. The first performance of the *Concierto* took place in Barcelona on November 9, 1940, with Sáinz de la Maza as the soloist accompanied by the Orquesta Filarmónica de Barcelona under César Mendoza Lassalle.
2. Federico Sopeña, *Historia de la música española contemporánea* (Madrid: Rialp, 1958), 196 and 246–247.
3. Sopeña, "Vicente Salas Viu," *Cuadernos Hispanoamericanos*, no. 216 (1967), 650.
4. According to Sopeña's own narrative, he was initially conscripted by the Republican side but eventually deserted and spent the rest of the war in Madrid in hiding; see Sopeña, *Defensa de una generación* (Madrid: Ediciones Taurus, 1970), 20; Sopeña, *Escrito de noche* (Madrid: Espasa Calpe, 1985), 63–65.
5. Sopeña, *Escrito*, 174.
6. Ibid., 174.
7. Ibid., 175.
8. Joaquín Turina, unpublished diary, Jan. 1–Dec. 31, 1940, 13 April.
9. Federico Sopeña, *Vida y obra de Manuel de Falla* (Madrid: Turner Música, 1988), 229.

10. Santos Juliá, "¿Falange liberal o intelectuales fascistas?" *Claves de razón práctica*, no. 121 (2002), 2.

11. Dionisio Ridruejo, "Excluyentes y comprensivos," *El Ateneo*, no. 8 (1952), 5.

12. Ibid.

13. The first retrospective study attempting to portray the Falange Liberal as internal dissidents within the regime can be considered to be José Carlos Mainer, *Falange y literatura* (Barcelona: Labor, 1971). More recent studies reject this hypothesis, arguing instead that the Falange Liberal was fully aligned with the ideology and goals of early Francoism; see Santos Juliá, "La Falange liberal o de cómo la memoria inventa el pasado," in *Autobiografía en España: un balance*, ed. María Ángeles Hermosilla Álvarez and Celia Fernández Prieto (Madrid: Visor Libros, 2004), 127–144; Juliá, "¿Falange liberal o intelectuales fascistas?" 4–13; Eduardo Iáñez, *No parar hasta conquistar: propaganda y política cultural falangista: el grupo de "Escorial", de la ocupación del Nuevo Estado a la posteridad (1936–1986)* (Gijón: Trea, 2011).

14. Sopeña, *Defensa*, 20; Sopeña, *Escrito*, 175.

15. Sopeña, *Defensa*, 20.

16. Sopeña, *Escrito*, 169.

17. For example, Sopeña's 1958 history of Spanish music is explicitly presented as a sequel to Salazar's 1930 *La música española contemporánea*: Sopeña, *Historia de la música española*, 13. Sopeña also gave a *laudatio* of Salazar at the Academia de Bellas Artes de San Fernando on the occasion of Salazar's death: Anonymous, "Crónica de la Academia," *Academia*, no. 7 (1958), 109.

18. Letter from Julio Gómez to José Subirá, Mar. 24, 1941, unpublished [BNE, M.SUBIRÁ/1/105].

19. Sopeña, *Defensa*, 20.

20. Sopeña, *Escrito*, 85.

21. These include not only the three Hispanic-German art music festivals in 1941 and 1942, but also a visit to Vienna to participate in the celebrations of the 150th anniversary of Mozart's death in 1941, organized by the Nazi government; Sopeña was joined by Turina, Rodrigo, and José Forns (see Federico Sopeña, "El 150 aniversario de la muerte de Mozart," *Arriba*, Dec. 9, 1941, 6; Sopeña, "El 150 aniversario de la muerte de Mozart," *Arriba*, Dec. 16, 1941, 7). Sopeña also visited Lisbon in 1943 and 1944 with the Orquesta Nacional, to participate in events aimed at promoting Spanish music.

22. See, for example, Federico Sopeña, "Sobre el Conservatorio Nacional," *Arriba*, Oct. 26, 1939, 7; Sopeña, "Otra vez sobre el Conservatorio Nacional," *Arriba*, Nov. 2, 1939, 7.

23. Anonymous, "Crónica cultural. La musicología en España," *Arbor*, vol. 7, no. 20 (1947), 209.

24. Anonymous, "Federico Sopeña," *Arriba*, Oct. 6, 1943, 7.

25. Sopeña, *Escrito*, 176.

26. Adolfo Salazar, "Musicología," *El Sol*, Feb. 20, 1934, 5. See also Salazar, "El estado de la música española al terminar el primer año de la República," *El Sol*, Jan. 1, 1932, 6; Salazar, "La República y el Cancionero de Barbieri," *El Sol*, Apr. 14, 1933, 35.

27. Mario Castelnuovo-Tedesco's first guitar concerto was completed in 1939 and first performed by Andrés Segovia that same year in Uruguay; nevertheless, most critics referred to Rodrigo's concerto as the first guitar concerto ever, suggesting that they were unfamiliar with Castelnuovo-Tedesco's work.

28. Gerardo Diego, "Notas teatrales," *ABC*, Dec. 12, 1940, 10; José María Franco, "Música," *Ya*, Dec. 12, 1940, 6; Joaquín Turina, "Rodrigo de Vivar," *Dígame*, Dec. 17, 1940, 7; Antonio de las Heras, "Música," *Informaciones*, Dec. 12, 1940, 6; Víctor Ruiz Albéniz [as Chispero], "Canta la guitarra," *Informaciones*, Dec. 12, 1940, 6; Anonymous, "Concierto de Aranjuez," *Radio Nacional*, no. 108 (1940), 5.

29. Letter from Nemesio Otaño to Manuel de Falla, Aug. 20, 1941, unpublished [AHSL, 004/010.014].

30. Letter from Julio Gómez to José Subirá, Dec. 25, 1940, unpublished [BNE, M.SUBIRÁ/1/105].

31. Examples written while still under Francoism include Antonio de las Heras, "La música en el año que termina," *Informaciones*, Dec. 31, 1940, 7; Joaquín Rodrigo, "La música en 1940," *Pueblo*, Dec. 31, 1940, 8; de las Heras, "Música," *Informaciones*, June 12, 1942, 6; Regino Sáinz de la Maza, "Informaciones musicales," *ABC*, June 12, 1942, 13.

32. See Tomás Marco, *Spanish Music in the Twentieth Century* (Cambridge and London: Harvard University Press, 1993), 130–131; Pérez Zalduondo, "Continuidades y rupturas en la música española durante el primer franquismo." In *Joaquín Rodrigo y la música española de los años cuarenta*, ed Javier Suárez-Pajares," 70.

33. Suárez-Pajares, "Adolfo Salazar: luz y sombras," in *Música y cultura en la Edad de Plata 1915–1939*, ed. María Nagore, Leticia Sánchez de Andrés, and Elena Torres (Madrid: ICCMU, 2009), 209.

34. Anonymous, "La Orquesta Nacional, en Lisboa," *Arriba*, Apr. 3, 1943, 7.

35. Federico Sopeña, "La música de estos años," *Arriba*, Oct. 1 1943, 3.

36. Sopeña, *Joaquín Rodrigo* (Madrid: Ediciones y Publicaciones Españolas, 1946).

37. Ibid., 9–10 and 39.

38. Federico Sopeña, *Joaquín Turina* (Madrid: Ediciones y Publicaciones Españolas, 1946).

39. Manuel de Falla, *Escritos sobre música y músicos* (Buenos Aires: Espasa Calpe, 1950).

40. Gilbert Chase's *The Music of Spain* was originally published in 1941, and the Spanish translation (done by a Spanish exile, Jaume Pahissa) was published in Buenos Aires in 1943; however, there is no evidence of either having been circulated in early Francoist Spain. See Gilbert Chase, *The Music of Spain* (New York: Norton, 1941); Chase, *La música de España* (Buenos Aires: Hachette, 1943).

41. Sopeña, *Joaquín Rodrigo,* 40.

42. Sopeña, *Diez años*, 147.

43. Sopeña, *Joaquín Rodrigo,* 39.

44. Sopeña, *Diez años*, 174.

45. Sopeña, *Joaquín Rodrigo,* 40.

46. Sopeña, *Diez años*, 156–159.

47. Ibid., 178.

48. María Palacios, "El *Grupo de los Ocho* bajo el prisma de Adolfo Salazar," in *Música y cultura en la Edad de Plata 1915–1939*, ed. María Nagore, Leticia Sánchez de Andrés, and Elena Torres (Madrid: ICCMU, 2009), 290–292.

49. Sopeña, *Diez años*, 189.

50. Among *los jóvenes* ("the younger ones"), Sopeña named Muñoz Molleda, García Leoz, Vicente Asencio, Miguel Asíns Arbó, Moreno Gans, Matilde Salvador, Montsalvatge, Carlos Suriñach, and Francisco Escudero. *Diez años*, 172.

51. Sopeña, *Joaquín Rodrigo*, 10 and 15.

52. Ibid., 13.

53. Sopeña, *Diez años*, 185.
54. Sopeña, *Joaquín Rodrigo*, 41.
55. Ibid., 84.
56. Ruth Piquer Sanclemente, "Clasicismo, nuevo clasicismo y neoclasicismo. Aproximación al concepto estético de neoclasicismo musical en España," *Revista de Musicología*, no. 28 (2005), 987–989.
57. Sopeña, *Diez años*, 189. See also Sopeña, *Joaquín Rodrigo*, 90.
58. For example, Federico Sopeña, "El nacionalismo en la música de estos años," *Arbor*, vol. 9, no. 27 (1948), 405; Conrado del Campo, "La música," *El Alcázar*, Oct. 31, 1941, 7; Joaquín Rodrigo, "Gran semana de música hispanoalemana," *Pueblo*, Jan. 27, 1942, 7.
59. Joaquín Rodrigo, "Concierto homenaje a Manuel de Falla," *Pueblo*, Oct. 16, 1941, 3.
60. Rodolfo Halffter, "Manuel de Falla y los compositores del Grupo de Madrid de la Generación del 27." In *Rodolfo Halffter. Tema, nueve décadas y final*, ed. Antonio Iglesias (Madrid: Fundación Banco Exterior, 1991), 412; María Palacios, *La renovación musical en Madrid durante la dictadura de Primo de Rivera. El Grupo de los Ocho (1923–1931)* (Madrid: Sociedad Española de Musicología, 2008), 263; Carol A. Hess, *Manuel de Falla and Modernism in Spain, 1898–1936* (Chicago: Chicago University Press, 2001), 270.
61. Rodrigo, "Concierto homenaje," 3.
62. Ibid., 3; Joaquín Rodrigo, "En torno al homenaje a Falla," *Escorial*, no. 12 (1941), 120–124. On Falla's mysticism, see Moreda Rodríguez, "A Catholic, a Patriot, a Good Modernist: Manuel de Falla and the Francoist Musical Press," *Hispanic Research Journal*, vol. 14, no. 3 (2013), 217–220. On Collet's concept of Spanish musical mysticism, see Samuel Llano, *Whose Spain? Negotiating Spanish Music in Paris, 1908–1929* (New York: Oxford University Press, 2012), 69–77; Pilar Ramos López, "Mysticism as a Key Concept of Spanish Early Music Historiography," in *Early Music—Context and Ideas II. International Conference in Musicology* (Cracow: University of Cracow, 2008), campusvirtual.unirioja.es/titulaciones/musica/fotos/13_ramos.pdf (accessed April 2014).
63. Federico Sopeña, "Homenaje a Falla," *Arriba*, Oct. 16, 1941, 3.
64. Anonymous, "La Orquesta Nacional, en Lisboa," 4.
65. Federico Sopeña, "Música, ausencias y homenaje," *Arriba*, Oct. 17, 1939, 6.
66. Federico Sopeña, "Igor Strawinsky," *Radio Nacional*, no. 163 (1941), 5. See also Sopeña, "Igor Strawinsky," *Radio Nacional*, no. 161 (1941), 7; and Sopeña, "Igor Strawinsky," *Radio Nacional*, no. 162 (1941), 6.
67. Sopeña, *Dos años de música en Europa* (Madrid: Espasa Calpe, 1942), 65–66.
68. Sopeña, "*Strawinsky*, de Alexandre Tansman," *Arbor*, vol. 12, no. 37 (1949), 152–153.
69. See, for example, in the visual arts María Isabel García Cabrera, *Tradición y vanguardia en el pensamiento artístico español (1939–1959)* (Granada: Universidad de Granada, 1998); for playwriting, Sultana Wahnón, "The Theatre Aesthetics of the Falange," in *Fascism and Theatre: Comparative Studies on the Aesthetics and Politics of Performance in Europe, 1925–45*, ed. Gunter Berghaus (Providence, RI, and Oxford: Berghahn, 1996), 191–209.
70. Douglas W. Foard, *The Revolt of the Aesthetes: Ernesto Giménez Caballero and the Origins of Spanish Fascism* (New York: Lang, 1989), 25; Aránzazu Ascunce Arenas, *Barcelona and Madrid: Social Networks of the Avant-Garde* (Lewisburg, PA: Bucknell University Press, 2012), 158.
71. Douglas W. Foard, "The Forgotten Falangist: Ernesto Giménez Caballero," *Journal of Contemporary History*, vol. 10, no. 1 (1975), 10.

72. Ibid., 10–11.
73. Ernesto Giménez Caballero, *La nueva Catolicidad. Teoría general del Fascismo en Europa, en España* (Madrid: Ediciones de La Gaceta Literaria, 1933), 107.
74. Foard, "The Forgotten Falangist," 5.
75. Giménez Caballero, *La nueva Catolicidad*, 210.
76. Foard, *The Revolt*, 205–206.
77. Ernesto Giménez Caballero, *Arte y estado* (Madrid: Ediciones de La Gaceta Literaria, 1935), 124.
78. Ibid., 54.
79. Ibid., 129.
80. Ibid., 57.
81. Ibid., 54.
82. Ibid., 201.
83. Ibid., 185–190, 202.
84. Ibid., 161.
85. Ibid., 126.
86. Ibid., 193 and 195.
87. Peter Davies and Derek Lynch, *The Routledge Companion to Fascism and the Far Right* (London: Routledge, 2002), 90.
88. Giménez Caballero, *Arte y estado*, 54 and 153.
89. Giménez Caballero, *La nueva Catolicidad*, 107.
90. Giménez Caballero, *Arte y estado*, 263.
91. Ibid., 204. See also Ernesto Giménez Caballero, "Por la radio se va derecho al cielo," *Radio Nacional*, no. 17 (1939), 5.
92. Federico Sopeña, "La música europea de estos años," *Arbor*, vol. 8, no. 23 (1947) 165–177; Sopeña, "El nacionalismo en la música," 401–476; Sopeña, "El problema de la música contemporánea," *Arbor*, vol. 19, no. 67–68 (1951), 449–456.
93. Anonymous, "Crónica," *Anuario Musical*, 6 (1951), 230. On Sopeña's tenure at the Conservatoire, see Contreras, "El 'empeño apostólico-literario' de Federico Sopeña," in *Los señores de la crítica. Periodismo musical e ideología del modernismo en Madrid (1900–1950)*, ed. Teresa Cascudo and María Palacios (Sevilla: Doble J, 2011), 331–335.
94. A well-known example was Laín Entralgo's essay *España como problema*, published in 1948, which argued that utopian visions of Spain had not thus far materialized in a project for Spain, to which Calvo Serer replied in *España, sin problema* that such tensions between utopian visions had already been resolved by the Franco regime through regeneration of Catholicism. See Pedro Laín Entralgo, *España como problema* (Madrid: Seminario de Problemas Hispanoamericanos, 1948); Rafael Calvo Serer, *España, sin problema* (Madrid: Rialp, 1949).
95. Federico Sopeña, "Joaquín Rodrigo, crítico musical," *Música. Revista Quincenal*, no. 16 (1945), 6.
96. For example, Sopeña, "La música en la Generación del 98," *Arbor*, vol. 11, no. 36 (1948), 459–464.
97. Sopeña, "Notas sobre la música contemporánea," *Escorial*, no. 3 (1941), 101–122; Sopeña "Joaquín Turina," *Escorial*, no. 7 (1941), 244–288.
98. Foard, "The Forgotten Falangist," 4.
99. Sopeña, "La música europea," 165.
100. Ibid., 177.
101. Ibid., 167.
102. Ibid., 168.

103. Ibid., 177.
104. Ibid., 173.
105. Sopeña, "El nacionalismo en la música," 404.
106. Ibid., 474–475.
107. Sopeña, "El problema de la música contemporánea," 450–452.
108. Ibid., 454.
109. Such a paradigm of the music of early Francoism as not only a conservative but specifically an antimodernist nadir has certainly been predominant in many studies about the period. See, for example, Gemma Pérez Zalduondo, "La utilización de la figura y la obra de Felip Pedrell en el marco de la exaltación nacionalista de posguerra (1939–1945)," *Recerca Musicològica*, no. 11–12 (1991), 467–487; Ignacio Henares Cuéllar and María Isabel Cabrera García, "El conflicto modernidad-tradición. La fundamentación crítica en la preguerra y su culminación en el Franquismo," in *Dos décadas de cultura artística en el Franquismo*, ed. Ignacio Henares Cuéllar, María Isabel Cabrera García, Gemma Pérez Zalduondo, and José Castillo Ruiz (Granada: Universidad de Granada, 1991), 31–57; Michael Walter, "Music of Seriousness and Commitment: The 1930s and Beyond," in *The Cambridge History of Twentieth-Century Music*, ed. Nicholas Cook and Anthony Pople (Cambridge: Cambridge University Press, 2004), 286–305.
110. These are indeed the words critics most frequently employed to refer to the music of their time, with *modernista* and *vanguardista* being used mostly in a derogatory manner (Antonio Fernández-Cid, "Música," *Arriba*, Mar. 1, 1949, 7; Joaquín Turina, "La nueva España musical," *Radio Nacional*, no. 50 (1939), 13.
111. A. Albert Torrellas, *Historia de la música* (Barcelona: Seix Barral, 1942), 80–84; Rafael Benedito, *Historia de la música* (Madrid: Sección Femenina de FET y de las JONS, 1946), 180–190; José Subirá [as Jesús A. Ribó], *Historia universal de la música* (Madrid: Plus Ultra, 1945), 462–473.
112. Pedro Carré, "Shostakovich, el compositor enigma," *Ritmo*, no. 208 (1948), 8; Federico Sopeña, "Una sinfonía rusa," *Alférez*, no. 1 (1947). Further examples of news stories focusing on Shostakovich's situation under the Zhdanov decree but not making any reference to Shostakovich's music are Anonymous, "Música 'capitalista y retrógrada' se estrenará en el Metropolitan," *Pueblo*, Feb. 14, 1948, 5; Anonymous, "Reacciones anticomunistas de Hollywood," *La Vanguardia*, May 8, 1948, 7; M. Blanco Tobío, "Música antidemocrática," *Pueblo*, Feb. 12, 1948, 5.
113. Carlos Suriñach, "Estados que intervienen en las creaciones musicales," *Música. Revista Quincenal*, no. 27 (1946), 14. Suriñach, a composer himself, admitted that he did not know Shostakovich's symphonies but hypothesized that they were "long, innocent bores in the style of Bruckner and Tchaikovsky."
114. Xavier Montsalvatge, "Strawinsky y Shostakovich, polos opuestos," *La Vanguardia Española*, Aug. 7, 1948, 8.
115. The exceptions were Vaughan Williams's *Fantasia on a Theme by Thomas Tallis* (performed by the Orquesta Nacional in March 1943) and *London Symphony* (again by the Orquesta Nacional in November 1944), which were generally praised for their respect for English folk and art music; see Regino Sáinz de la Maza, "Informaciones musicales," *ABC*, Mar. 25, 1943, 16; Joaquín Rodrigo, "Música," *Pueblo*, Mar. 25, 1943, 7; Rodrigo, "Música," *Pueblo*, Nov. 25, 1944, 7.
116. For example, José Forns, "La sociedad internacional para la música contemporánea ha reanudado sus actividades," *Harmonía*, no. 32 (1947), 11; Regino Sáinz de la Maza, "Informaciones musicales," *ABC*, Nov. 11, 1947, 16.

117. Manuel Quesada, "La música y su influencia en la cultura nacional," *Ideal de Granada*, Dec. 27, 1936, 2.
118. Joaquín Rodrigo, "La música en la radiodifusión," *Radio Nacional*, no. 52 (1939), 12.
119. Ibid., 12.
120. For example, Ramón Serrano Suñer in an interview, Anonymous, "Una conversación sobre Radio con el Excelentísimo sr. Ministro del Interior," *Radio Nacional*, no. 1 (1939), 3; Nemesio Otaño, "La música de las emisoras de radio," *Ritmo*, no. 145 (1941), 3; Anonymous, "La radio como factor de educación musical," *Radio Nacional*, no. 34 (1939), 3; Anonymous, "Sobre la educación musical de la radio," *Música. Revista Quincenal*, no. 8 (1945), 3.
121. Conrado del Campo, cited by Juan de Alcaraz, "Nuevos juicios sobre la música pura y la música de programa," *Radio Nacional*, no. 237 (1943), 5.
122. P. Yáñez, "César Frank," *Radio Nacional*, no. 42 (1939), 13.
123. Antonio de las Heras, "Música," *Arriba*, Apr. 15, 1942, 7.
124. These included Domingo Santa Cruz's *Canción de cuna*; Alfonso Leng's *Preludio* and *Cima*; Alfonso Letelier's *Canción de cuna*, *Balada*, and *Suite grotesca*; and Próspero Bisquert's *Piezas*.
125. Regino Sáinz de la Maza, "Noticias musicales," *ABC*, Feb. 28, 1947, 17.
126. Antonio de las Heras, "El primer problema que plantea la música española," *Arriba*, Nov. 7, 1943, 7.
127. José Forns, "Siluetas radiofónicas de grandes músicos. El moderno renacimiento italiano," *Radio Nacional*, 136 (1941), 14.
128. José María García Laborda, "Compositores de la Segunda Escuela de Viena en Barcelona," *Revista de Musicología*, vol. 23, no. 1 (2000), 187–220; Diego Alonso Tomás, "Música nacional de categoría universal: catalanismo, modernidad y folclore en el ideario estético de Roberto Gerhard tras el magisterio Schönberguiano (1929–31)," in *Discursos y prácticas musicales nacionalistas (1900–1970)*, ed. Pilar Ramos López (Logroño: Universidad de La Rioja, 2012), 255–275.
129. Javier Suárez-Pajares, "Adolfo Salazar: luz y sombras." In *Música y cultura en la Edad de Plata 1915–1939*, ed. María Nagore, Leticia Sánchez de Andrés, and Elena Torres (Madrid: ICCMU, 2009), 211.
130. Anonymous, "Schönberg," *Ritmo*, no. 69 (1933), 7–9.
131. Arnold Schoenberg, "Mi evolución," *Nuestra música*, no. 16 (1949).
132. For example, Federico Sopeña, "Schönberg-Bartok," *Arriba*, Oct. 26, 1950, 7.
133. Xavier Montsalvatge, "Schoenberg o la música atomizada," *La Vanguardia Española*, July 25, 1951, 5.
134. José Forns, "Arnold Schoenberg," *La Vanguardia Española*, Sep. 6, 1944, 7.
135. Norberto Almandoz, "Leyendo libros," *Ritmo*, no. 136 (1940), 8.
136. Joaquín Turina, "La arquitectura en música," reprinted in *Escritos de Joaquín Turina*, ed. Antonio Iglesias (Madrid: Alpuerto, 1982), 45–47.
137. Montsalvatge, "Strawinsky y Shostakovich," 17.
138. Regino Sáinz de la Maza, "Informaciones musicales," *ABC*, Apr. 1, 1948, 17.
139. Victorino Echevarría, "Aspectos: tema con variaciones," *Boletín del Colegio de Directores de Bandas de Música Civiles*, no. 29 (1945), 8.
140. Conrado del Campo, "Música," *El Alcázar*, Mar. 13, 1946, 8.
141. Rafael Sánchez Mazas, "Ha muerto en la Argentina el maestro Falla," *Arriba*, Nov. 15, 1946, 3.
142. A recent example is Walter Aaron Clark and William Craig Krause, *Federico Moreno Torroba: A Musical Life in Three Acts* (New York: Oxford University Press, 2013), 240.

143. Federico Sopeña, "Música," *Arriba*, Mar. 1, 1949, 6; José Luis Pinillas, "Crónica cultural," *Arbor*, vol. 12, no. 40 (1949), 611; see also Germán Gan Quesada, "Three Decades of Messiaen's Music in Spain: A Brief Survey, 1945–1978," in *Messiaen Perspectives 2: Techniques, Influence and Reception*, ed. Christopher Dingle and Robert Fallon (Farnham: Ashgate, 2013), 301–322.

144. Tomás Marco, *Spanish Music in the Twentieth Century* (Cambridge and London: Harvard University Press, 1993), 155–157.

145. Ibid., 156; Tomás Marco, *Música española de vanguardia* (Madrid: Guadarrama, 1970), 15–19.

146. Ibid., 27–28; Germán Gan Quesada, "A la altura de las circunstancias … Continuidad y pautas de renovación en la música española," in *Historia de la música en España e Hispanoamérica, vol. 7: La música en España en el siglo XX*, ed. Alberto González Lapuente (Ciudad de México: Fondo de Cultura Económica, 2012), 169.

147. Stanley G. Payne, *Fascism in Spain, 1923–1977* (Madison: University of Wisconsin Press, 1999), 398.

148. Sopeña, *Joaquín Rodrigo*, 29.

CHAPTER 3

The Sound of *Hispanidad*

Reviewing Early Music

In November 1939, the mortal remains of José Antonio Primo de Rivera were carried on falangists' shoulders from Alicante, where Primo de Rivera had been executed on November 20, 1936, to the sixteenth-century monastery of El Escorial, some thirty miles northwest of Madrid. The solemn state funerals confirmed José Antonio, as he was commonly referred to under the regime, as the most conspicuous martyr of the Civil War and further stimulated his personality cult, which lasted through the Franco regime to our day. It was not by chance that the monastery of El Escorial had been chosen to host José Antonio's tomb: a magnificent work of architecture, it was built by Philip II as a burial place for his father, Charles V, with both monarchs having been behind Spain's colonial expansion in America and the Pacific; it had been described by Giménez Caballero as the ultimate artwork and a symbol of Spanish genius[1]; and its architecture was considered to be monumental yet austere, said to mirror the Spanish character.[2] Franco himself had been given the keys of the monastery, and he walked into and out of it under a canopy in a ceremony aimed at confirming him as the head of state, legitimized by the grace of God, shortly after the end of the Civil War.[3]

The music for Primo de Rivera's state funeral was not left to chance either. Nemesio Otaño, who both organized the event and reviewed it for *Radio Nacional*, selected Tomás Luis de Victoria's *Officium Defunctorum* ("the eternal voice of the Church, one, holy, Catholic and apostolic") and sixteenth- and seventeenth-century trumpet fanfares ("the war sounds of imperial Spain, the sounds which accompanied our deeds in the highest peak of our military power and conquests") as the background music for the funeral.[4] Both Victoria's work and the trumpet fanfares had been composed in the years of the Spanish Empire, which the Franco regime, consonant with principles of *Hispanidad*, was trying to revive. Indeed, the music of the Spanish empire occupied a privileged position not only in José Antonio's funeral, but also in Francoist music criticism more generally: polyphonists (Victoria, Morales, Guerrero), organists (Cabezón, Cabanilles), *vihuelistas* (Narváez, Millán, Fuenllana), and theoreticians (Ramos de Pareja) had all composed their music and written their works in the same period in which Spain, under the rule of the Austrias, became the most powerful nation in the world and a bulwark of Catholic orthodoxy in the face of the rise of Protestantism. This does not mean that Spanish early music was constantly played in state-sponsored concerts and on Spanish radio, on the contrary, whereas Martínez Torner had complained that there were precious few opportunities to hear Spanish early music live in Spain under the Second Republic,[5] the situation had all but changed under Francoism, and critics were well aware of it.[6] Exceptions were few and included the guitar recitals of Sáinz de la Maza performing the *vihuela* repertoire and the visits to Madrid of a few choirs and *escolanías* (children's choirs) from the provinces performing Spanish polyphony.

Nevertheless, there were other ways in which Spanish early music could be disseminated among generalist audiences, thus escaping the boundaries of academic monographs and journals. Otaño regularly wrote for nonspecialist publications as a music critic, and so did Anglès, also a priest and a musicologist. Though not a full-time, professional musicologist, Julio Gómez also regularly expressed his thoughts and concerns about Spanish early music and its research under the new regime. These three writers on Spanish early music, united by a shared love of the repertoires and the belief that such repertoires were a milestone in shaping Spanish identity, and coming from contrasting backgrounds and political positions, differed in their understanding of the link between Spanish early music and national identity, and how could it be better researched and promoted.

NEMESIO OTAÑO: UNVEILING THE EPIC OF SPANISH EARLY MUSIC

Of the three men, Otaño was most actively involved in government musical policies. Born in 1880, he had enjoyed a successful career in church music both in his native Basque Country and in Castile, as an organist, choir master, researcher of liturgical music, composer of the *Motu Proprio* movement, and music critic; he founded and from 1907 to 1922 directed *Música Sacra Hispana,* a magazine specializing in church music. But he never engaged in high-level arts management until the Franco side gave him the opportunity to do so; he spent the first five months of the war in his native Azkoitia, still under the control of the Republican government. As soon as the Francoist troops gained control of the city, Otaño showed his commitment to the cause by giving talks about Spanish music in various cities on the national side.[7] This, together with his efforts in organizing musical life, soon garnered him an influential position, which he kept in the years following the war. Musicians of all kinds and ideologies regularly wrote to Otaño, imploring his protection, pleading with him to give positive reports about them to the Francoist authorities so that they would be allowed to work again, asking for a leg up in the various *oposiciones* and state exams.[8] Even Falla asked for protection for his former student, Ernesto Halffter, and his friend Miguel Salvador[9]; and Enrique Casals managed to enlist Otaño's support to procure a Spanish passport for his exiled brother, Pau Casals.[10]

Otaño's research interests before 1936 focused mostly on liturgical music. During the Civil War, however, he developed expertise in a new area: the military music of Spain, mostly from the time of the Austrias. This was not simply a scholarly pursuit; Otaño explicitly regarded his skills and involvement in musicological research as both a patriotic duty and part of his pastoral mission as a priest. In a letter to Falla in 1938 he announced that he was "stirring up the whole history of Spanish music" to disseminate it "as broadly as possible"; specifically, he was interested in early Spanish military music, "splendid, but known by very few." Otaño felt more at ease (and more attuned with his desire to help the Francoist army win the war) conducting research in the archives than being in charge of the nitty-gritty of organizing musical life on the National side, which he scornfully described as "that fuss which is patriotic music."[11] Otaño's choice of military music as his latest research interest was not at all casual: with Franco himself being a general of the Spanish army and the army having a crucial part in defeating the Second Republic and literally creating the new Spain by military conquest, it is no surprise that militarism played a more significant role under Francoism than it did in the German and Italian fascist regimes. Similarly, some of the key ideas that eventually came together under the concept of *Hispanidad,* such as longing for national regeneration by returning to the past and a providentialist view of the history of Spain, had been significant in military circles since at least the late nineteenth century.[12]

Otaño soon started giving public talks and lecture recitals on Spanish early military music in various Spanish cities on the nationalist side, with local newspapers and the newly created magazines of the Francoist side disseminating and amplifying Otaño's ideas. His archival research soon bore fruit as well, and Spanish military hymns from the past were performed in public again; this led *Radio Nacional* to praise Otaño for having refuted "the legendary claim that Spain's instrumental music was of poor quality" and to compare Antonio Rodríguez de Hita—a seventeenth-century composer of religious, theatrical, and military music—with Gluck and Händel.[13]

Otaño's mission, however, was not to simply inform the public about the forgotten treasures of Spanish military music; consonant with the ideas of *Hispanidad* and national resurrection, the military hymns of the past had to help construct the new Spain of the future. Otaño himself composed a hymn for Franco (*¡Franco! ¡Franco!*) in the style of the music he had been researching in the archives, which Norberto Almandoz, also a priest and Otaño's student, praised in these terms: "The vigorous inspiration of Father Otaño, at the service of such a noble cause, has produced this work. . . . After God and His saints, there is nothing more sacred than the cult to the Fatherland and its heroes."[14] Another significant effort to make archival research relevant for constructing the new Spain was Otaño's campaign to have the *Marcha de Granaderos* readopted as the Spanish national anthem; it had functioned as the national anthem since the 1770s and was replaced by *Himno de Riego* during the Second Republic. By referring to it as *Marcha de Granaderos* instead of the more common *Marcha real*, Otaño (and the press) emphasized the military nature of the march instead of its monarchist implications.[15]

After the war ended, apart from his successive appointments at the Comisaría de Música and the Conservatorio de Madrid, Otaño contributed to reconstructing musical life under the new regime by taking over the directorship of the magazine *Ritmo* after negotiations with Fernando Rodríguez del Río, who had headed the editorial committee after Rogelio Villar's death.[16] The appointment certainly allowed Otaño to extend his already considerable influence into the realm of music criticism, but he admitted in a letter to Anglès that the new appointment was a chore he was taking over simply for the sake of Spanish music:

> I have agreed to take over the directorship because that was the only solution which allowed the magazine to be published and paper to be procured—my colleagues at Prensa y Propaganda will not be able to say no. Moreover, although I have very little time for such things, it was advisable to make an effort so that we musicians can at least have a modest newsletter.[17]

Ritmo, which in the years 1929–1936 focused on concert life in various Spanish cities and general news about contemporary Spanish music, was probably not the most obvious publication from which to disseminate Spanish early music. Nevertheless, under Otaño's directorship, early music did become a significant topic in *Ritmo,* as it was in *Radio Nacional* and *Vértice*; not by chance, the latter two were published by the Delegación Nacional de Prensa, under the control of the Falange. *Ritmo*'s new focus was obvious from its very first issue after the war: Otaño followed the editorial in which the newly relaunched magazine announced its intention of serving the new regime, as has been discussed in Chapter 1, with his own research on the *Marcha de Granaderos*[18]—as if to suggest that reconstruction of the country had started by restoring the national anthem itself. Thanks to his efforts, the *Marcha de Granaderos* was readopted as the national anthem right after the end of the war. Otaño was quick to point out in the article that his research was groundbreaking: no Spanish musicologist, he claimed, had so far devoted any attention to the *Marcha,* "this very transcendental factor of unification and affirmation of our patriotic faith." Spanish musicology had thus failed, he implied, to fulfill its patriotic duties during "the greatest period of decadence of our history, with our long-lived institutions and our centers of spiritual education in decline thanks to nonsensical revolutions and foolish ideas."[19] In a second article for *Ritmo* a few months later, he called for introduction of sixteenth-to-nineteenth-century military music into the Falange-led military training of Spanish boys and young men; every nation, Otaño argued, needed "the military spirit, which means discipline, order, organized strength, safety and defense of the fatherland," and the best way to achieve this in the new Spain was, precisely, by looking back at the past.[20]

Contributors to *Ritmo* other than Otaño also found in the magazine an environment receptive to Spanish early music, including its most characteristic instruments. Just as Sáinz de la Maza and others presented the guitar as the successor of the *vihuela* and therefore an artifact for national regeneration, the organ-building company Organería Española attempted to do the same with its instrument by means of a paid advertisement in *Ritmo*[21]:

When the Glorioso Movimiento Nacional[22] ended and we saw before ourselves the immense load of work which remained to be done after the Marxist destruction, one of the concerns of the shareholders of this business was whether organ building should continue as it had been before the Movimiento, completely subjected to foreign influences, using deficient tubular organs which demanded constant repairs, with only a few exceptions; with incomplete equipment, in a way which is completely contrary to the Spanish taste and soul and the organists of the present days; with nineteenth-century misbalanced, tasteless harmonization, etc.; or whether the time had come to introduce a revolution in our organs in a completely SPANISH sense, creating an entirely SPANISH organ-building industry.

The aftermath of the Civil War was certainly a time of rebirth for Organería Española. The company was founded in 1941 in Azpeitia (very near Otaño's home town of Azkoitia) by Ramón G. Amezúa to continue the legacy of his relative Aquilino Amezúa, a well-known local organ builder deceased in 1912. In the late nineteenth century, Aquilino Amezúa himself had defended the notion of a purely Spanish way of building organs, and wrote a pamphlet on the subject on the occasion of the 1890 Universal Exhibition in Barcelona. Amezúa was, at the time, reacting against the increasing commercial success of French organ builders, who were exporting their organs into the Basque Country and Navarra.[23] What was originally a mixture of nationalism and commercial protectionism in Amezúa's pamphlet was adapted by the newly established Organería Española to fit into the framework of *Hispanidad*: first, the advertisement reflected the notion of the Civil War as a process of cleansing and purification during which all those elements alien to the perceived Spanish essence (Marxism, leftism, etc.) were swept away by the Francoist army, or even expurgated, like illness from a sick body; then, the need for regeneration and reconstruction carefully avoiding foreign influences was highlighted. A few months later, Ramón G. Amezúa made the connection between organ building and *Hispanidad* even clearer in an article published in *Radio Nacional*. Amezúa called for eliminating foreign influences from Spanish organ building as a return to the imperial past; it was indeed under the Spanish empire that Spanish organ music and performance had flourished, with Antonio de Cabezón (1510–1556), Francisco Correa de Arauxo (1584–1654), and Juan Bautista Cabanilles (1644–1712). Again, for Amezúa, revival of the organ was not merely a matter of nostalgia or tradition. He asserted that, after an authentically Spanish school of organ building was established, a blooming national school of composition would soon follow:[24]

> After the Liberation Crusade, now that all our efforts must be aimed at the resurgence of our Fatherland and the dissemination of our imperial tradition to revive the glorious past and return to our greatness, now it is the time to start an energetic campaign to get rid of foreign influences and return to the legitimately Spanish organ.

Ritmo also offered extensive coverage of the centenary of Victoria in 1940,[25] starting with an editorial article in June that encouraged all Spanish musicologists to take advantage of the centenary to thoroughly research the composer's life and works, because "such a great and exemplary figure of universal art and the highest glory of Spanish musical history deserves to admired by everybody, once and for all."[26] Some Spanish musicologists and, more generally, writers and politicians with an interest in Victoria responded to *Ritmo*'s call; subsequent issues of *Ritmo*, until November 1940, all contained at least one article on him,[27] and the year ended with a 112-page themed issue on Victoria, complete with an edition of four of his motets.[28] Otaño was prominently involved in the official celebrations as well, again showing his belief that musicological research had to serve practical ends: government officers for education and the arts travelled to Victoria's hometown of Ávila, in Castile; a mass was celebrated in honor of Victoria; Otaño gave a lecture on Victoria's life and works; and some of Victoria's music was performed. Jesús Rubio, who was then subsecretary for education, gave a speech that illustrates why Victoria was so appealing for the early Franco regime. Rubio defined the notion of empire as "the domination over elements which are, by nature, different to each other," thus referring to the role of Spain in ostensibly bringing together, linguistically, culturally, and religiously, the diverse populations of America and other parts of the world, all the while establishing itself as the bulwark of Catholicism against expansion of Protestantism. Polyphony, Rubio argued, was the musical expression of empire—because polyphony was about bringing disparate melodies together as a unity.[29] Rubio further argued that El Escorial was the best place to listen to Victoria's polyphony, because they both were symbols of the unity of Spain. His polyphony, however, was again not simply a memory from the past, a symbol from a bygone empire; another reason Victoria's music was profoundly Spanish, according to Rubio, was that "a characteristic of Spanish culture is the reproduction of archaic ideals which acquire unexpected novelty and brilliance after having been reshaped in a modern environment."[30]

The Victoria celebrations, however, may not seem as significant as would be expected of a composer of international standing and one so obviously illustrative of *Hispanidad*; they can certainly be considered modest compared with the large Bach, Wagner, or Bruckner festivals of Nazi Germany, or with the celebratory military parades of the Franco regime itself. Even *Ritmo* acknowledged that the celebrations in Ávila were anything but lavish ("There were no impressive official commemorations"[31]), and the only other events to commemorate Victoria's centenary were lectures and lecture recitals by Sopeña in a few cities of the Spanish provinces[32]; but there was no large Victoria festival or concert in Madrid. Nor was the centenary very successful in terms of encouraging performance of Victoria's works: Sopeña complained that the high-profile music festival Quincena Musical de San Sebastián did not include any performances of Victoria's works,[33] and Gómez deplored the centenary not having encouraged Spanish choirs to include more of Victoria's works in their repertoire.[34] Events in Ávila and elsewhere were not extensively featured in the Madrid newspapers and magazines, which did not even send correspondents to cover the events.

The reasons for this relative disinterest must be sought in the fact that the Civil War had only recently ended; with Otaño and other members of the Comisaría busy elsewhere reorganizing musical life in Madrid, it is understandable that preparations for the Victoria celebrations in Ávila had to be rushed. Audiences, however, could still familiarize themselves with Victoria and his role within *Hispanidad* through *Ritmo*. The magazine had originally called for "an in-depth study of Victoria's life and works"[35]; a number of contributors chose to research Victoria's family origins and national identity. Some attention was devoted to the question of whether he should be considered a Spanish or a Roman composer. F. Barberá claimed that other researchers had exaggerated Palestrina's influences on Victoria, whose style, he argued, could not be Palestrinian because he had spent his formative years in Spain, absorbing the "expressivist" principles and technique of what he called the Spanish school of polyphony. Barberá also alluded to Collet's thesis of Spanish musical mysticism to establish a further reason for Victoria being considered Spanish rather than Roman.[36]

Nevertheless, most of the contributors' efforts to establish Victoria's standing as "a genius of the Race"[37] did not focus on whether his years in Rome had turned him into an Italian composer, but rather on whether his family lineage was Castilian and "old" enough—"old" here meaning Christian, not only in the religious but also in the racial sense. Indeed, although the word *raza* had been frequently used in the debates about musical nationalism predating the Civil War, referring to national spirit, essence, or identity rather than to genetic makeup, under the Franco regime *raza* became literal in meaning.[38] Whereas *Hispanidad* was inseparable from Catholicism, it was not enough to simply be a Catholic; one had to be descended from generations of Catholics. *Hispanidad* fully materialized not only after the religious and political unity of Spain was achieved by the Catholic monarchs in 1492; the defeat of Granada, the last Muslim kingdom to survive in the Iberian Peninsula, and the expulsion of the Jews resulted in ethnic unity as well. From then on, *limpieza de sangre* (cleanliness of blood), or being a *cristiano viejo* (old Christian), came to denote not only pure Christian descent but a sign of social status as a true Spanish citizen. Although no longer used to formally discriminate against minorities, *limpieza de sangre* enjoyed a revival in Francoist mythology; for example,

Saint Theresa of Ávila, the sixteenth-century nun, writer, and founder of the Carmelite order, was hailed during the Franco regime as the Saint of the Race (*la santa de la raza*).[39]

Contributors to *Ritmo* were also concerned with establishing Victoria's status as *cristiano viejo*. Although they may simply have been aware that being a *cristiano viejo* was a prerequisite for presenting Victoria as a symbol of *Hispanidad*, it is likely they were trying to respond explicitly to the widespread notion that Victoria had Muslim blood. This claim was first made by the Italian priest and musicologist Giuseppe Baini, in 1828; he apparently mistranslated the "more" in "more hispano" (literally, "in the Spanish style," a formula that was often appended to Victoria's compositions, meaning that the plainchant hymn melody came from the Spanish and not the Roman rite) as "moro" (Moor).[40] None of the authors contributing to *Ritmo* named Baini, although some of them mentioned cryptically other musicologists holding mistaken ideas about Victoria's family origins. The Marquis of Lozoya wrote two articles exploring the genealogy, concluding that although he did not come from an aristocratic family, his ancestors had been "rich merchants" on both maternal and paternal sides; he also paid special attention to those of Victoria's ancestors who had been members of the Church.[41] Ferreol Hernández wrote about Victoria's bloodline, arguing that his Castilian background—and, therefore, his Christian background as well—went back several generations,[42] whereas Fernando del Valle Lersundi rejected the hypothesis that Victoria had been born in poverty; rather, the family had been one of the richest and most respected of sixteenth-century Ávila, which, according to del Valle Lersundi, should be enough to dispel any suspicions about the purity and antiquity of his lineage,[43] with purity and antiquity referring, again, to a *pure* and *old* Christian background.

HIGINIO ANGLÈS: *HISPANIDAD* MEETS PEDRELL

Otaño was not the only priest-musicologist to occupy a prominent position under the Franco regime and write, in the nonspecialist press, about his research and the role of early music in constructing the *Nuevo Estado*. Unlike Otaño, Anglès, as founding director of the Instituto Español de Musicología since 1943, was engaged in musicology full-time, whereas for Otaño it was one of several roles. Although both men came from similar church music backgrounds, had research interests in early music, and held offices in early Francoism, it must not be assumed that their views on Spanish early music and its dissemination to lay audiences were identical;

indeed, although both managed to adapt to the Franco regime and sub-
stantially develop their careers under it, this was probably easier for Otaño
than it was for Anglès.

Born in 1888 in Maspujols (Tarragona, Catalonia), Anglès was ordained
at the Tarragona seminary and then studied musicology in Barcelona under
Felipe Pedrell, regarded as the father of Spanish musicology and a pioneer
in collecting and editing both Spanish traditional and early music. It was
Pedrell who in 1917 got Anglès a position as head of the Music Department
at the Biblioteca Nacional de Catalunya.[44] Until 1936, Anglès developed
his career in Catalonia, with occasional research stays at German universities, such as Freiburg and Göttingen in 1923–24, and Göttingen again
in 1928. He was also committed to defending and promoting Catalan culture at a time in which social support for Catalan self-government was on
the rise. He was a member of the Institut d'Estudis Catalans, he regularly
used his native Catalan in publications and private correspondence, and
his research also focused, to a considerable extent, on Catalan early music
(mostly Medieval and Renaissance),[45] although he also published a few
works of importance on Spanish topics (most notably his 1935 edition of
the Las Huelgas codex).

Anglès fled Barcelona at the beginning of the Civil War; being a priest, he
was concerned about his personal safety under the Republican side, which
was well known for its anticlericalism. He used his professional contacts
abroad to settle in Munich, living at a convent and conducting academic
research in collaboration with German musicologists.[46] In early 1938,
however, he asked Otaño to help him go back to Spain and reconstruct his
career there. Although Otaño was hardly sympathetic to those who had
fled Spain, he agreed to give good references for Anglès to Francoist officers to help dissipate doubts about Anglès's commitment to Franco's project
for the new Spain.[47] The relationship between the two men was not free of
difficulties: when Otaño mentioned that Anglès' past Catalan nationalist
sympathies could be a problem in the new regime[48] and that Anglès would
not be officially invited to return to Spain but would instead have to submit
an application to the authorities for its examination, Anglès felt offended.[49]

Anglès eventually returned to Spain in summer 1938 after Otaño and
the Spanish prelate Isidro Gomá provided positive references for him.
He first entered the country as a guest speaker of the Cursos de Verano
Internacionales de Santander, a summer school organized by Franco's
Ministry of Education in order to help the regime strengthen its international prestige in the arts and sciences.[50] The relationship—and the
tensions—between the two men did not end there; Anglès now needed further help from Otaño to reestablish his career under the new regime, given

that the Catalan institutions in which he thrived had now been dismantled. Eventually, in January 1939 Otaño put forward Anglès's name to head a "department of musicology" within the newly founded Consejo Superior de Investigaciones Científicas (CSIC).[51] The Department of Musicology was finally founded in 1943 under the name Instituto Español de Musicología (IEM), and Anglès was appointed as its first director. The appointment allowed Otaño to retain his influence on most of the institutions that had relatively high impact on musical life and music policies (the Conservatorio de Madrid, *Ritmo*, and in part the Comisaría de Música), whereas Anglès remained in charge of the less-influential area of musicological research. Otaño, however, was adamant that the directorship of the IEM was an excellent opportunity for Anglès and the best option available for relaunching his career after the Civil War, particularly taking into account that he was, Otaño argued, practically unknown in Madrid.[52]

Under the new regime, Anglès was torn between his own sympathies and preferences, both political and scholarly, and the conditions in which he now had to work. As a conservative Roman Catholic, it is understandable that Anglès harbored sympathies for Francoism versus the Second Republic. There were other aspects of the new regime, however, with which Anglès arguably felt less comfortable: his strong sense of Catalan self-identity clashed with Francoist centralism, and, unlike Otaño, he certainly never expressed any satisfaction at the death or exile of those who opposed the Franco regime.[53] On the contrary, during the Franco era he remained friends with some of the exiles, among them Jesús Bal y Gay and Roberto Gerhard, who had worked with him at the Biblioteca Nacional de Catalunya. Anglès was similarly conflicted about his professional status: in public, he repeatedly expressed his gratitude to the regime for providing support for academic research in music,[54] but in private he was considerably more skeptic about the conditions he had to work in. For example, he felt overwhelmed by Otaño's attempts to control every aspect of Spanish musical life, and he had to assert himself to be allowed to appoint people of his choosing as IEM staff members.[55]

The two flagship projects of the IEM similarly proved problematic for Anglès. *Monumentos de la música española*, a series of editions of Spanish early music, was launched in 1941, even before the IEM was founded; the CSIC clearly realized the importance such a project could have for cultural reconstruction of the country. Anglès did contribute a significant number of volumes, although this time his focus on composers from the Catalan-speaking regions was less conspicuous than it was before the Civil War; his editions included the music of the courts of the Catholic monarchs and of Charles V, sonnets and *villancicos* by Juan Vázquez, and the complete works by Victoria and Morales.[56] Nevertheless, because of the perceived strategic importance of the project, Anglès was given rather tight deadlines he was not happy with, as he felt it did not allow him to properly conduct archival work[57]; he also resented the fact that, with paper supplies being scarce, he was not given sufficient allocation to print his personal, non-IEM projects, such as his edition of *Cantigas de Santa María*.[58] The second flagship project of the IEM was an annual music journal, *Anuario Musical*, first launched in 1946. From at least 1932, Anglès had harbored hopes of founding an academic periodical focusing on Spanish music from the Middle Ages to the nineteenth century, and from the start he wanted to name it *Anuario Musical*.[59] When the journal was finally founded under the Franco regime, however, Anglès was not entirely enthusiastic about it. He confided in his friend Subirá that there were not enough good music scholars in Spain to guarantee solid articles for every issue, and he suspected that the CSIC was pushing the idea "just to give the impression that some serious work is happening: we quickly write some articles, and that's already the great musicology periodical!"[60] Similarly, despite Anglès's original intentions, few non-Spanish scholars published their work in *Anuario Musical* during the 1940s, possibly owing to the isolation of the Franco regime.

Nevertheless, leaving aside Anglès's discomfort with the Francoist apparatus, his way of understanding music history could potentially fit relatively well with the dominant concept of *Hispanidad*—which therefore made him suitable to direct the IEM and to write about Spanish music history for a nonspecialist audience. The roots of Anglès's understanding of Spanish music history have to be sought in the writings of his teacher, Pedrell, a pioneer in gathering and researching both Spanish early and traditional music with the aim of turning it into the foundation of a national school of composition.[61] Pedrell's attempts at renovation and his narrative of Spanish music history were based, to a great extent, on the assumption that Italian opera had had a negative effect on eighteenth- and nineteenth-century Spain and thus prevented a truly national school of music from fully developing; therefore, Pedrell argued, the true essence of Spanish music must be sought before the eighteenth century. Pedrell regarded his activity as a musicologist as a scientific pursuit, thus relying on what he considered scientific tools and methods (editions, transcriptions, organological studies) to accomplish his mission.[62] Although research into a country's musical past with the aim of promoting ideas of national identity is certainly not an inherently right-wing pursuit—several of the exiles, for example, conducted research on early music with similar aims—Pedrell's approach to music history was adopted almost verbatim by the IEM in its research program.[63] The IEM's goals focused on rediscovering and promoting the "treasures" (*tesoros*) of Spanish early and traditional music, and the tools of the IEM for rediscovering and recovering these treasures were, essentially, the same as Pedrell's: its foundational goals named cataloguing, collection, transcription, and edition as the main tools Spanish musicologists had available to rediscover these treasures. The IEM's focus on Spanish music was therefore presented as a patriotic duty, which fit well with Francoist nationalism.

Pedrell's understanding of Spanish music also fit imperial nostalgia: the decline he described in eighteenth- and nineteenth-century music matched almost perfectly the putative decline of *Hispanidad* after the Austrias, and foreign influences were similarly regarded with suspicion both by Pedrell and in narratives of *Hispanidad*. It is therefore not surprising that Pedrell's narrative of Spanish music history, strengthened with allusions to *Hispanidad* to explain periods of splendor or decline, soon became commonplace in music criticism. Sopeña even claimed in a talk that "Spanish music in the first half of the nineteenth century can be summed up in one word: nothing."[64] Tomás Andrade de Silva wrote that, after the seventeenth century, "Spanish music went down a path of decline which was as fast as it was deplorable. Music became impersonal, conformist and vulgar, and welcomed all kinds of influences from foreign fashions and tastes, to the point that it lost, in all of its variations, its clear national physiognomy."[65] It was again a racial force equivalent to *Hispanidad*, according to music critics, that forced Spanish music out of its decline; Eduardo López-Chavarri claimed that a "powerful instinct" led Granados and Albéniz to react against the foreign-dominated panorama of nineteenth-century Spanish music,[66] and Mariano Daranos wrote that "Before 1800, the Spanish musical landscape vanished, but it reappeared a century later, more energetic, more communicative, and, above all, closer to the purest Iberian tradition."[67]

Following Pedrell, Italian opera was frequently named as the cause of the decline of Spanish nineteenth-century music. Composer and conductor Victoriano Echevarría accused Philip V of having severely harmed Spanish theatrical music by employing an Italian theater company in his court.[68] In particular, *zarzuela* was considered to have been almost irreparably wounded by Italian influences—and by a free-market, mercantilist approach to music that allegedly came with them.[69] It was not that nineteenth-century *zarzuelistas* (Francisco Asenjo Barbieri, Federico Chueca, Emilio Arrieta, Gerónimo Giménez, Tomás Bretón) were entirely despicable; on the contrary, some critics praised them for having created a genre with a national, Spanish component at a time in which Italian influences were overwhelming. Sopeña claimed that 80 percent of Barbieri's musical personality was Italian, but the remaining 20 percent, in being Spanish, was "pure and original."[70] At the same time, the *zarzuelistas* were to be blamed, or at least pitied, for having missed the chance to create a truly Spanish opera.[71] Again, some critics saw the Franco regime as an opportunity to revive *zarzuela* and turn it into a true Spanish opera tradition, in the same way other areas of national culture were being brought back to life after the war. A few critics rushed to suggest government measures, which, however, were never put into practice: Fernández-Cid, one of the most conspicuous supporters of *zarzuela*, called for a state-owned company devoted to production and promotion of the genre[72]; he argued that its staff should be paid only minimum wage, to ensure they would be working for the sake of the nation and not for personal profit. *Revista Literaria Musical* urged the government to pass a law to regulate *zarzuela*, and to protect impresarios so that composers could focus on writing music without having to worry about anything else.[73] Victor Ruiz Albéniz also called for more government support, and he suggested that the government should establish a national *zarzuela* company and grant tax exemptions to such entities.[74]

Among the many critics who brought Spanish early music into the musical press, Anglès was one of the most conspicuous voices to write on the topic in nonspecialist publications, namely in *Radio Nacional*, to which he first contributed in December 1939. Given that he had very rarely engaged in this kind of writing before, and that, at the time, he still had not been confirmed as founding director of the IEM, it is plausible that he was looking to increase his visibility outside his native Catalonia—as suggested by Otaño—and to establish himself as a supporter of the new regime. Indeed, in his very first article he implicitly presented his status as a professional musicologist as crucial for the newly established regime: it was of pressing importance, Anglès claimed, to establish, once and for all, the role Spain had in universal music history, because in the past many amateur musicologists had severely harmed Spain's musical prestige with their insufficiently researched writings.[75] Certainly, no one could accuse Anglès of not having properly researched the topic he chose for his first *Radio Nacional* article: the *Cantigas de Santa María*, which he had been studying since the late 1910s.[76] Anglès made use of his expertise to dispel a myth disseminated by amateur musicologists that did not fit well with the new ideals of *Hispanidad:* there were some medieval melodies in the *cantigas*, Anglès argued, that such musicologists had been unable to identify, and they thus hypothesized that these melodies were of Arab origin. This was, in Anglès's opinion, totally wrong; he thought they were purely Spanish.[77] With the *cantigas* being, according to Anglès, sufficiently important by themselves to give Spain a "prominent place" in the history of monody,[78] Anglès's intention was to define the work as purely Spanish in the racial sense and the religious.

In a subsequent article, Anglès focused on a similarly crucial topic for musical construction of *Hispanidad*: music in the court of the Catholic monarchs, on which he was conducting research for *Monumentos de la música española*. He credited Ferdinand and Isabella with having expelled all foreign musicians from their chapels and having hired Spanish musicians only, who dedicated themselves to "shaping, once and for all, a typically Spanish musical repertoire."[79] In a later article for *Arbor* covering the entirety of Spanish music history, Anglès repeated that it was the duty of Spanish musicology under the new regime to unveil and rightly appraise the musical past to make sure that Spanish modern music attained "the place it deserves in the modern destiny of our Fatherland."[80] And the place he thought Spain deserved was that of being a pioneer in all eras of music history: the Hispanic proto-Christian communities of the sixth and seventh centuries had already made significant contributions to the nascent liturgical music of the Middle Ages,[81] the Iberian Peninsula had also been home to the first secular songs in Latin,[82] and Spanish Renaissance polyphonists and *vihuelistas* had been at the forefront of European music.[83]

Anglès's writings for *Radio Nacional* and *Arbor* were not the only project he was involved in to disseminate Spanish early music among general audiences. In May 1941, again as he was awaiting his appointment at the IEM, he curated an exhibition to celebrate the centenary of Pedrell's death at the Biblioteca Nacional de Catalunya (renamed under the Franco regime as Biblioteca Central de la Diputación de Barcelona). Archival material donated by Pedrell to the Biblioteca was put on display to present the history of Spanish music from the Visigoth era, that is, several centuries before Spain came to exist as a modern nation. "Spain had a peculiar chant and musical notation as early as the seventh century," claimed the exhibition's catalogue, suggesting, as Giménez Caballero and others had done on the topic of *Hispanidad*, that a distinct Spanish identity existed already in the years of the Visigoth kingdom.[84] The Marquis of Lozoya and several local and provincial government officers attended the opening of the exhibition, thus making it clear that the new regime was willing to support musicological research as well. It is worth mentioning, however, that, both the exhibition and Anglès's writings for specialized and nonspecialist publications avoided using the word *Hispanidad* in the sense of eternal essence of spirit, and similarly shied away from mentioning race. Instead, Anglès chose to emphasize the scientific nature of his scholarly criteria; in his *Arbor* article, for example, he wrote that Spain "does not need to indulge in the fantasy of ennobling its musical past," because simply unveiling and properly presenting the hidden treasures of Spain, without any unnecessary embellishments, would suffice.[85] This was certainly consonant with Anglès's training in Germany during the 1920s and with the allegedly scientific, objective approach he generally adopted in his work.[86] Nevertheless, the claim that Spain needed not embellish its musical past may also hide Anglès's reluctance in collaborating with a regime that so clearly clashed with his commitment to Catalonia, especially given that *Hispanidad* pretty much obliterated all pretensions to cultural and linguistic diversity within Spain.

JULIO GÓMEZ: A DISSIDENT VOICE?

Despite Anglès's and Otaño's personal differences and their contrasting approaches when it came to presenting Spain's musical past to the general public, both of them felt equally outraged when Julio Gómez published an article in the magazine *Harmonía* in which he was critical of the newly founded Instituto Español de Musicología. According to Anglès, indignation erupted at the Conservatorio de Madrid, and Otaño visited the minister for national education in order to express his discomfort with Gómez's article; indignation, similarly, flared up at the IEM in Barcelona, and its staff members "could not believe [there was] such ignorance and such carelessness from people who seemed to be far more cultured than that."[87]

Gómez's article, however, comes across as rather mild compared with the controversies that had been so conspicuous in music criticism before the Civil War and that Gómez himself had taken part in. Indeed, he did not name the IEM, or Otaño or Anglès, in his *Harmonía* article.[88] Nevertheless, it is understandable that his rather subdued criticism was all the more visible in a climate in which any mildly negative comment about musical life in Spain was normally paired with enthusiastic praise of the government's efforts. As Gómez pointed out:

> It is very common to say that the State has never done anything; that it is only *now* that the State is starting to concern itself with this matter [referring to editions of musical works], and that in the future everything will be perfectly fine. This *now* is always whenever someone who is interested in editing something in particular—which is, almost always, the most useless music—achieves his goal.[89]

Gómez argued that the various Spanish governments since the nineteenth century had in fact supported publication of musical works (he named Hilarión Eslava's *Lírica Sacra Hispana* and Martínez Torner's *Cancionero musical de la lírica popular asturiana* as examples), and that editions of wind band music in Spain—in which he was involved through *Harmonía*—were of the highest quality, even without government support.[90] It is not likely that Gómez was referring to Anglès's interests when he mentioned "useless" music; Gómez believed, and said so in his article, that the liturgical music from the court of the Catholic monarchs was worth editing.[91] Rather, it was probably Gómez's skepticism toward the overenthusiasm with which the IEM's project had been presented in the press that caused outrage at both the Conservatorio de Madrid and the IEM itself.

This was not the first time, nor it would be the last, that Gómez was critical of the policies of the new regime, particularly those concerning research and dissemination of early music, within the narrow boundaries where press censorship left him to do so. This is not to say that he opposed early music research per se in any way; on the contrary, as a music librarian and musicologist, he was a specialist in the eighteenth-century *tonadilla escénica*. Gómez's writings in the 1940s are a reminder that interest in early music flourished in early twentieth-century Spain across the whole political spectrum and adopted numerous approaches. After Francoism, however, some of those approaches revealed themselves as more easily adaptable to the new regime than others.

Born in 1886, Gómez studied composition under Bretón at the Conservatorio de Madrid and concurrently graduated with a doctorate in history from the Universidad Central. From the 1910s onward, he held various full-time jobs as a music librarian and archivist, most significantly at the Conservatorio from 1915. In his spare time, he composed music, his first success in the Madrid musical scene being *Suite en la* in 1917; he conducted musicological research, and he wrote music criticism for various periodicals and newspapers, most significantly *El liberal*. A self-confessed nineteenth-century nationalist composer, Gómez repeatedly expressed his disapproval of Salazar's Europeanist solutions for Spanish music, arguing instead that Spanish composers should reabsorb their own national traditions (particularly in theatrical music) as the path to national regeneration[92]; he was similarly critical of the Grupo de los Ocho and their ironic approach to music.[93]

In spite of his dislike for Salazar and the Grupo de los Ocho, which theoretically should have helped him fit in the musical life of the early Franco regime, Gómez's attempts at reestablishing himself as a critic, composer, and musicologist after the war initially met with difficulties. Although the Republican government had urged all civil servants to leave Madrid at the beginning of the Civil War and join the government in Valencia, Gómez decided to stay in Madrid, unwilling to abandon the library of the conservatoire. After the war, however, some of his colleagues there accused Gómez of having worked for *El liberal* and having been a member of various left-wing organizations and trade unions (Izquierda Republicana, UGT, Frente Popular). Gómez had to undergo an investigation—including eleven days in prison in April 1939 and being removed from his job as a librarian—which lasted until the end of 1939.[94] However, he eventually managed to dissipate the suspicions about his loyalty to the new regime by minimizing his involvement in the leftist organizations.[95]

Though he avoided major punishment for his political sympathies, a year after the end of the war Gómez was still not particularly optimistic about his professional future. In a letter to Subirá, he complained that all his efforts in favor of Spanish music and musicology had not been rewarded by the new regime: it is true that Gómez had been reappointed to his music librarian position at the Conservatorio and claimed he felt respected as such, but he lamented that he was still forced to compose his music in his free time, without receiving any support or recognition from the government. His claims may seem surprising considering that his personal politics were closer to the Second Republic's than to Francoism, but musically he felt more at home in the new regime than among Salazar and the Grupo de los Ocho, and he confessed to Subirá that he had hoped "to flourish again as a composer and a critic, because of the natural tendency which music should have experienced towards a conservative style ... which is, I believe, what I have always defended in my works and my music criticism."[96] However, broadly considered, Gómez's career as a composer certainly advanced during the 1940s. It was under Francoism that he was appointed, for the first time in his life, to a full-time teaching position at the Conservatorio de Madrid, having occasionally covered for his former teaching Bretón during the 1910s; he was first made a professor of literary and musical culture in 1944, a professorship created expressly for him, given his lifelong interest in helping music students develop a humanistic and literary background.[97] On Turina's death in 1949, Gómez replaced him as a professor of composition. His visibility as a composer also picked up. In June 1940, for the first time after the war, he managed to have a work of his given its first performance (two choral works, actually, in Ávila and Salamanca, by the Zamora Choral Society), and he was awarded a composition prize by the Ateneo de Sevilla for his cantata *Maese Pérez, el organista*.[98] During the rest of the decade, a number of Gómez's works were premiered by the Madrid orchestras.[99] Moreover, generally speaking, Gómez's creativity peaked in the Franco era, with some forty works completed between 1940 and 1962.[100]

It is more complicated to determine whether Gómez equally managed to reconstruct his career as a music critic under Francoism. Once his investigation had been resolved, Gómez was invited to write for *Harmonía* again—a periodical addressed to wind band conductors to which Gómez had already contributed since its founding in 1916, and until it was temporarily suspended because of the Civil War.[101] Gómez's pre- and postwar contributions both took the same form: rather than reviewing specific music works, he wrote a section under the name *Comentarios del presente y del pasado* (commentaries about the present and the past) focusing on a range of problems in Spanish musical life and on aspects of Spain's musical past that interested him from his work as a librarian and researcher.

In despite of *Harmonía* being a niche magazine that certainly could not boast the circulation of *Ritmo* or *Música. Revista Quincenal Ilustrada,* Gómez was clearly committed to his task of discussing various musical problems for a readership of wind band conductors. Indeed, he did not see them as a lesser audience: in line with his interest in spreading musical culture to all levels of Spanish society, he considered wind conductors "the most active and efficient section of our musical culture"[102] and the only ones who had significantly improved as a group over the last sixty years.[103] He also thought that, in medium-sized and small Spanish cities, good wind bands were more efficient than mediocre symphony orchestras in making the orchestral repertoire known among the population.[104] Nevertheless, he sometimes could not hide his disappointment that he had not been able to get a staff music critic position in a newspaper, comparable to the appointment at *El liberal*, and in one of his *Harmonía* articles he claimed that he had been a music critic and would be happy to become one again if someone paid him to do so.[105] However, Gómez's writings for *Harmonía*—and his occasional contributions to *Ritmo*—allowed him to express, within the constraints of Francoist press censorship and the expectations of triumphalism placed on music critics, opinions on Spanish early music and its research that dissented from the official views pressed by Otaño, and to some extent by Anglès.

Gómez certainly seemed aware of the expectations placed on him as a writer on music—and specifically on early music—by the newly established regime. Shortly after *Ritmo* was relaunched, Otaño commissioned an article for the magazine. Gómez would have rather published some of his latest research, but he acquiesced to Otaño's request that he publish on the *vihuelistas*, including some photogravure prints of the *vihuela* books kept at the Biblioteca Nacional; Otaño wanted at all costs to feature images of the *vihuela* books for reasons of "archeological prestige," in Gómez's words.[106] Nevertheless, in the article Gómez still expressed opinions that dissented from the perspectives Otaño and Anglès were introducing in the historiography of Spanish early music. Referring vaguely to "Spanish music criticism" but without naming any historians or critics, Gómez expressed his disagreement with the widespread pretense that the Spanish *vihuelistas* had been ahead of their European counterparts and, more generally, that Spanish musicians had historically been pioneers "in all matters"[107]—as Anglès had argued in Spanish music exhibition in 1941 and, later on, in his 1948 article in *Arbor*. Similarly, unlike Anglès, Gómez did not hesitate to accept that Spanish music could have absorbed Arab influences; he claimed that one of the reasons the *vihuela* developed in Spain was because the Muslims had first introduced the lute there.[108]

Gómez's articles for *Harmonía* again avoided naming Anglès, Otaño, or any other music critic he disagreed with, but he did not hesitate to point out what he considered to be the flaws of research into early music, which would be easily recognizable to anyone familiar with the IEM's work. Although writing from a self-confessed nationalist and regenerationist perspective, Gómez was wary of narrating the history of Spanish music as a story of triumph, defeat, and regeneration animated by *Hispanidad*, national identity, rejection of foreign influences, or any other presumably unifying but undefined force. Instead of focusing on an abstract idea of national art, he preferred to focus on the artists who produced it ("Although Art may not have a fatherland, we artists do—and if Art does not eat, unfortunately we artists do have to eat. And the splendor of a country depends, in the first instance, on the splendor of its artists."[109]). Gómez claimed it was a common mistake among Spanish historians (not only musicologists) to "attribute to a particular era ideas, feelings, passions and concerns which pertain to a later time"; for example, he wrote, it was common for Spanish musicologists to "speak of Spanish music and vigorous reactions of Spanish nationalism against the invasion of foreign music in times in which no one considered the national character of music,"[110] which Gómez considered acceptable for "simple minds," but not sound enough for construction of a historical argument.[111]

Again, he named no names, but it is not difficult to imagine him referring to Anglès; indeed, at the end of the article, he proceeded to question Pedrell, or rather the prevailing understanding of Pedrell among Spanish musicologists, which of course the IEM, being based to a great extent on Pedrell's postulates, had been keen to promote. In Gómez's opinion, Pedrell's musicological research had not really been the foundation of the national school of composition of Albéniz, Falla, and Granados because "fruitful artistic schools are not based upon theories, pedagogy or advice; they are based upon works."[112] He similarly argued that "the Spanish school that Pedrell wanted to found with all his theories and works was already founded and lived next to him, without him noticing it—and not only did he not help the members of that school, but rather fought against them with all of his energy."[113] Gómez was obviously referring to the *zarzuelistas*, such as Chapí, Giménez, and his own teacher, Bretón.[114]

Consonant with his role as a composer-musicologist-librarian, Gómez also saw musicology as a means rather than an end in itself, and in a likely veiled attack on *Ritmo* and Otaño, he was remarkably critical of how the newly established regime had chosen to celebrate Victoria's centenary: on one hand, he claimed, the musicologists who had been publishing articles about the life and works of Victoria were not adding much to public knowledge; on the other, and more importantly, interest in musicological research had not encouraged Spanish musicians to perform Victoria's works, which should be the ultimate goal of such musicological research ("Speeches, books, newspaper articles, are only words").[115] He similarly complained that it had been impossible to perform Pedrell's works on the occasion of the centenary in 1941, given that musicologists had not even thought about producing performing editions of his works.[116] Musicology, he claimed, was ancillary to music composition and performance; music research should focus on one's own country as a way of being "useful" to composers and performers.[117] Gómez thought that Spanish musicologists should focus on Spanish music, not because it was better than other nations' but because a musicologist needed firsthand knowledge of his musical environment (to which Gómez referred ironically as "the telephone handbook") rather than of "Egyptian hieroglyphics, cuneiform scripts, palimpsests and medieval parchments."[118]

Gómez's critical approach to early music research under Francoist Spain extended to other aspects of musical life; it was, after all, informed not only by his particular expertise and interests as a music librarian and musicologist, but also by his view, as a nationalist composer, that early music research was one of several aspects necessary for cultural and musical regeneration of the country. He wrote extensively about how the state should protect musical composition (but disagreed that the Franco regime had been the first government to do so)[119]; about the need to unify the curriculum of all Spanish conservatoires[120]; and about both the excessive optimism and excessive pessimism that simultaneously plagued contemporary Spanish composition, which led critics and musical authorities to consider that all Spanish contemporary music was either similarly excellent or similarly despicable.[121] Although his opinions were normally cautiously expressed and he, like other critics, sometimes felt the need to soften his criticism with enthusiastic praise of the government or specific officers,[122] his writings for *Harmonía* reveal the quest of a writer on music to find a space of dissent, however mild, within the regime.

NOTES

1. Ernesto Giménez Caballero, *Arte y estado* (Madrid: Ediciones de La Gaceta Literaria, 1935), 254.
2. María Isabel García Cabrera, *Tradición y vanguardia en el pensamiento artístico español (1939-1959)* (Granada: Universidad de Granada, 1998), 297–298.
3. Giuliana di Febo, *Ritos de guerra y de victoria en la España Franquista* (Bilbao: Desclée de Brouwer, 2002), 116.
4. Nemesio Otaño, "Los solemnísimos funerales de José Antonio en El Escorial," *Radio Nacional*, no. 57 (1939), 12–13. The score for the trumpet fanfares, which Otaño had researched, was reprinted in the magazine, under the generic name of "toque militar español," without indication of the composer.
5. Letter from Eduardo Martínez Torner to Adolfo Salazar, Feb. 12, 1924, reprinted in Emilio Casares Rodicio (ed.), *La música en la Generación del 27. Homenaje a Lorca 1915-1939*, ed. Emilio Casares Rodicio, 20–34 (Madrid: Ministerio de Cultura/ INAEM, 1986), 164.
6. For example, both Sopeña and Rodrigo complained that Spanish early music for organ was not performed often enough. Federico Sopeña, "Madrigalistas," *Arriba*, Apr. 10, 1945, 7; Joaquín Rodrigo, "Música," *Pueblo*, Apr. 22, 1943, 7.
7. Letter from Nemesio Otaño to Valentín Ruiz Aznar, Jan. 20, 1937, unpublished [AHSL, 009/001.011]; letter from Antonio Mompeón to Nemesio Otaño, Feb. 21, 1937, unpublished [AHSL, 005.068]; letter from Agustín Cadarso García de Jalón to Nemesio Otaño, Feb. 22, 1937, unpublished [AHSL, 005.070]; letter from José Múgica to Nemesio Otaño, Feb. 2, 1937, unpublished [AHSL, 005.067]; letter from Nemesio Otaño to Manuel de Falla, Nov. 17, 1938 [AHSL, 004/010.008].
8. Letter from Ignacio Fernández Eleizgaray to Nemesio Otaño, unpublished, day and month unknown, 1937 [AHSL, 003/014.001]; letter from Nemesio Otaño to Manuel de Falla, Mar. 1, 1939, unpublished [AHSL, 004/010.011]; letter from César Figuerido to Nemesio Otaño, Apr. 18, 1940, unpublished [AHSL, 004/ 008.034]; letter from Jesús García Leoz to Joaquín Turina, May 2, 1940, unpublished [AHSL, 007/009.02]; letter from Manuel García Matos to Nemesio Otaño, July 17, 1940, unpublished [AHSL, 002/003.008]; letter from Domingo Lázaro to Eduardo López-Chavarri, May 12, 1941, reprinted in *Eduardo López-Chavarri. Correspondencia*, ed. Rafael Díaz Gómez and Vicente Galbis López (Valencia: Generalitat Valenciana, 1996), 323.
9. Letter from Nemesio Otaño to Manuel de Falla, July 1, 1940, unpublished; letter from Otaño to Falla, Aug. 20, 1941, unpublished.
10. Letter from Juan Puiggrós to Nemesio Otaño, Apr. 11, 1940, unpublished [AHSL, 003/024.001]; letter from Enrique Casals to Nemesio Otaño, Aug. 19, 1940 [AHSL, 003/024.003]; letter from Casals to Otaño, Dec. 2, 1940 [AHSL, 003/024.005].
11. Letter from Nemesio Otaño to Manuel de Falla, Nov. 17, 1938, unpublished.
12. Geoffrey Jensen, *Irrational Triumph: Cultural Despair, Military Nationalism, and the Ideological Origins of Franco's Spain* (Reno: University of Nevada Press, 2002), 80–114.
13. Anonymous, "Música militar española," *Radio Nacional*, no. 2 (1939), 7.
14. Norberto Almandoz, "Música," *Heraldo de Aragón*, Aug. 22, 1938.
15. For example, Fernando Irigaz, "Cómo transformar la Marcha Granadera en himno nacional," *Heraldo de Aragón*, Jan. 6, 1937; Anonymous, "Música," *Heraldo de Aragón*, Jan. 30, 1937; Anonymous, "Música," *Heraldo de Aragón*, Feb. 18, 1937.

16. Letter from Fernando Rodríguez del Río to Nemesio Otaño, July 22, 1940, unpublished [AHSL, 017/003.005]; letter from Rodríguez del Río to Otaño, Oct. 18, 1940, unpublished [AHSL, 017/003.006].

17. Letter from Nemesio Otaño to Higinio Anglès, Apr. 21, 1940, unpublished [BNC, Fons Higini Anglès, uncatalogued].

18. Nemesio Otaño, "El himno nacional español," *Ritmo* (1940), no. 133, 4–5.

19. Ibid., 4.

20. Otaño, "El himno nacional y la música militar," 3.

21. "Organería Española S.A.," *Ritmo*, no. 146 (1941), 11.

22. Refers to the Spanish Civil War.

23. Françoise Clastrier and Oscar Candendo, "Órganos franceses en el País Vasco y Navarra (1855–1925)," *Cuadernos de la sección de música*, no. 7 (1994), 155 and 200–201.

24. Ramón G. Amezúa, "El órgano, artísticamente," *Radio Nacional*, no. 133 (1941), 14–15.

25. At the time, Victoria was commonly thought to have been born in 1540. It was not until 1960 that Ferreol Hernández established that his birth was in 1548, as is commonly accepted today.

26. Anonymous, "Tres centenarios," *Ritmo*, no. 135 (1940), 3.

27. Such articles include Juan de Contreras y López de Ayala [as Marquis de Lozoya], "Algunas noticias familiares de Tomás Luis de Victoria," *Ritmo*, no. 135 (1940), 4; José Artero, "La pobreza de Tomás Luis de Victoria," *Ritmo*, no. 136 (1940), 4–5; Artero, "Dos problemas psicológicos de Victoria," *Ritmo*, no. 137 (1940), 4–5; Artero, "Obras históricas de Victoria," *Ritmo*, no. 138 (1940), 6–7; Artero, "Obras históricas de Victoria," *Ritmo*, no. 139 (1940), 4–5; Artero, "Obras históricas de Victoria," *Ritmo*, no. 139 (1940), 7–8.

28. Articles in the special issue include Juan de Contreras y López de Ayala [as Marqués de Lozoya], "Algunas noticias familiares de Tomás Luis de Victoria," *Ritmo*, no. 141 (1940), 17–25; Ferreol Hernández, "La cuna y la escuela de Tomás L. de Victoria," *Ritmo*, no. 141 (1940), 28–34; Fernando del Valle Lersundi, "La supuesta pobreza de Victoria," *Ritmo*, no. 141 (1940), 35–37; Nemesio Otaño, "Fundamentos de las tendencias espirituales y artísticas de Victoria," *Ritmo*, no. 141 (1940), 39–60; Francisco Pujol, "La estética en la obra de Tomás Luis de Victoria," *Ritmo*, no. 141 (1940), 61–72; F. Barberá, "Tomás Luis de Victoria, músico español," *Ritmo*, no. 141 (1940), 73–77; David Pujol, "Ideas estéticas de T. L. de Victoria," *Ritmo*, no. 141 (1940), 79–86; Luis Millet, "Recuerdos sobre Victoria," *Ritmo*, no. 141 (1940), 87–90; Higinio Anglès, "A propósito de las ediciones originales de Victoria," *Ritmo*, no. 141 (1940), 91–101; Nemesio Otaño, "Los últimos años de Victoria en Madrid," *Ritmo*, no. 141 (1940), 103–110.

29. Jesús Rubio, "Discurso del Ilmo. Sr. Subsecretario de Educación Nacional D. Jesús Rubio en el día de la inauguración del Centenario en Ávila (7 de mayo de 1940)," *Ritmo*, no. 141 (1940), 9. On the idea of empire as a unifying force, and the ramifications of this conception in Francoist cultural relations with Latin America, see Lorenzo Delgado Gómez-Escalonilla, *Imperio de papel. Acción cultural y política exterior durante el primer Franquismo* (Madrid: Consejo Superior de Investigaciones Científicas, 1992), 123.

30. Ibid., 15.

31. Anonymous, "El centenario de T. L. de Victoria," *Ritmo*, no. 135 (1940), 12.

32. Anonymous, "Breve reseña de los actos celebrados en España con motivo del Cuarto Centenario oficial de Tomás Luis de Victoria," *Ritmo*, no. 141 (1940), 111–112.

33. Federico Sopeña, "Prólogo a la quincena musical," *Arriba*, Sep. 8, 1940, 7.

34. Julio Gómez, "Los vihuelistas españoles del siglo XVI," *Ritmo*, no. 134 (1940), 4–5.

35. Anonymous, "Tres centenarios," 3.

36. Barberá, "Tomás Luis de Victoria," 75.

37. Anonymous, "Nuestro número extraordinario," *Ritmo*, no. 141 (1940), 5. Other examples of music criticism naming Victoria as a composer or musician of the Race are Antonio de las Heras, "Mística y música de un imperio," *Vértice*, no. 29 (1939), 5; Tomás Andrade de Silva, "La canción española fuera de España," *Revista Literaria Musical*, no. 34 (1947), 4.

38. For discussions of the concept of race in pre-1939 music criticism, see Carol A. Hess, *Manuel de Falla and Modernism in Spain, 1898–1936* (Chicago: University of Chicago Press, 2001), 65–71; Gemma Pérez Zalduondo, "Racial Discourses in Spanish Musical Literature, 1915–1939," in *Western Music and Race*, ed. Julie Brown (Cambridge: Cambridge University Press, 2007), 216–229.

39. Di Febo, *Ritos de guerra*, 86–91. Ironically, Saint Theresa was not *cristiana vieja*; she was instead descended from *conversos*, or Jews who nominally converted to Christianity to avoid being expelled from Spain in 1492, but kept their faith and rituals in private.

40. Robert M. Stevenson, *Spanish Cathedral Music in the Golden Age* (Berkeley and Los Angeles: University of California Press, 1961), 455.

41. Contreras López de Ayala, "Algunas noticias familiares," 4.

42. Hernández, "La cuna y la escuela," 27–34.

43. Valle Lersundi, "La supuesta pobreza de Victoria," 35–37.

44. Anonymous, *Miscelánea en homenaje a Monseñor Higinio Anglés* (Barcelona: Consejo Superior de Investigaciones Científicas, 1958–1961), ix.

45. Publications and editions (all of them published by the Music Department of the Biblioteca de Catalunya, Barcelona) include *Els madrigals i la missa de difunts d'en Brudieu* (1921, with Pedrell); *Johannis Pujol. Opera omnia* (1927–1932); *Musici organici Iohannis Cabanilles: Opera omnia* (1927–1956); *A. Soler: Sis quintets per a instruments d'arc i orgue o clave obligat* (1933, with Gerhard); *La música a Catalunya fins al segle XIII* (1935). Catalan topics on which Anglés published articles during these years include the Epístola farcida de Sant Esteve, the Cant del la Sibilla, Mateu Flecha, and Pedrell.

46. Letters from Higinio Anglès to Josep Maria Lamaña, Nov. 1 and 13, 1938, unpublished [BNC, Fons Higini Anglès, uncatalogued].

47. Letter from Nemesio Otaño to Higinio Anglès, Jan. 25, 1938, unpublished [BNC, Fons Higini Anglès, uncatalogued].

48. Ibid.

49. Letter from Nemesio Otaño to Higinio Anglès, Mar. 14, 1938, unpublished [BNC, Fons Higini Anglès, uncatalogued].

50. Letters from Nemesio Otaño to Higinio Anglès, May 19 and 22, 1938, unpublished [BNC, Fons Higini Anglès, uncatalogued].

51. Letters from Nemesio Otaño to Higinio Anglès, Jan. 8, 1939, and Apr. 21, 1940, unpublished [BNC, Fons Higini Anglès, uncatalogued].

52. Letter from Nemesio Otaño to Higinio Anglès, Jan. 8, 1939.

53. Letter from Nemesio Otaño to Higinio Anglès, July 29, 1937, unpublished [BNC, Fons Higini Anglès, uncatalogued].

54. For example, Higinio Anglès (ed.), *La música en la corte de Carlos V* (Barcelona: Consejo Superior de Investigaciones Científicas, 1944), 9.

55. Letters from Higinio Anglès to José Subirá, Nov. 6, 1943, unpublished [BNE, M.SUBIRÁ/1/11]; and Feb. 9, 1944, unpublished [BNE, M.SUBIRÁ/1/11].

56. *La música en la corte de los Reyes Católicos*, vol. I (1941); *La música en la corte de Carlos V* (1944); *La música en la corte de los Reyes Católicos*, vol. II (1946); *Recopilación de sonetos y villancicos a quatro y a cinco* (1946); *La música en la corte de los Reyes Católicos*, vol. III (1951); *Opera Omnia de Cristóbal de Morales*, 8 vols. (1952–1971); *Opera Omnia de Tomás Luis de Victoria*, 4 vols. (1965–1968).

57. Letter from Higinio Anglès to Diego Angulo, Sep. 2, 1940, unpublished [BNE, M.SUBIRÁ/1/11].

58. Letter from Higinio Anglès to José Subirá, Mar. 4, 1942, unpublished [BNE, M.SUBIRÁ/1/11].

59. Letter from Higinio Anglès to José Subirá, Jan. 27, 1932, unpublished [BNE, M.SUBIRÁ/1/11].

60. Letter from Higinio Anglès to José Subirá, Nov. 6, 1943, unpublished [BNE, M.SUBIRÁ/1/11].

61. Felipe Pedrell, *Por nuestra música* (Barcelona: Heinrich, 1891), 17.

62. Juan José Carreras, "Hijos de Pedrell: la historiografía musical española y sus orígenes nacionalistas," *Il Saggiatore Musicale*, no. 8 (2001), 135.

63. For the research program of the IEM at the time of its foundation, see Anonymous, "Nuevos institutos," *Arbor*, vol. 1, no. 1 (1944), 1. Pedrell's influence extended beyond musicological research to other aspects of musical policy under Francoism; see Gemma Pérez Zalduondo, "La utilización de la figura y la obra de Felip Pedrell en el marco de la exaltación nacionalista de posguerra (1939–1945)," *Recerca Musicològica*, no. 11–12 (1991), 476–480.

64. Federico Sopeña, quoted in Anonymous, "Homenaje a Barbieri en la Asociación de Cultura Musical," *Pueblo*, May 5, 1942, 7.

65. Tomás Andrade de Silva, "Labor musical de la Delegación nacional de propaganda," *Arriba*, Nov. 7, 1943, 2.

66. Eduardo López-Chavarri, "Orientaciones," *Ritmo*, no. 182 (1944), 23.

67. Mariano Daranos, "Abolengo de nuestra música de cámara," *ABC*, Jan. 16 1942, 3.

68. Victoriano Echevarría, "Orígenes de la zarzuela," *Boletín del Colegio de Directores de Banda de Música Civiles*, no. 34 (1946), 3–5.

69. Federico Sopeña, "Un estreno de Ramón Usandizaga," *Arriba*, Sep. 15, 1940, 7.

70. Sopeña, quoted in Anonymous, "Homenaje a Barbieri," 7.

71. For example, Rafael Villaseca, "De 'Guzmán el Bueno' a la 'Verbena de la Paloma'," *ABC*, Mar. 10, 1951, 15; Rodrigo A. de Santiago, "Tomás Bretón," *Boletín del Colegio de Directores de Bandas de Música Civiles*, no. 80 (1950), 6.

72. Antonio Fernández-Cid, "El teatro lírico en España. Al margen de una campaña de género chico," *Música. Revista Quincenal Ilustrada*, 14 (1945), 22.

73. Anonymous, "Editorial," *Revista Literaria Musical*, no. 27 (1945), 3

74. Víctor Ruiz Albéniz, [as Acorde], "Zarzuela española," *Arriba*, Nov. 7, 1943, 11.

75. Higinio Anglès, "Las cantigas de Santa María del Rey don Alfonso el Sabio," *Radio Nacional*, no. 59 (1939), 4–5. A second article was published as Anglès, "Las cantigas de Santa María del Rey don Alfonso el Sabio," *Radio Nacional*, no. 87 (1940), 4–5.

76. Higinio Anglès (ed.), *La música de las cantigas de Santa María del Rey Alfonso el Sabio. Facsímil, transcripción y estudio crítico*, vol. 1 (Barcelona: Diputación Provincial de Barcelona/Biblioteca Central, 1943), ix.

77. Recent research, however, has unveiled instances of Arab influence on the *cantigas*, specially in the rhythm; see Manuel Pedro Ferreira, "Andalusian Music and the *Cantigas de Santa Maria*," in *Cobras e Son. Papers on the text, music and manuscripts of the "Cantigas de Santa María*," ed. Stephen Parkinson (Oxford: Legenda, 2000), 10–11.

78. Anglès, "Las cantigas de Santa María" (1939), 4.

79. Higinio Anglès, "La música española en la España imperial," *Radio Nacional*, no. 140 (1941), 6–7.

80. Higinio Anglès, "España en la historia de la música universal," *Arbor*, vol. 11, no. 30 (1948), 50.

81. Ibid., 8.

82. Ibid., 13.

83. Ibid., 18.

84. Higinio Anglès, *La música española desde la Edad Media hasta nuestros días: Catálogo de la exposición histórica celebrada en conmemoración del primer centenario del maestro Felipe Pedrell (18 mayo–25 junio 1941)* (Barcelona: Diputación provincial de Barcelona, 1941), 3.

85. Anglès, "España en la historia de la música universal," 51.

86. Anglès, *La música de las Cantigas*, ix–x.

87. Letter from Higinio Anglès to José Subirá, Dec. 29, 1943, unpublished [BNE, M.SUBIRÁ/1/11].

88. Julio Gómez, "Comentarios del presente y del pasado," *Harmonía*, October–December (1943), 5.

89. Ibid., 5.

90. Ibid., 4.

91. Ibid.

92. Beatriz Martínez del Fresno, *Julio Gómez. Una época de la música española* (Madrid: ICCMU, 1999), 23.

93. Ibid., 28.

94. Ibid., 377.

95. Ibid., 381.

96. Unpublished letter from Julio Gómez to José Subirá, Apr. 9, 1940.

97. Julio Gómez, "Comentarios del presente y del pasado," *Harmonía*, July–September issue (1946), 2; Gómez, "Cultura literaria aplicada a la música. Concepto y plan de la asignatura," *Harmonía*, April–June (1947), 1–9.

98. Letter from Julio Gómez to José Subirá, June 23, 1940, unpublished [BNE, M.SUBIRÁ/1/105].

99. These include *Maese Pérez* in 1941 by the Orquesta Filarmónica, *La gacela de Almoctamid* in 1942 by the Orquesta Sinfónica, a piano concerto in 1944 by the Orquesta Nacional, and *Concierto lírico* in 1945 by the Orquesta Nacional.

100. Martínez del Fresno, *Julio Gómez*, 20.

101. Gómez contributed to *Harmonía* from 1916 to 1916, and then from 1929 to 1935. See Martínez del Fresno, *Julio Gómez*, 215.

102. Julio Gómez, "Comentarios del presente y del pasado," *Harmonía*, April–June (1941), 4.

103. Gómez, "Comentarios del presente y del pasado," *Harmonía*, January–March (1946), 1.

104. Gómez, "Comentarios del presente y del pasado," *Harmonía*, October–December (1941), 3; Gómez, "Comentarios del presente y del pasado," *Harmonía*, April–June (1945), 1.

105. Julio Gómez, "Comentarios del presente y del pasado," *Harmonía*, April–June (1944), 3.

106. Letter from Julio Gómez to José Subirá, June 23, 1940.

107. Gómez, "Los vihuelistas españoles," 4.

108. Ibid., 8. During the remainder of the decade, Gómez only occasionally contributed to *Ritmo*, mostly on music bibliography topics he was familiar with thanks to his work as a librarian; see Julio Gómez, "Un autógrafo de Bizet en la Biblioteca del Conservatorio," *Ritmo*, no. 138 (1940), 4–6; Gómez, "Un concierto sinfónico español en 1875," *Ritmo*, no. 155 (1942), 4–5; Gómez, "La biblioteca del conservatorio," *Ritmo*, no. 160 (1942), 30–32; Gómez, "Pedagogía y autoanálisis," *Ritmo*, no. 176 (1944), 4–6.

109. Gómez, "Comentarios," April–June (1945), 4. See also, on Falla's Spanishness, Gómez, "Comentarios del presente y del pasado," *Harmonía*, January–March (1947), 2.

110. Julio Gómez, "Comentarios del presente y del pasado," *Harmonía*, October–December (1947), 3.

111. Ibid., 5.

112. Ibid., 5.

113. Ibid., 5.

114. Bretón and Pedrell indeed had significant differences over their approaches to founding a Spanish operatic tradition. See Martínez del Fresno, *Julio Gómez*, 49.

115. Gómez, "Comentarios," April–June (1941), 4.

116. Gómez, "Comentarios del presente y del pasado," *Harmonía*, July–September (1941), 3–4.

117. Gómez, "Comentarios," January–March (1946), 1.

118. Gómez, "Comentarios," July–September (1946), 3.

119. Gómez, "Comentarios," October–December (1943), 1–2; Gómez, "Comentarios del presente y del pasado," *Harmonía*, July–September (1944), 1.

120. Gómez, "Comentarios," April–June (1944), 1; Gómez, "Comentarios del presente y del pasado," *Harmonía*, July–September (1945), 1–3.

121. Gómez, "Comentarios del presente y del pasado," *Harmonía*, April–June (1943), 3–4.

122. Gómez, "Comentarios," July–September (1944), 1; Gómez, "Comentarios del presente y del pasado," *Harmonía*, April–June (1946), 1.

CHAPTER 4

Reviewing Traditional Music

Toward Unity of the Men and the Land of Spain

In his 1948 article for *Arbor* on the history of Spanish music, Anglès did not only write about the musicians working for the Catholic monarchs, the music of the *vihuelistas*, and Renaissance polyphony to exemplify how the spirit or essence behind Spanish identity had expressed itself in sound through the centuries. Traditional music had also been crucial, according to Anglès, in granting Spain a significant role in universal music. Anglès argued, following Pedrell's concept of *música natural*,[1] that Spanish art and traditional music—in other words, Spanish high and low culture—were in constant synergy, with Spanish folklore showing traits derived from Greek culture, Provencal lyric poetry, and medieval religious plays.[2] There were no legacies, however, from the music of Al-Andalus, as written by Anglès when he was trying to refute the theory that the *melismae* typical of the music of southern Spain had Arab origins[3]; as with Spanish early music, traditional music also had to be fitted within *Hispanidad*, and this made it necessary to minimize or excise any connections to religions other than Catholicism.

Anglès had a lifelong interest in traditional music. In his youth he collected traditional songs in his home province of Tarragona.[4] Nevertheless, he soon found himself focusing mostly on Spanish early music during his years at the Biblioteca Nacional de Catalunya, and his interest in traditional music was not rekindled by the Franco regime in any significant way. His contributions to *Monumentos* and *Anuario Musical* all focused on Spanish art music, and he was at first skeptical about founding a department of folk music within the IEM: Otaño intended to create, and direct himself, a section of folklore within the IEM, but as Anglès, unhappy about Otaño's interference, confided to Subirá, "let us focus first on the *Monumentos* and the catalogues, and then, little by little, we will start to think about folklore."[5] The folklore department of the IEM was eventually founded in 1944, under the direction not of Otaño but of Marius Schneider, a German folklorist fleeing the Nazi regime whom Anglès personally selected for the job while he focused on the *Monumentos*. Schneider remained in office until 1951; during his tenure, he organized fieldwork expeditions, or *misiones folklóricas*, in which several researchers collected folk material in various regions of Spain, with the aim of creating and publishing a corpus of Spanish folk music. The IEM also organized regular contests to distinguish the best compilations of folklore, usually from specific regions.[6]

It was, however, not the IEM but rather the Sección Femenina that allowed Spanish traditional music to repeatedly make the headlines in newspapers and magazines during the early Franco regime. This is because, according to Sopeña in his 1949 account of the first ten years of music under Francoism, it was thanks to the Sección Femenina that "authentic and genuine folklore now regularly visits Madrid, that is, the song, the dance, the costumes, the 'atmosphere', thoroughly reconstructed following detailed study. It is only this living folklore that can bring us something with substantial and effective consequences."[7] The Sección Femenina was founded in 1934 as the women's department of the Falange under the direction of José Antonio Primo de Rivera's sister Pilar, who remained its leader through the Civil War and all of the dictatorship until 1977. It was already during the Civil War that the Sección Femenina developed a strong interest in traditional music, with its first cohort of *instructoras* being trained in 1938.[8] These were young women sent by the organization to villages and rural areas to collect traditional dances and songs, which would then be published and taught throughout the country by the *instructoras* themselves, mainly to children and other young women.

After Franco's victory, the Sección Femenina was put in charge of organizing education and leisure activities for Spanish girls and young women throughout the country. Traditional music was, from the beginning, a crucial part of its program: it was in 1939 that local ensembles of amateur female performers specializing in traditional song and dance were established under the name of *Coros y Danzas* (literally, "choirs and dances"). More significantly, on May 30, 1939, the national committee of the Sección Femenina, in its first significant meeting after the war, which was held in Medina del Campo with Franco in attendance, named traditional music as one of the three elements that would ensure the unity of Spain in the future (the other two were Spanish soil and national-syndicalism). In the meeting itself, traditional song and dance were given the utmost importance, with thousands of women attending from all regions of Spain and singing traditional songs as they paraded before Franco.[9] The strong presence of traditional music in large-scale political events demonstrates how the Sección Femenina did not regard collecting, publishing, and teaching traditional music as a mere pastime or a nostalgic attempt at rescuing the music from the past. On the contrary, such activities had a clear political intention and were meant to address a specific problem: separatism, particularly in the Basque Country, Catalonia, and to a lesser extent Galicia. Members of the Sección Femenina were required to learn and perform songs and dances from all over Spain; eventually (or such was the rationale), all Spaniards would be acquainted with traditional music from all Spanish regions and would also come to regard all of them as their own, thus eroding regional differences and making traditional music uniform throughout the country. The *cancioneros*, or collections of popular songs mainly aimed at nonprofessional performance and teaching, pursued the same end.[10] As Pilar Primo de Rivera put it in a well-known quotation from 1942:

> When the Catalans can sing the songs of Castile, when all Castilians know the *sardana*[11] and can play the *txistu*,[12] when Andalusian *cante*[13] shows all its depth and philosophy, when the songs of Galicia get to be known in Levante, when 50,000 or 60,000 voices raise to sing the same song, then we will be able to say that we have achieved unity among all men and lands of Spain.[14]

Moreover, with the Sección Femenina being an all-women institution, the Franco regime introduced a hitherto unknown gender divide into collection, promotion, and performance of folklore. Although the equivalent organizations for boys and young men—the Frente de Juventudes and, from 1960 onward, the Organización Juvenil Española—also included singing of traditional songs in their training programs, in no way was it as ubiquitous as within the Sección Femenina. There certainly were other entities catering to both genres, such as the Organización Sindical de Educación y Descanso (Trade Organization for Education and Leisure) within the government-controlled workers' association Sindicato Vertical. The Organización Sindical convened and managed choirs and other traditional music ensembles throughout the country with the aim of promoting a way of entertainment for the population that was healthy and morally appropriate; even so, it did not enjoy the nationwide presence or the press coverage of the Sección Femenina.

Through song and dance, the Sección Femenina strongly codified the bodies and gender roles of women,[15] but at the same time it gave them a political role in construction of the nation, at least nominally; through their involvement with traditional music, women could, and should, help achieve and preserve the unity of Spain and educate men and children following traditional Spanish values.[16] From the 1940s onward, the political role of women involved in folklore extended to supporting Spain's diplomatic relations with countries in the Western Bloc. *Coros y Danzas* toured abroad for the first time in 1948, under the auspices of the Foreign Service of the Sección Femenina, giving performances at embassies and cultural associations in Argentina and Brazil. In the following years they performed in Peru and Colombia (1949), at the Llangollen festival in Wales (1950), in the Middle East and the United States (1950), and in Paris, Rome, and Venice (1951).[17] Through numerous reports on the musical activities of the Sección Femenina and other organizations, or simply by enthusiastically defending folklore, newspapers and magazines under the early Franco regime helped establish a connection between Spanish traditional music and the values of *Hispanidad*. Writings on Spanish traditional music were also intended to reach a broader audience than those on early or new music; indeed, news stories about the Sección Femenina were not confined to the music columns of newspapers, but appeared in other sections and even on the front page, and some magazines outside the Madrid mainstream circles—such as *Boletín del Colegio de Directores de Bandas de Música Civiles* or *Revista Literaria Musical*—devoted considerable attention to traditional music events.

Although it was thanks to these writings that traditional music was made into an essential component of *Hispanidad*, interest in traditional music was by no means a novelty under the Franco regime. The first collections of Spanish folklore were published in the early nineteenth century; many more appeared during the remainder of the century.[18] As products of the various nationalist and regionalist movements that flourished during this time, most collections aimed to present either the folklore of a particular region (usually the Basque Country, Catalonia, and Galicia) as a differential trait setting that region apart from the rest of Spain and asserting its national identity against the perceived cultural monopoly of Castile, or regional and local differences in traditional music not as an expression of the existence of differing national identities within Spain but rather as a manifestation of diversity within unity.[19] Pedrell's *Cancionero musical popular español*, published between 1918 and 1922, is an example of the latter; not surprisingly, it was published during the years in which debates about national regeneration of Spain were at a peak.

As was the case with research into Spanish early music, during the first three decades of the twentieth century, interest in traditional music was not the province of one particular political ideology; governments of various sorts supported research and dissemination of folklore under one form or another, informed by ideas of national self-awareness and regeneration. The Junta para Ampliación de Estudios (Society for Extension of Studies) and the Centro de Estudios Históricos (Center for Historical Studies) were founded by Spanish liberal governments in 1907 and 1910 respectively, with the aim of promoting scientific research into all disciplines as a source of regeneration and progress for the country. They both supported research into Spanish traditional music, with Eduardo Martínez Torner collecting Spanish folklore in numerous field trips for the Junta[20] and also contributing to the Centro together with another future exile, Jesús Bal y Gay. Under the Second Republic, Martínez Torner also found a welcoming environment for his interest in traditional music: he took part, together with other well-known intellectuals such as Federico García Lorca, Antonio Machado, and the future exile Óscar Esplá in the Republic's Misiones Pedagógicas, aimed at introducing a range of cultural experiences to the Spanish rural population through series of talks, workshops, lectures, itinerant libraries, cinema screenings, concerts and recitals, and theater performances.[21] Similarly, most of the Grupo de los Ocho and other composers committed to modernization of Spanish music, such as Roberto Gerhard, showed an interest in folklore both before and after exile; this was normally coupled with concern and reflection on how to best make use of Spanish traditional music as a renovating force for Spanish music, all the while escaping clichéd uses of folklore. In this, Falla was a model for many.[22]

Under Francoism, traditional music had to be adapted to the new understandings of Spanish identity promoted by the regime. Music journalism and criticism played an important role in this; for example, a folk song was now not simply a folk song, but a symbol of the unity of the country and of the military prowess of the Francoist army. After all, it was surely not by chance that the first of April—the same day the Civil War ended in 1939—was turned, shortly after the war, into the Día de la Canción (Day of the Song), perhaps because when Franco announced that the war had ended "the Spanish population demonstrated their joy by organizing patriotic demonstrations and singing cheerful songs. Song is a spontaneous expression of joy, optimism and hope, and at that time Spaniards felt these three emotions because the war had ended and because a triumphant dawn was awaiting the Fatherland."[23] Folk songs were not just an expression of joy, but also a force that crucially helped the military triumph, with Francoist soldiers often singing them to gather courage and stimulate patriotism ("the same songs which, not long ago, sounded in the battlefields, sacrificed for the homeland, of Teruel, Ebro, Brunete").[24]

Conversely, some military and war hymns composed during the Spanish Civil War or shortly before, such as *Cara al sol* and *Montañas nevadas,* were printed in the *cancioneros* of the Sección Femenina next to bona fide traditional songs, so as to emphasize that both genres ultimately served the same aims. The patriotic role of traditional song, however, did not end with the war effort. After the Civil War, traditional song was to continue exerting a crucial influence in the cultural and symbolic construction of Spain, now that physical construction had been achieved; Joaquín Turina described the Día de la Canción as an impulse for yearlong efforts to achieve national construction and unity, especially for younger Spaniards.[25] Similarly, Adelaida (believed to be a pseudonym for the identity of a female primary school teacher) named in *Radio Nacional* the folk song as the basis of the system of musical instruction that the regime should put in place to satisfy its aim of "constructing a new Spain." Musical education at the primary school level should thus aim to cater for the "emotional and spiritual needs" of the students, and the best way to do so would be through use of Spanish folklore in schools.[26]

Ideas of national unity were, of course, an important part of what Spanish children should absorb through learning traditional songs, consonant with Pilar Primo de Rivera's well-known quote. On the occasion of the Día de la Canción of 1943, Fernando Rodríguez del Río specifically addressed the therapeutic power traditional music could have against separatism because "[the Día de la Canción] prevents, with rhythms born out of the community, the spiritual isolation, so disintegrating and lethal, of our people and our beautiful regions."[27] The task of the Sección Femenina was, according to Rodríguez del Río, not only to overcome such isolation, but also to counterbalance individual talent, thus submerging the individual in the mass: "They do not aim for spectacular successes, nor for the revelation of outstanding artists; on the contrary, they want the villages, the towns, the regions, to get to know each other, and, in so doing, to understand and love each other."[28]

Focus on national unity, however, did not mean that all Spanish traditional music was perceived as totally homogeneous, by the Sección Femenina or by the critics writing on traditional music; their discourse left a space to acknowledge regional differences, which sometimes adopted the form of long-lasting stereotypes. For example, Julieta Mateo Box characterized the music of several Spanish regions in these terms: "gracious Andalusia, noble Aragon, refined Galicia, most beautiful Asturias, industrious Catalonia, aristocratic Castile."[29] Diversity, however, was not considered a trait to be celebrated per se, but rather as nothing other than a further expression of unity; Eduardo López-Chavarri named Spain as "the world's richest nation in folklore" and stated that the reason for this was to be found in Spain's history, with its succession of invasions and its varied geography.[30] Such historical and geographical diversity, however, argued López-Chavarri, had shaped the Hispanic race in a unique way, and thus the diversity of traditional music, arising from the same historical and geographical circumstances, was nothing other than a expression of national identity, or, in his words, the "reintegration of the conscience of the race."[31] López-Chavarri explicitly praised Franco for his efforts to keep folk song alive "in order to avoid the disappearance of the soul of our race."

"Canción popular" (popular song) or simply "canción" (song) was the term most frequently used by music critics under Francoism to refer to popular music; folklore, for its part, could have negative connotations, as will be discussed later. The word *song* emphasized the vocal nature of the music, its simplicity (no instruments were needed; the human voice was enough to recreate popular music), and its potential to be an expression of both the individual and the community; a monophonic song could indeed be sung by as few or as many voices as required. Traditional music, although deemed suitable to provide solutions to the specific problems of post–Civil War Spain, was also thought to be atemporal and fundamentally rural; it was regarded as a fossilized repertoire rather than a living reality, mirroring general notions that had influenced the compilation and study of European folklore since the nineteenth century and that were already becoming outdated in other countries by the 1930s.[32] Such notions of traditional music operated not only in musical criticism or the popular imaginary; they also had a crucial influence on traditional music research. The IEM organized in 1948 a competition aiming to distinguish the best creative and scholarly works in a number of disciplines, including traditional music, and it had very precise entry requirements: "The music of modern forms of entertainment (cinema, *cuplé, zarzuela,* etc.) which have grown popular among the masses will not be taken into account, but only the music which is undoubtedly popular." The examples named by the Instituto were primarily urban, thus suggesting the notion that true popular music could be found only in rural settings, following Pedrell's view of traditional music as *música natural.*[33]

Some critics even claimed that geographical isolation was necessary for preservation of the purest and most original features of the music, without fear of external contamination: when reviewing a concert of the local choral society of Tarrasa, in Catalonia, José María Franco praised the purity of villages "constrained in valleys" because they could "keep their traditions unaltered."[34] It was not only geography, though, that guaranteed that traditional music remained faithful to its rural origins, but also a whole culture of transmission and learning. For example, spontaneous learning of music through folklore was implicitly (and sometimes explicitly) compared to the traditional, stricter, and more strongly regulated learning methods and procedures of Western art music. In an extended article about the training of the *instructoras* in a school of the Sección Femenina, the journalist María Dolores Pérez Camarero commented that "they [the *instructoras*] are now learning to feel the music, to know it spiritually" because, despite the majority of them being conservatory graduates in music, "they used to know music only mechanically."[35] Pérez Camarero also claimed that women were more suited than men to the type of work *instructoras* did; after all, she argued, the first music ever heard by every human being was the *canción de cuna* (cradle song) of his or her mother. This particular brand of musical purity, supposedly achieved through physical isolation and loyalty to traditional values, was compared to the purity of the race, which should also remain isolated in order to avoid foreign contamination; Mateo Box was precisely referring to this perceived contamination by asking rhetorically, "Why do you sing those terrible, extravagant, blackish rhythms and forget the purity and beauty of our songs?"[36]

For all the efforts of the Spanish government to promote and disseminate traditional music, it was often portrayed by music critics as fragile and threatened by a multiplicity of dangers. In the 1940s, separatism was supposed to be under control after Franco's victory, but there were other pressing dangers: foreign influence (as reflected in Mateo Box's article), industrialization, and generally speaking everything threatening the rural lifestyle in which traditional music was said to flourish. Disruption of rural space—by way of being urbanized or the inhabitants leaving for the cities—was a threat in itself, and a particularly real one: not only was the Spanish countryside being depopulated, but the early Franco regime itself, for all the rhetoric in defense of the past, regarded industrialization as a pillar in regenerating post–Civil War Spain.[37] Eduardo López-Chavarri did not of course explicitly criticize the government's industrializing measures, but he lamented that "[the common man] has lost contact with nature, has forgotten that there is dawn, and morning stars, and streams, and agriculture tasks: the machine turned him into a pleb. His songs to life became mean political satires or cabaret eroticism."[38] Urban and industrial life, López-Chavarri argued, were a threat to the diversity and distinctiveness that constituted the main feature of Spanish musical essence, for urban popular music was the same "in New York as in Istanbul, in Bilbao as in Buenos Aires." And it would not be long, warned the journalist Javier del Valle, until those still living in the countryside demanded "fox trots, tangos and *corridos*," because this was the music that was in fashion in the cities.[39]

It was the urban population and especially the working classes who were considered more likely to succumb to negative influence, much of which was supposedly coming from abroad. In this regard, the traditional-music events organized by Educación Sindical were repeatedly praised in the musical press for allowing workers to entertain themselves by singing together and socializing, and therefore preventing them from giving in to more dangerous forms of entertainment. Or as Santiago Riopérez y Milá put it, "[Educación Sindical] steal the leisure time of workers away from pernicious vices and forms of entertainment." Such vices included consumerism, which, paradoxically, can be considered to go hand-in-hand with the nascent capitalism fostered by the regime: Riopérez y Milá congratulated himself that "the working class has abandoned its materialism and is now busy with spiritual aspirations."[40]

Similarly, Sáinz de la Maza praised Educación Sindical for "teaching the young citizens, who used to pervert the good qualities of the song in absurd and dull *cuplés*,[41] how to sing the great, good and noble things of life: Fatherland, love and soil."[42] Sáinz de la Maza thus implicitly recognized that without the guidance of overarching, ubiquitous state institutions, the young population could be easily misled by the appeal of the urban and sophisticated *cuplé* rather than remain faithful to rural song. Nonmilitary wind bands, which also received state support, were regarded as potential vehicles of expression of the "true character of the race," ideal for performing arrangements of popular songs originally conceived for voice alone.[43] The composer and wind band conductor Eduardo S. Morell similarly highlighted the importance of bands and choirs for spiritual development of the rural population, especially children, to "educate and purify our feelings." He also deplored that some villages had abandoned these practices, attracted by more mundane forms of entertainment.[44] Bands and especially choirs could also safeguard moral values as dictated by Catholicism, in particular those concerning family and sexual mores: Rafael Benedito, conductor of the Masa Coral de Madrid and a collaborator with the Sección Femenina, established a connection between choral singing and formation of patriarchal, traditional, Catholic families in 1945, on the occasion of the twenty-fifth anniversary of the Masa: "Our task is so full of moral significance and so pure that some of our current singers are the sons and daughters of the couples who met years ago while singing."[45]

Capitalism and consumerism could allegedly also harm traditional music by turning it into a commercial product dissociated from its values and essence; in this regard, warned some music critics, it was essential that traditional music remain an amateur pursuit, such as in the *Coros y Danzas* both in Spain[46] and abroad. Members of the *Coros y Danzas* did not receive any payment for their work, but instead gave to the state any money the ensemble earned during international tours.[47] Santiago Riopérez y Milá highlighted the altruistic nature of the *Coros y Danzas* and claimed, "There is nothing more convenient to make the different countries embrace each other, to unite their frontiers, than the cultural missions which they undertake."[48] The other side of the coin were the dance troupes, which, in the critics' opinion, commercially exploited folklore by reducing it to a few clichéd, exotic traits, such as flamenco *café cantantes*, about which critic Dámaso Torres wrote, "Popular song, which has been transmitted from one generation to another through the centuries, as soon as it gets distorted and put on *tablados*[49] and stages, stops being popular and loses its scent and freshness."[50] In a language heavily reminiscent of Giménez Caballero's reservations about the commercialization of art, Torres argued that traditional music should be dissociated from any kind of financial goal in order to conserve its purity and ability to shape the national conscience of the country, and also to guarantee that it was indeed a collective, anonymous enterprise rather than an opportunity for particular individuals to enjoy undue prominence.

Another example of the commercialization of traditional music was the so-called *género folklórico* or simply *folklore*—an early twentieth-century derivation of *zarzuela*'s *género chico* formulaically based on traditional music, specially from Andalusia.[51] In *Ritmo*, José Rivera Centeno called the *género folklórico* "the monstrosities and caricatures of our true folklore," divulged abroad by ensembles and impresarios with "mercantilist" aims.[52] The only antidote against the *género folkórico*, argued Rivera Centeno, was the *Coros y Danzas*, who altruistically disseminated Spanish authentic traditional music abroad. In order to overcome the problem, Rivera Centeno, as others had done before, suggested stronger intervention of the state in regulating folklore, namely, to appoint a teacher in every conservatory or music academy who would be responsible for "preserving the purity and conservation of the music, instruments and dances of each region."[53]

THE DANGERS AND SEDUCTIONS OF JAZZ

Other musical genres could also be a threat to traditional music and the national values it embodied, especially jazz, whose popularity was on the rise in 1940s Spain.[54] It must be taken into account that, when Spanish critics used the word, they were referring not only to Dixieland, bebop, and the like but, more generally, to any genre of popular urban music, especially those intended for dancing.[55] Not surprisingly, during the Civil War and the first years thereafter until approximately 1945, racist and anti-Semitic arguments informed the discourse on jazz in music criticism: Giménez Caballero's views on art were still influential, and the Spanish government was still close to Nazi Germany, besides echoing the long-standing right-wing ideas that a Jewish-Freemason conspiracy (*contubernio judeo-masónico*) was damaging Spain's international prestige.[56] Many of the writings on jazz used the derogatory terms "negro" or "negroid" music; the critic Sebastián Méndez, for example, deplored that many Spanish conservatoire graduates, having been trained in the Western art music tradition, chose to play "negroid or foreign music."[57] Derogatory references to the African origins of jazz were also commonplace, as in *El Alcázar*, which complained that hot jazz was so popular in Belgium that "the whole nation dances to the rhythms imported from the jungle,"[58] thus elevating the popularity of jazz to the scale of national tragedy.

For some critics, it was not simply a matter of jazz displacing indigenous genres, but rather of it fatally altering the national racial traits in the process. Francisco Padín, who was staff music critic at *El Diario de Cádiz* and a frequent contributor to *Ritmo*, was in this regard one of the most vocal detractors of jazz, frequently warning his readers about the negative consequences that a clash between African music and Spanish society would have for preservation of the race: "[Jazz musicians] offend our ears with the rhythm of this black, wild music, even when there is so much to retrieve and disseminate in the everlasting archive of Spanish folklore."[59] The fact that jazz remained popular among Spanish audiences in spite of governmental and journalistic contempt was perceived by Padín as an aberrant reversal of the natural order established by the intrinsic qualities of the different races; it was now the colonized, Padín argued, who were attacking the colonizers instead of showing them gratitude ("We Spaniards . . . should not be so fond of imitating the *negroes*, who received baptism and Christian civilization from the hands of our conquerors and evangelizers"[60]). This reversal of the natural order could, warned Padín, have extremely negative effects on gender roles as well, and he accused African music and jazz of producing effeminate behavior ("There is nothing more opposed to our masculine racial features than those sweet, decadent, monotone melodies, which, like an impotent lament, effeminate our souls; there is nothing more unworthy of our spiritual dignity than those crazy dances"[61]). Other writers were less critical than Padín, but they still understood jazz predominantly in terms of race. Joaquín Rodrigo wrote for *El Español* an article about "black music and white music" as part of a special feature on "negro" (sic) culture.[62] He commented on the presence of "black music" in Western art music, citing the examples of Ravel and Debussy and their jazz-influenced compositions, and even attempted to describe the characteristics of this vaguely defined "black music": in Rodrigo's opinion, "black" music was characterized by the presence of rhythm, which "tries to replace the very soul of white music: the melody."

Other texts echo early Francoism's obsession with the *conspiración judeo-masónica*, with jazz portrayed as a further tool of the Jewish community to domesticate the Western nations. As seen in one example written during the Civil War, this meant specifically Spain, Germany, and Italy:

> Spain, Germany and Italy happen to be the greatest musical nations of the world. Why should we continue paying attention to music which is only suitable for the *negros* and American barbarians, but damages the sensibility of those peoples which have reached the highest peaks even in their popular art? Let *fox-trots* die at once. They are part of the arsenal of the Jewish soul to degenerate the selected races.[63]

The idea that jazz was an element of the *conspiración* did certainly resonate with some critics; this quotation was first printed in 1938 at the *Periódico de San Sebastián*, but Eduardo López-Chavarri considered its words so relevant in 1942 that he quoted them in an article about jazz versions of works of the mainstream art music repertoire, which he compared to "a slaughter of the great masters."[64] Nevertheless, anti-Semitism was not necessarily the norm in writings about jazz, and articles such as López-Chavarri's are the exception rather than the norm; further, most openly anti-Semitic articles date from the Civil War and the few years thereafter. Even López-Chavarri himself did not explain in detail how exactly this Jewish attack was orchestrated, and who was facilitating it in Spain and how. With no significant Jewish community in Spain, let alone a community of Jewish musicians, anti-Semitism was hardly an articulating force in the discourses of Francoist music critics about jazz; rather, it can be regarded as a particular expression of racial discourses that typically found a more present, threatening enemy in the United States and capitalism, especially in the years before 1945. Critics thus regarded jazz as a symptom of the rising cultural hegemony of the United States, which would corrupt Spanish traditional values with cosmopolitanism and immorality. Otaño argued that all music genres should be represented except for one: "That artistically and morally reviling music, so insisting and tiresome, which is modern jazz and its derivations.[65]" He resorted to the usual racial tropes to describe jazz as "those exotic dances of the negroes, the product of the African jungles, transformed artistically, often in a way which is morally wrong, by the orchestras of the cabarets of the city." Otaño complained that the Americans had "flooded the world with their wild folklore," which had taken them "back to the primitive caves in morals and good taste," therefore accusing the American government of using jazz as propaganda.

As with Spanish early music or contemporary music, however, slightly dissenting opinions about jazz can be found in the musical press even before 1945. It is not that particular publications or authors wholeheartedly embraced jazz, but rather that their arguments to reject it were pragmatic rather than based on racial understandings of music.[66] This was the case with *Boletín del Colegio de Directores de Bandas de Música Civiles* and *Revista Literaria Musical,* which were primarily directed to working musicians, not only from Madrid but also in the provinces, who presumably had to respond to the demands of their audiences. Therefore, *Boletín del Colegio* and *Revista Literaria Musical* did not focus so much on the racial origins of jazz—as *Ritmo,* for example, did—but rather on how the increasing popularity of jazz had changed the marketplace for Spanish composers. Conductor and composer Rodrigo A. de Santiago complained that Spanish composers did not have any incentive to submit entries to government-sponsored composition contests (*premios nacionales de música*) and chose to compose light music instead because "they can easily earn more money by playing a couple of swing songs."[67] *Revista Literaria Musical* encouraged young Spanish composers, in a somewhat bitter tone, to write jazz and dance music because "this is where the money is"; the writer complained that foreign genres (referred to as "foxtrots") already amounted to 75 percent of the music being played in Spain, which either destroyed job opportunities for Spanish composers of popular music or forced them to turn to foreign genres.[68]

Professional protectionism and racial rhetoric, however, were not mutually exclusive and could indeed complement each other rather well. Indeed, some of the measures taken by professional associations presumably with the aim of protecting job opportunities for Spanish musicians were exaggeratedly praised in the musical press for their role in preserving Spanish racial values. For example, *Ritmo* published in 1942 an anonymous editorial supporting recent measures against foreign music adopted by the Sindicato Nacional del Espectáculo,[69] which had banned the "jazzy" or merely "modern" versions of art music composers.[70] The editorial framed the conflict again in racial terms, labeling such versions as "an invasion of negroid music, with its performances which profaned the great ideas, treasures of the musical goldsmithing, and which were a serious threaten to Western culture and civilization." It also encouraged readers to denounce transgressions of such regulations, therefore inviting audiences to take an active part in preserving the purity of the Spanish race. But although the Sindicato did adopt some measures such as the ban and also demanded that song titles be translated from foreign languages into Spanish, requests for governmental control coming from music critics and made on the premise of preserving the purity of the race went largely unheard.[71]

But even such suggestions for measures of government control based on racial premises were hard to find past 1945, as the Franco regime was trying to minimize its past associations with the Axis countries and approach the Western powers instead. In a very different tone from López-Chavarri when he was complaining about the "slaughter of the great masters," some critics now appreciated the hybridization of jazz and art music, with positive comments about Gershwin's and Copland's works.[72] *Ritmo* itself, which in the first half of the decade had repeatedly attacked jazz on racial grounds, was redesigned in December 1950 to accommodate a whole section on jazz music. In the previous years, *Ritmo* had already given some space to jazz through the writings of the pioneer jazzman and music journalist Luis Araque, who argued that jazz was not the product of putatively inferior races, but rather the natural evolution of art music in the twentieth century, and as such it was just as spiritual as art music genres of the past.[73] Also in *Ritmo*, P. C. Hernández praised jazz because "it is a popular genre, warmly human, alive and free."[74] Nevertheless, although it is reasonable to think that *Ritmo* was responding to the change of direction of the regime's international politics, this should not be regarded as proof that the government had an official line on jazz disseminated through the musical press. It is even doubtful that *Ritmo* itself had an official line on jazz, since these examples still coexisted with criticism of jazz on racial grounds, as in this comment from 1949[75]: "The influence of negroid music has penetrated alarmingly into the sentimental or romantic souls of the Latin race.... There are few musicologists and composers among us who defend the Hispanoamericanism of our indigenous music. Let the *negros* alone play, sing and dance their African dances."

The first Spanish periodical ever specializing in jazz, *Ritmo y Melodía*, also occupies an interesting position in the landscape of music criticism in early Francoism. It was founded in 1944 by Araque, with contributions from other Spanish pioneering jazzmen such as Alfredo Papó, and ceased publication in 1950. In its first issues, *Ritmo y Melodía* did include information about art music in Spain, as well as interviews with art music composers and performers.[76] But most prominently, it provided information on the jazz scene and latest record releases in foreign countries, as well as on the activities of Spanish hot clubs, associations of jazz enthusiasts in the main Spanish cities who met regularly to listen to jazz recordings imported from abroad or to actually play jazz themselves. Nevertheless, it would not be accurate to portray *Ritmo y Melodía* as a voice of dissent in a milieu hostile to jazz music, as was the case in Germany,[77] in the same way as jazz itself in early Francoism cannot unequivocally be considered a music of subversion.[78] In the first place, as has been discussed before, in the mid-to-late 1940s hostility against jazz was less widespread than it was in the first half of the decade; and second, with a print run of seven thousand in the years 1945–46, *Ritmo y Melodía* was the most widely circulated music magazine in Spain, followed by *Ritmo* (with a print run of six thousand) and *Música. Revista Quincenal* (print run five thousand), which hardly makes it a semiclandestine publication for a small minority. Moreover, contributors to *Ritmo y Melodía* did not often complain about widespread hostility about jazz; an exception was Papó, in his response to an article published elsewhere by the writer and journalist Wenceslao Fernández Flórez.[79] Papó argued that Fernández Flórez, who referred to jazz as "negroid music," had a simplistic and inaccurate understanding of the genre, and he asked the journalist to listen to jazz without preconceived ideas based on racial notions. However, he agreed with Fernández Flórez in arguing that the government should ask for a minimum percentage of Spanish music to be played on radio stations for the sake of protecting the livelihood of Spanish musicians.[80] Other contributors complained that art music critics attacked jazz on the basis of inaccurate and illogical arguments, but they did not explain who those critics might be.[81]

Nevertheless, more often than not, contributors to *Ritmo y Melodía* agreed with detractors of jazz in regarding the great popularity of the genre as a threat—not because it would harm the purity of the Spanish race, but rather because it would dilute the purity of jazz. Indeed, in the same way that other publications used the word *jazz* loosely, contributors to *Ritmo y Melodía* typically chose "hot jazz" to refer to their object of interest, presumably to differentiate themselves from other popular music genres. *Ritmo y Melodía* contributors complained that Spaniards were not genuinely interested in jazz and that its popularity was rather "a fashion"[82]; that the "excesses" of swing dancing attracted toward jazz people who did not really care about the music[83]; that the Spanish listeners were "an amorphous audience, deprived of a personality—we mean, of a jazzistic personality"[84]; or that jazz musicians, in an effort to be commercially successful, were introducing alien elements into jazz.[85] From September 1949 onward, however, *Ritmo y Melodía* softened some of these criticisms and tried to broaden its readership: the magazine was redesigned to allocate more than half of every issue to entertainment forms other than jazz, including cinema, theater, musical theater, and dance music; in one of its last issues before it eventually ceased publication in November 1950, critic

Eugenio S. Mendo encouraged all jazz enthusiasts in Spain to publicly present their music and others' and thus definitely persuade those who judged jazz on the basis of racial prejudices that were disseminated through music that was not even jazz in the first place.[86]

At first sight, Mendo's words do not paint a very different picture from the racially based attacks on jazz during the Civil War and shortly thereafter; in the late 1940s and early 1950s traditional music was still regarded—and perhaps more so than in the early 1940s—as an expression of national values to be preserved and protected from foreign influence, thanks to the popularity of the *Coros y Danzas* abroad. But, ultimately, before it ceased publication, *Ritmo y Melodía* provided a means of expression for jazz enthusiasts in Spain. And perhaps out of the tensions generated by the way in which other critics opposed traditional and jazz music, it was from the ranks of *Ritmo y Melodía* that some criticism of traditional music research politics emerged. In an article for *Ritmo*, Araque questioned whether such opposition should exist in the same place, as, he claimed, it was perfectly possible to enjoy both traditional music and jazz; he challenged the argument that, were it not for jazz and musical theater, traditional music would flourish in every Spanish household, as it had in the past centuries.[87] He furthermore argued that compilations of traditional music were not as "pure and clean" as its authors claimed, thus tacitly questioning the prevailing notion of traditional music as a fossilized being rather than a living one.[88] Although Araque's article did not amount to full-fledged criticism of the politics of traditional music of the Spanish government—and indeed, he did not explicitly name any of the individuals or institutions he was arguing against—it is illustrative of how individual critics and publications could sometimes create a space to express dissent or disagreement with the politics promoted by the government.

TRADITIONAL MUSIC IN ART MUSIC: JOAQUÍN RODRIGO AS A MUSIC CRITIC

With traditional music being so frequently featured in various types of publications and transformed into one of the pillars of national regeneration, it could be expected that most young and not-so-young Spanish composers would make ample use of Spanish traditional music in their compositions to ensure they would be performed and positively reviewed. Some writers on music supported use of traditional music without showing much subtlety, or discussing in detail what would be the best way to do so; for example, the wind band conductor Sergio Valbuena Esgueva wrote that new compositions for this ensemble should be "built upon a solid racial support" and always stay "within the Hispanic soul."[89] Victoriano Echevarría regarded traditional music as an antidote against Stravinsky's and Schoenberg's dehumanization, arguing that the only path for Spanish music was "to find its foundation in the sincerest expression of our eternal values, that is, in the essence of our popular music, focusing on the spirit rather than on the literal use."[90] Similarly, it is true that Sopeña, for all his hopes that traditional music would be the solution to the crisis of Spanish contemporary music, did not devote much time to discussing what distinguished sincere from nonsincere use of traditional music, apart from repeatedly naming Falla as the model all Spanish composers should follow. A significant number of works by Spanish composers, both newcomers and the more established, were given their first performances by the Madrid orchestras during the 1940s,[91] and they were generally positively reviewed in newspapers, although not always with much engagement with the techniques composers used and how they treated traditional music. Nevertheless, although these and similar approaches to use of folklore in art music have sometimes led to the claim that the music of 1940s *neocasticismo* (a Spanish version of *neoclasicismo*, based on Spain's own eighteenth-century music) was scarcely innovative and was formulaic and based only superficially on Falla's legacy, without an attempt to create a musical language of one's own,[92] a few music critics were in fact concerned with helping composers find the best ways to integrate folklore into art music as a truly regenerative force under the newly established regime.

As with other prominent topics in music criticism during the 1940s, some of the debates that occupied music critics were hardly new; Spanish musicians had been discussing them for years, or even decades. A long-standing debate was whether the traditional music of some Spanish regions was more suitable than that of others in providing the foundation for a truly Spanish school of composition; specifically, should Andalusian music, which had been repeatedly used by nineteenth-century composers, Spanish and foreign, be embraced or avoided? Pedrell had advised composers to avoid relying on Andalusian music only,[93] but Albéniz and Granados, although knowledgeable about a variety of Spanish traditional and European art music traditions, eventually became best known for their works based on Andalusian folklore.[94] Falla's shift from *andalucismo* to *castellanismo* in the 1920s was widely commented on and magnified in Spain,[95] with composers of the Grupo de los Ocho choosing to embrace, at least theoretically, the latter rather than the former for purportedly being more suitable to realizing their modernist ideals and avoiding sentimentalism and clichés.[96] In early Francoism, however, some critics had a more pragmatic outlook: Rodrigo A. de Santiago, who predominantly used in his compositions for wind band and other ensembles traditional music from his native Basque Country and Galicia, where he settled in 1947, nevertheless advised Spanish composers to use Andalusian music, because, among the regions of Spain, he felt it was "the only one which can travel abroad with possibilities of success."[97] He also complained that there was too much "regionalism" in Spanish music—that is, composers were using only the music from their home region—and this was thought to be breaking up the unity of Spanish music.[98] Castile, however, remained a serious contender, after having received a strong push from the Falange as the embodiment of traditional Spanish values; Sáinz de la Maza advised Spanish composers to use predominantly Castilian folklore because "among all manifestations of popular art, [Castilian] music is the one that keeps and preserves the feeling of the race."[99]

One of the critics to show sustained interest in use of traditional music in Spanish art music was Joaquín Rodrigo. This is not surprising, given that his success as a composer during the 1940s was partly based on his use of well-known Spanish sources, both high-brow and low-brow, interspersed with well-known Western art music models to which Rodrigo added a Spanish twist[100]—and sometimes even a Spanish twist closely related to, or even celebratory of, the Franco regime.[101] In the 1940s, critical success and recognition was a new experience for Rodrigo; he did not have a work published until 1940, for one thing. Born in 1901 in Sagunto and suffering from blindness since his early childhood, Rodrigo studied in Paris under Paul Dukas from 1927 to 1932 and achieved some moderate success in the French capital. On his return to Spain, he settled in Valencia, where his works were generally well received by López-Chavarri and other prominent local critics. Nevertheless, in Madrid, with Salazar enthusiastically supporting Ernesto Halffter and the Grupo de los Ocho eliciting the strongest reactions—in one sense or another—from music critics, Rodrigo found himself practically being ignored, and Salazar even wrote about him dismissively.[102]

Rodrigo and his wife were not in Spain when the Civil War started: Rodrigo moved back to Paris in 1935 to study musicology at the Sorbonne, supported by a scholarship awarded by the Count of Romanones. At the Sorbonne, Rodrigo specialized in early music and particularly the *vihuelistas*, but he also developed an interest in traditional music.[103] When the Civil War started, he decided not to return to Spain and moved instead, with his wife, to Freiburg, where they lived in a residence hall for the blind.[104] Like Anglès, Rodrigo first returned to Spain in 1938 as a guest speaker of the Cursos Internacionales de Verano de Santander, but the couple subsequently left for Paris again.[105] They returned to Madrid permanently in September 1939 after Antonio Tovar offered Rodrigo a job as music advisor at Radio Nacional.[106]

The 1940s were a busy decade for Rodrigo: apart from his successes as a composer,[107] he taught music and was in charge of organizing concerts at the Organización Nacional de Ciegos Españoles (Spanish National Organization for the Blind), served a guest lecturer in composition at the Conservatorio de Madrid, was appointed to the Manuel de Falla Professorship in Music at the Universidad Central de Madrid in 1947, and also started his career as a music critic. Like other music professionals who took up staff music critic posts at the end of the Civil War, such as Conrado del Campo and Sáinz de la Maza, Rodrigo did not have significant experience in writing music criticism; nevertheless, in 1940 he was offered, and accepted, a position as staff music critic at *Pueblo*. As an employee of Radio Nacional, he also regularly contributed to the station's newsletter, *Radio Nacional*, and occasionally to other publications such as *Vértice* and *Música. Revista Quincenal*. Rodrigo lost his job at *Pueblo* in summer 1946, allegedly after his colleague, Emiliano Aguado, a member of the Falange Liberal, maneuvered to have him fired so that the post could go to Aguado's wife, Dolores Palá Berdejo.[108] After his dismissal from *Pueblo,* Rodrigo went on to write a weekly music column ("La semana musical") for the sports newspaper *Marca*, a post he held until 1949.

Most critics writing in the early Franco era regularly called for more Spanish contemporary music to be included in concert programs in Spain, especially orchestral concerts. Even by those standards, however, Rodrigo's protectionism of Spanish music may sometimes appear to border on chauvinism. Indeed, instead of simply asking for an increase in the amount of Spanish works performed in Madrid, on several occasions he went as far as to calculate how much music of various nations was performed in Madrid during October 1944, concluding that only 24 percent of it was Spanish. Rodrigo deemed this unacceptable, claiming that the minimum of Spanish music should be 33 percent.[109] During the following months, he single-handedly continued his campaign in favor of Spanish music, including in his concert reviews a breakdown of percentages by composer nationality, to illustrate a concern other critics had voiced, that Spanish music was insufficiently present in Madrid's concert life.[110] Similarly, when a Spanish work was included in a concert program together with non-Spanish works, Rodrigo would typically devote much more space to the former than to the latter.[111]

Nevertheless, it would be inaccurate to consider Rodrigo's protectionism of Spanish music as predominantly chauvinistic, or as an example of an isolating brand of nationalism in line with the *autarquía* promoted by the Francoist government during the early-to-mid-1940s. His defense of Spanish music, in reality, was often accompanied by a concern for his fellow composers' working conditions, including low royalty payments and the obligation to fund the orchestral parts themselves; the solutions Rodrigo suggested typically included financial support from the government and protectionism, notably forcing orchestras to play a minimum amount of Spanish music.[112] As with other similar measures suggested by critics, however, there is no evidence that Rodrigo's ideas were ever given serious consideration by the Comisaría de Música or otherwise. As well, he often encouraged fellow composers to look outside Spain to the mainstream Austro-Germanic canon. Composers, he argued, should write more works in the genres underrepresented in Spanish music, such as the piano sonata or the string quartet[113]; he himself set an example by writing a *Concierto heroico* for piano.

What is perhaps more relevant, Rodrigo's concert reviews show engagement with the music of his contemporaries well above the norm for music critics of the time, exhibiting a distinct concern for performance practice and for discussion of the musical language. Although it would not be accurate to claim that Rodrigo, unlike Sopeña, formulated something approaching a full-blown theory of what new music, or Spanish new music, should sound like, he certainly left telling commentaries in his daily music reviews for *Pueblo*, showing his concern for renovating Spanish music and for reflecting on the role traditional music should play in it. It is not that Rodrigo, as the most successful young Spanish composer in early Francoism, determined an official line in music criticism regarding the use of traditional music; but his nuanced discussions of the use of folklore in Spanish art music are interesting because they certainly go beyond the level of detail and engagement that was the norm among his contemporaries. Indeed, although sometimes his articles are simply founded, without much critical elaboration, on some of the tropes about traditional music so ubiquitous in music criticism of early Francoism, such as the touted exceptional wealth of Spanish traditional music, superior to that of any other country,[114] Rodrigo's writings were also in some ways a continuation of the debates and opinions on traditional music that had informed Spanish art music since the late nineteenth century, from Pedrell and Falla to the Grupo de los Ocho.

More precisely, Rodrigo's positions on Spanish nationalism can be read as an extension of the *castellanismo* versus *andalucismo* debate that so profoundly affected Spanish music (and elsewhere), and particularly the Grupo de los Ocho, after Falla turned his back on Andalusian folklore in the 1920s.[115] In the 1920s and 1930s, Falla's *castellanismo* was perceived in Spain and abroad not only (and not predominantly) as a celebration of the essence of Spain, consonant with appreciation on the part of the Generation of '98 for Castile: much of the popularity of *castellanismo* came from the notion that those values of purity attached to Castile fitted well within neoclassicism. When positively reviewing del Campo's symphonic poem *Evocación de Castilla* on the occasion of its first performance in 1943, Rodrigo was not necessarily following, say, Sáinz de la Maza's focus on Castile as the essence of Spain and the embodiment of the values that should shape the *Nuevo Estado*; he seemed more drawn to the neoclassical values of simplicity and spirituality ("spiritual," "austerity," "broad and large horizon").[116] The same can be said of Rodrigo's review of the performance of Falla's *Retablo* sponsored by the Comisaría de Música in 1941, which was discussed in Chapter 2. Rodrigo himself coined the word *neocasticismo* after *neoclasicismo* (neoclassicism), but replacing *classical* with *castizo*—that is, the intrinsically Spanish—because, he claimed, Spanish musicians had not had a proper classical era in the same way French and German composers did.[117]

As the Grupo de los Ocho, and then Sopeña, had done, Rodrigo expressed his preference for Falla's *Retablo* over "picturesque Andalusia, which is the least interesting Andalusia."[118] Though not dismissive of *andalucismo* per se, Rodrigo found it more difficult to give positive reviews to those composers who chose to take inspiration from Andalusian rather than Castilian folklore. In the same way Falla had warned against literally quoting traditional melodies without making an effort to capture the spirit of the people and translating it into original music,[119] Rodrigo valued above all the skill of the composer in reflecting the "fragrance,"[120] all the while adapting it to his own particular style, without using clichés; he was quite aware of the centurylong popularity of Andalusian music as a marker of exoticism and Spanishness, which, he argued, put pressure on Spanish composers "to be staunch nationalists."[121] Thus, Rodrigo's review of Bonifacio Gil's *En una aldea extremeña* was reasonably positive, for Gil had "avoided excessively populist themes."[122] Nevertheless, he wrote on Emilio Lehmberg's *Suite andaluza* that "this way of understanding Andalusian music, which is just the usual one, does not need a large symphonic orchestra"[123] and labeled José Muñoz Molleda's use of Andalusian folklore in the *Suite de danza* as "gracious and authentic, but not very personal, *andalucismo*."[124]

Rodrigo was aware that his reluctance around *andalucismo* connected him to the Grupo de los Ocho and similar composers, to whom he referred as "my generation" ("My generation was European, we were . . . against nationalism—we did not like *andalucismo*—but we lovingly had to go back to it").[125] On the occasion of Adolfo Salazar's death in 1958, Rodrigo again claimed that he belonged to the same generation as the Grupo de los Ocho—that is, those composers who had come of age and started their careers between the 1910s and the 1930s and for whom Rodrigo chose the term "generation of '25"—and as such he felt deeply moved by Salazar's death.[126]

Whereas it is true that Rodrigo was never part of the Grupo de los Ocho environment, the successive critical interpretations of Rodrigo's music and his significance, first with Sopeña (as discussed in Chapter 2) and then less sympathetically with Tomás Marco,[127] have tended to separate or even oppose the Grupo de los Ocho and Rodrigo. In the case of Marco, this opposition is established by Marco defining *neocasticismo* as neoclassicism without the avant-garde elements,[128] thus effectively portraying the 1940s—the era of *neocasticismo*—as a period of artistic stagnation preceded by the *Edad de Plata* and followed by the Generation of '51, with Rodrigo being the most representative symbol of such stagnation. Rodrigo's critical writings, however, show how some of the same concerns that had preoccupied Falla, Salazar, and the Grupo de los Ocho survived in 1940s criticism, without being totally superseded by ideas of traditional music promoted by the regime through the Sección Femenina and the IEM.

NOTES

1. *Música natural* (natural music) is, according to Pedrell, music that is not subjected to a historical context or to artifice, but is rather born spontaneously to express emotion between individuals and between generations. *Música natural*, according to Pedrell, should also be the inspiration for *música artificial* (artificial music). See Felipe Pedrell, *Cancionero musical popular español* (Valls: E. Castells, 1922), I.9–11 and II.83–86.

2. Higinio Anglès, "España en la historia de la música universal." *Arbor*, vol. 11, no. 30 (1948), 9–10.

3. Ibid., 10.

4. Robert Stevenson, "Tributo a Higinio Anglès," *Revista musical chilena*, vol. 24, no. 112 (1970), 7.

5. Letter from Higinio Anglès to José Subirá, Nov. 6, 1943.

6. Josep Martí i Pérez, "Folk Music Studies and Ethnomusicology in Spain," *Yearbook for Traditional Music*, no. 29 (1997), 113–114.

7. Gerardo Diego, Joaquín Rodrigo, and Federico Sopeña, *Diez años de música en España* (Madrid: Espasa Calpe, 1949), 171.

8. María Asunción Lizarazu de Mesa, "En torno al folklore musical y su utilización. El caso de las Misiones Pedagógicas y la Sección Femenina," *Anuario Musical*, no. 51 (1996), 234–235.

9. Beatriz Martínez del Fresno, "Mujeres, tierra y nación. Las danzas de la Sección Femenina en el mapa politico de la España franquista (1939–1952)," in *Discursos y prácticas musicales nacionalistas (1900–1970)*, ed. Pilar Ramos López (Logroño: Universidad de La Rioja, 2012), 233–235.

10. Such publications include *Cancionero de la Sección Femenina de F.E.T. y de las J.O.N.S.* (1943); *Breves notas sobre algunas de las danzas populares españolas* (1947); *Spanish Songs and Folk Dances* (1952, for distribution abroad); *Música. Teoría de Solfeo y Canciones* (1958); *Villancicos y canciones religiosas de Navidad* (1958); *Canciones populares para escolares* (1959); *Canciones infantiles* (1964); *1000 canciones* (1966); *Cancionero popular español* (1968); *Audiciones musicales para niños* (1974).

11. The most distinctive dance of Catalonia, a region in northeastern Spain.

12. A wind instrument typical of the Basque Country.

13. Referring to flamenco.

14. Cited in Anonymous, *Cancionero* (Madrid: Departamento de Publicaciones de la Delegación Nacional del Frente de Juventudes, 1943), 5.

15. Beatriz Busto Miramontes, "El poder en el folklore: los cuerpos en NO-DO (1943–1948)," *Trans. Revista Transcultural de Música*, no. 16 (2012), 14–16; Isabel Ferrer Senabre, "Cant i quotidianitat: visibilitat i gènere durant el primer franquisme," *Trans. Revista Transcultural de Música*, no. 15 (2011), 7–18; Aurora Morcillo, *True Catholic Womanhood Gender Ideology in Franco's Spain* (DeKalb: Northern Illinois University Press, 2000); Kathleen Richmond, *Women and Spanish Fascism: The Women's Section of the Falange 1934–1959* (London and New York: Routledge, 2003), 14.

16. Eva Moreda Rodríguez, "'La mujer que no canta no es … ¡ni mujer española!': Folklore and Gender in the Earlier Franco Regime," *Bulletin of Hispanic Studies*, vol. 89, no. 6 (2012), 635–638.

17. Ibid., 639–641.

18. The first one was a collection of *seguidillas* published by J. A. Iza Zamácola in 1799, followed by Iztueta's collection of Basque dances in 1826. In the following decades, Serafín Estébanez Calderón, Manuel Murguía, Marià Aguiló, and of special importance Manuel Milà i Fontanals and Antonio Machado y Álvarez published collections focusing mainly on the texts. Toward the end of the century, José de Manterola, Francisco Rodríguez Marín, Pau Bertran y Bros, F. P. Briz, José Inzenga, Eduardo Ocón, R. M. de Azkue, and Casto Sampedro Folgar published new collections in which music became more important.

19. Francesc Cortés i Mir, "El nacionalisme en el context català entre 1875 i 1936," *Recerca musicològica*, no. 14–15, 27–45; Emilio Rey García, "La etnomusicología en España. Pasado, presente y futuro," *Revista de musicología*, no. 20, 877–886.

20. Susana Asensio Llamas, "Eduardo Martínez Torner y la Junta para Ampliación de Estudios en España," *Arbor*, vol. 187, no. 851 (2011), 857–874.

21. Francisco Canés Garrido, "Las misiones pedagógicas: educación y tiempo libre en la Segunda República," *Revista Complutense de Educación*, vol. 4 no. 1 (1993), 150–152.

22. Julián Bautista, "Lo típico y la producción sinfónica," *Música*, no. 3 (1938), 23–27; María Palacios, *La renovación musical en Madrid durante la dictadura de Primo de Rivera. El Grupo de los Ocho (1923–1931)* (Madrid: Sociedad Española de Musicología, 2008), 15–16; Elena Torres Clemente, "El 'nacionalismo de las esencias': ¿una categoría estética o ética?" in *Discursos y prácticas musicales nacionalistas (1900–1970)*, ed. Pilar Ramos López (Logroño: Universidad de La Rioja, 2012), 38–44; Julian White, "Promoting and Diffusing Catalan Musical Heritage: Roberto Gerhard and Catalan Folk Music," in *The Roberto Gerhard Research Companion*, ed. Monty Adkins and Michael Russ (Farnham: Ashgate, 2013), 49–77; Thomas Schmitt, "*Con las guitarras abiertas*. El neopopularismo como reacción y progreso en las canciones españolas de los años 30 del siglo XX," *Anuario Musical*, no. 66 (2011), 275–282.

23. Antonio Álvarez Pérez, *Enciclopedia* (Miñón: Valladolid, 1971), 1005.

24. R. Ortega León, "El primero de abril, Día de la Canción," *Pueblo*, Mar. 24, 1943, 3. Teruel, Ebro, and Brunete are the names of well-known victories of the Franco army during the Civil War.
25. Turina, quoted in Joaquín Rodrigo, "El Día de la Canción ha de ser el preludio alegre de una gran labor anual," *Pueblo*, Mar. 21, 1942, 7.
26. Adelaida, "Orientación general de la enseñanza de la música en los distintos grados de la escuela primaria," *Radio Nacional*, 52 (1939), 13.
27. Fernando Rodríguez del Río, "El Frente de Juventudes y sus competiciones artísticas," *Ritmo*, no. 166 (1943), 9.
28. Ibid., 9.
29. Julieta Mateo Box, "España por el arte," *Revista Literaria Musical*, no. 53 (1951), 11–12.
30. Eduardo López-Chavarri, "Nuestros músicos," *Radio Nacional*, no. 48 (1939), 10–11. Dividing nations into "rich" and "poor" according to the wealth of their traditional music was common practice in late-nineteenth-century studies of folklore, mirroring Darwinist ideas; folklorists thought that wealth (or lack thereof) was a sign of the potential and strength of the nation in question. See Joaquina Labajo Valdés, "Política y usos del folklore en el siglo XX español," *Revista de Musicología*, no. 16 (1993), 1995–96.
31. López-Chavarri, "Nuestros musicos," 11.
32. Josep Martí i Pérez, "Folk Music Studies," 115–116.
33. Josep Martí i Pérez, "Felip Pedrell i l'etnomusicologia," *Recerca musicològica*, no. 11–12 (1991), 211–229.
34. José María Franco, "Música," *Ya*, Jan. 11, 1944, 7.
35. María Dolores Pérez Camarero, "Una escuela de instructoras de música en la Ciudad Lineal," *Arriba*, Mar. 10, 1946, 7.
36. Mateo Box, "España por el arte," 11.
37. Richards, *A Time of Silence*, 104.
38. López-Chavarri, "Nuestros músicos," 10–11.
39. Javier del Valle, "Páginas folklóricas," *Revista literaria musical*, no 31 (1946), 4.
40. Santiago Riopérez y Milá, "Empresas nobles de nuestra España," *Revista Literaria Musical*, 49 (1950), 21–23.
41. *Cuplés* were a cabaret-style song genre that developed in Spain from the late nineteenth century onward; they were normally sung by women (or men in drag) to a male audience, and were often filled with sexual innuendo.
42. Regino Sáinz de la Maza, "La masa coral de Educación y Descanso de Lugo inicia el primer concurso folklórico," *ABC*, Mar. 2, 1943, 17.
43. Pedro Echevarría Bravo, "España canta a través de sus juventudes y sus bandas de música", *Boletín del Colegio de Directores de Bandas de Música Civiles*, no. 40 (1946), 13.
44. Eduardo S. Morell, "La cultura musical en algunos pueblos," *Boletín del Colegio de Directores de Bandas de Música Civiles*, no. 34 (1946), 14–15.
45. Rafael Benedito, quoted in L. V., "La Coral de Madrid celebra hoy su XXV aniversario," *Arriba*, Jan. 21, 1945, 6.
46. For example, Anonymous, "Editorial," *Revista Literaria Musical*, no. 27 (1945), 3; Cristóbal de Castro, "*Coros y Danzas* de las regiones españolas," *Revista Literaria Musical*, no. 30 (1946), 7.
47. For example, in 1950, after a *Coros y Danzas* tour to the United States, its unwaged members gave the Instituto de Moneda y Timbre $15,000 as a gift. See Anonymous, "Éxito de los *Coros y Danzas* como productores de divisas," *El Alcázar*, Oct. 10, 1950, 5.

48. Santiago Riopérez y Milá, Untitled article, *Revista Literaria Musical*, no. 41 (1949), 5–6.
49. *Tablado* is the name given to the typical stage for flamenco performances.
50. Dámaso Torres, "El gusto y su fabricación," *Boletín del Colegio de Directores de Bandas de Música Civiles*, no. 90 (1951), 8.
51. Víctor García Ruiz and Gregorio Torres Nebra, *Historia y antología del teatro español de posguerra*, vol. 1 (Madrid: Fundamentos, 2003), 128.
52. José Rivera Centeno, "Triste paradoja. Dos facetas de nuestro Folklore," *Ritmo*, no. 229 (1950), 8.
53. Ibid., 8.
54. Iván Iglesias, "(Re)construyendo la identidad musical española: el jazz y el discurso cultural del Franquismo durante la Segunda Guerra Mundial," *Historia Actual Online*, no. 23 (2010), 121–122.
55. Ibid., 120.
56. José Luis Rodríguez Jiménez, "El antisemitismo en el Franquismo y en la Transición," in *El antisemitismo en España*, ed. Gonzalo Álvarez Chillida and Ricardo Izquierdo Benito (Cuenca: Ediciones de la Universidad de Castilla-La Mancha, 2007), 245–247.
57. Sebastián Méndez, "Música negroide o extranjera," *Boletín del Colegio de Directores de Bandas de Música Civiles*, 31 (1945), 7.
58. Anonymous, "Consternación en Bélgica," *ABC*, 24 May, 1951, 16.
59. Francisco Padín, "A propósito de una campaña a favor de la Música española," *Ritmo*, no. 147 (1941), 15.
60. Padín, "Nuevamente en favor de la buena música," *Ritmo*, no. 157 (1942), 8.
61. Padín, "La música de jazz y sus estragos," *Ritmo*, no. 170 (1943), 7–8.
62. Joaquín Rodrigo, "Música negra y música blanca," *El Español*, Jan. 29, 1944, 6.
63. Quoted in Eduardo López-Chavarri, "Sigue la matanza de los grandes maestros," *Ritmo*, no. 153 (1942), 4.
64. Ibid., 4.
65. Nemesio Otaño, "La música en las emisoras de radio," 3.
66. In this, I dissent from Iglesias, "(Re)construyendo la identidad musical española," 125–126, who regards racial discourse as the most important determinant in the reception of jazz in Spain during the years 1939–1945.
67. Rodrigo A. de Santiago, "Los concursos nacionales de música," *Boletín del Colegio de Directores de Bandas de Música Civiles*, no. 36 (1946), 7.
68. Anonymous, "Doctrinales," *Revista Literaria Musical*, no. 36 (1947). 5.
69. Literally, Performers' National Trade Union. The Sindicato Nacional del Espectáculo was a subsection of the Sindicato Vertical (Vertical Trade Union), the only trade union allowed to exist during the regime. It was controlled by the Falange, and it included both employees and their employers.
70. Anonymous, "El sindicato nacional del espectáculo y sus recientes disposiciones," *Ritmo*, no. 159 (1942), 3.
71. A rather popular suggestion was to ban jazz from radio stations, as suggested by Otaño, "La música en las emisoras de radio," 3; José Antonio Antequera, "La música clásica y la radiodifusión," *Radio Nacional*, no. 119 (1941), 5. Other critics proposed that jazz should not be banned completely, but instead all radio stations should be required to play a minimum percentage of Spanish music to prevent jazz from becoming hegemonic; see, for example, Francisco Casares, "Música 'de diario'," *ABC*, Oct. 2, 1941, 16.

72. For example, Antonio Fernández-Cid, "Música," *Arriba*, Apr. 10, 1948, 7; Anonymous [as Bill el repórter], "Aaron Copland el notable compositor norteamericano triunfa en Europa con su tercera sinfonía," *Revista Literaria Musical*, no. 40 (1948), 19–20.

73. Luis Araque, "El jazz como filosofía musical," *Ritmo*, no. 205 (1947), 18.

74. P. C. Hernández, "El jazz, música popular," *Ritmo*, no. 204 (1947), 7–8.

75. Luis A. Gaztambide, "El mundo musical invertido," *Ritmo*, no. 218 (1949), 4.

76. See, for example, Anonymous, "Entrevista con Carlos Suriñach Wrokona," *Ritmo y Melodía*, no. 12 (1945), 6; Anonymous, "Joaquín Rodrigo no cree en el hot," *Ritmo y Melodía*, no. 13 (1945), 5; Anonymous, "Conversación con Juan Manén sobre el jazz," *Ritmo y Melodía*, no. 8 (1945), 5.

77. See Michael H. Kater, "Forbidden Fruit? Jazz in the Third Reich," *American Historical Review*, no. 94 (1994), 11–43.

78. Iván Iglesias, "Hechicero de las pasiones del alma: El jazz y la subversión de la biopolítica franquista (1939–1959)," *Trans. Revista Transcultural de Música*, no. 17 (2013), 3.

79. Alfredo Papó, "Wenceslao Fernández Flórez y la música demente," *Ritmo y Melodía*, no. 30 (1948), 5.

80. Ibid., 5.

81. José M. Fonollosa, "Sobre el concierto de Willie Smith 'The Lion' en Barcelona," *Ritmo y Melodía*, no. 42 (1950), 4; Enrique Sanz de Madrid, "Verdadero valor del jazz," *Ritmo y Melodía*, no. 32 (1949), 9.

82. Anonymous [as El predicador en el desierto], "El jazz, tema de moda," *Ritmo y Melodía*, no. 9 (1945), 10.

83. Anonymous [as El predicador en el desierto], "La locura del swing," *Ritmo y Melodía*, no. 18 (1946), 7; Alfredo Papó, "Notas sueltas," *Ritmo y Melodía*, no. 23 (1947), 7.

84. Anonymous [as El predicador en el desierto], "¿Existe un público español de jazz?" *Ritmo y Melodía*, no. 20 (1947), 9.

85. Giancarlo Testoni, "El riff," *Ritmo y Melodía,* no. 26 (1948), 9; Anonymous, "Dos farsantes: James y Cugat; y una decepción: 'Casa de locos'," *Ritmo y Melodía*, no. 20 (1948), 10.

86. Eugenio S. Mendo, "Unificación del jazz," *Ritmo y Melodía*, no. 47 (1950), 5.

87. Luis Araque, "¡Dejemos en paz al folklore!," *Ritmo*, no. 213 (1948), 14.

88. Ibid., 14.

89. Sergio Valbuena Esgueva, "Orientaciones," *Boletín del Colegio de Directores de Bandas de Música Civiles,* no. 38 (1946), 4–5.

90. Victoriano Echevarría, "Aspectos: tema con variaciones," *Boletín del Colegio de Directores de Bandas de Música Civiles*, no. 29 (1945), 11.

91. These include *Suite Fantasi*, Victoriano Echevarría; *Evocaciones Castellanas*, Benito García de la Parra; *Diez Melodías Vascas*, Jesús Guridi; *Aires Viejos de Danza*, Joaquín Rodrigo (1941); *Castilla*, Jesús Arámbarri; *La Gacela de Almoctámid*, Julio Gómez; *Credos populares*, Jaime Menéndez; *Postales Madrileñas*, José Muñoz Molleda (1942); *Piano Concerto* (inspired by Castilian folklore) and *Paisajes castellanos*, Conrado del Campo; *Suite de Danza*, Muñoz Molleda (1943); *En la pradera*, del Campo; *Balada de Roncesvalles*, Joaquín Gasca; *Peñamariana*, Guridi (1944); cello concerto (inspired by Castilian folklore), del Campo; *Balada de Roncesvalles*, Gasca; *En una aldea extremeña*, Bonifacio Gil; *Sinfonía Pirenaica*, Guridi; *Suite Vasca*, Pablo Sorozábal; *Tonades d'amor*, Pedro Sosa (1946); *Cinco Canciones*, Jesús García Leoz; *Don Quijote velando las armas*, Gerardo Gombau; *Concierto Vasco*,

Rodrigo A. de Santiago (1947); guitar concerto, Manuel Palau; *Passacaglia*, Carlos Suriñach (1948); *Concierto Vasco*, Francisco Escudero (1949); *Fantasía Castellana*, Antonio Iglesias (1951).

92. Tomás Marco, *Spanish Music in the Twentieth Century* (Cambridge and London: Harvard University Press, 1993), 129–130; Marco, "Los años cuarenta," in *España en la música de Occidente*, ed. Emilio Casares Rodicio, Ismael Fernández de la Cuesta, and José López Calo, vol. 2 (Madrid: Instituto Nacional de las Artes Escénicas y de la Música, 1987), 400–401.

93. Felipe Pedrell, *Por nuestra música* (Barcelona: Heinrich, 1891), 42–43.

94. Walter Aaron Clark, *Enrique Granados: Poet of the Piano* (New York: Oxford University Press, 2005), 9; Clark, *Isaac Albéniz: Portrait of a Romantic* (New York: Oxford University Press, 1999), 67.

95. Carol A. Hess, *Manuel de Falla and Modernism in Spain, 1898–1936* (Chicago: Chicago University Press, 2001), 180 and 270–272.

96. Palacios, *La renovación musical en Madrid,* 263.

97. Rodrigo A. de Santiago, "El nacionalismo como antecedente de lo universal," *Boletín del Colegio de Directores de Bandas de Música Civiles*, no. 83 (1951), 6.

98. Ibid., 7.

99. Regino Sáinz de la Maza, "Canción de Castilla," *Vértice*, no. 67 (1943), 39.

100. Rodrigo, however, seemed more interested in high-brow Spanish musical culture than low-brow: works by him based on Spanish art rather than traditional music include *Zarabanda lejana y villancico* (1927–1930), *Concierto de Aranjuez* (1939), *Concierto en modo galante* (1949), *Soleriana* (1953). It was mostly in his vocal and solo guitar music that he more decidedly took inspiration in Spanish traditional music, including arrangements of Valencian folk songs for choir.

101. Namely, in his 1943 *Concerto heroico* for piano; see Eva Moreda Rodríguez, "Musical Commemorations in Post-Civil War Spain: Joaquín Rodrigo's *Concierto Heroico*," in *Twentieth-Century Music and Politics: Essays in Memory of Neil Edmunds*, ed. Pauline Fairclough (Farnham: Ashgate, 2012), 177–190.

102. Javier Suárez-Pajares, "Joaquín Rodrigo en la vida musical y la cultura española de los años cuarenta. Ficciones, realidades, verdades y mentiras de un tiempo extraño," in *Joaquín Rodrigo y la música española de los años cuarenta*, ed. Javier Suárez-Pajares (Valladolid: Glares, 2005), 31; Suárez-Pajares, "Adolfo Salazar: luz y sombras," in *Música y cultura en la Edad de Plata 1915–1939*, ed. María Nagore, Leticia Sánchez de Andrés, and Elena Torres (Madrid: ICCMU, 2009), 211.

103. Victoria Kamhi de Rodrigo, *Hand in Hand with Joaquín Rodrigo: My Life at the Maestro's Side*, transl. Ellen Wilkerson (Pittsburgh: Latin American Literary Review Press, 1992), 87.

104. Ibid., 92–93.

105. Ibid., 103–148.

106. Ibid., 109.

107. Rodrigo had four instrumental concertos premiered by the Orquesta Nacional in the period 1939–1951 (*Concierto de Aranjuez, Concierto de estío, Concierto heroico, Concierto en modo galante*)—certainly more than any other living Spanish composer—as well as several solo and chamber works.

108. Letter from Joaquín Rodrigo to Rafael Rodríguez Albert, June 10, 1946, unpublished [BNE, M. RALBERT/64/2/20].

109. Joaquín Rodrigo, "Estadísticas y comentarios," *Pueblo*, Nov. 1, 1944, 7.

110. For example, Rodrigo, "Agrupación Nacional de Música de Cámara," *Pueblo*, Jan. 19, 1945, 7; Rodrigo, "José Cubiles en el Español. Música española en el

programa: 23 por 100," *Pueblo*, Nov. 14, 1944, 7; Rodrigo, "Orquesta Sinfónica en el Monumental; director, Enrique Jordá. Música española en el programa: cero," *Pueblo*, Nov. 20, 1944, 6.

111. For example, Rodrigo, "Rosa Mas en la A.D.C.M. Interpretación de *El poema de una sanluqueña*," *Pueblo*, Nov. 1, 1941, 7.

112. For example, Rodrigo, "El dinero de los músicos sinfónicos," *Pueblo*, May 14, 1942, 7; Rodrigo, "Concierto de música española de la Vicesecretaría de Educación Popular," *Pueblo*, Oct. 13, 1944, 7.

113. Rodrigo, "Conferencia de Sainz de la Maza," *Pueblo*, Dec. 30, 1942, 7; Rodrigo, "Concurso de música de cámara," *Pueblo*, Jan. 26, 1943, 7.

114. Rodrigo, "Segundo concurso nacional de folklore," *Pueblo*, Oct. 18, 1943, 7.

115. Hess, *Manuel de Falla*, 180.

116. Joaquín Rodrigo, "Cuarto concierto de la Orquesta Nacional," *Pueblo*, Nov. 13, 1943, 7.

117. Antonio Iglesias, *Escritos de Joaquín Rodrigo* (Madrid: Alpuerto, 1999), 52.

118. Ibid., 23.

119. Falla's words were: "Some consider that one of the means to 'nationalize' our music is the strict use of popular material in a melodic way. In a general sense, I am afraid I do not agree, although in particular cases I think that procedure cannot be bettered. In popular song I think the spirit is more important than the letter. Rhythm, tonality and melodic intervals, which determine undulations and cadences are the essential constituents of these songs. . . . Inspiration, therefore, is to be found directly in the people, and those who do not see it so will only achieve a more or less ingenious imitation of what they originally set out to do." Originally published in 1917, reprinted in Manuel de Falla, *On Music and Musicians*, ed. by Federico Sopeña, trans. by David Urman and J. M. Thomson (London: Boyars, 1979), 31–32.

120. Joaquín Rodrigo, "Clausura del ciclo de conferencias," *Pueblo*, Jan. 5, 1943, 7; Rodrigo, "Orquesta Sinfónica con Enrique Jordá, estreno de 10 canciones populares vascas de Jesús Guridi. La pianista Ginette Doyen," *Pueblo*, Dec. 24, 1941, 7.

121. Quoted in Iglesias, *Escritos de Joaquín Rodrigo*, 23.

122. Joaquín Rodrigo, "Estreno de *En una aldea extremeña*," *Pueblo*, Sep. 25, 1944, 7.

123. Rodrigo, "La Orquesta Sinfónica, en el Monumental," *Pueblo*, Mar. 19, 1945, 7.

124. Rodrigo, "Conrado del Campo y la Orquesta Clásica, Orquesta Sinfónica con Jordá," *Pueblo*, Dec. 20, 1943, 6.

125. Rodrigo, quoted in Julián Navarro, "Rincón indiscreto," *El español*, June 16, 1956, reprinted in Iglesias, *Escritos de Joaquín Rodrigo*, 41.

126. Rodrigo, "Lo que fue para nosotros," *Arriba*, Oct. 7, 1958, 29.

127. Marco, *Spanish Music*, 129–130.

128. Ibid., 130.

Conclusion

It is a long-held assumption that music criticism in the period preceding the Spanish Civil War—that is, circa 1918 to 1936—was dominated by a single, quasi-hegemonic figure: Adolfo Salazar. Rather paradoxically, the beginnings of the Salazar legend can be traced back to Francoism, and even more precisely to the time around Salazar's death: in their obituaries of Salazar, a number of the most prominent figures of Spanish musical life praised him as a tireless champion of new music, a very effective mediator between young composers and audiences, an administrator fully committed to improving Spanish musical life, and an excellent writer.[1] Present-day writers often invoke similar notions to confirm Salazar's hegemony.[2] This is not to say that the legend has gone completely unchallenged: as early as 1958, on the occasion of Salazar's death, Julio Gómez called into question the idyllic picture other critics painted in their obituaries and refused to call Salazar "the best Spanish critic of all times," arguing that he had excellent writing skills but his judgment was not always reliable or impartial; nor was it unanimously embraced even by those who were, in principle, supporters of new music.[3] More recently, a few scholars have called into question the claim that Salazar's role was hegemonic in disseminating and regulating new music in Spain.[4] Nevertheless, it cannot be denied that Salazar is still, to a significant extent, the visible face of Spanish music criticism 1918–1936; studies of music criticism of that era, even when discussing the writings of other critics, still see in Salazar an important focus,[5] and he has been practically the only critic of the period to have some of his correspondence, as well as an anthology of his writings, published in book form, which further confirms his status as not simply a critic writing for the present, but someone whose opinions deserve to be preserved through time.[6]

Setting aside appraisals of Salazar's writing and stature, however, there are enough elements in his biography and career to make it relatively easy to turn him into a myth: his thus-far unknown dedication to music criticism, his excellent writing skills, and his polemic style. His political commitment and subsequent exile turned him into a symbol of the frustrated *Edad de Plata*. It would be difficult, however, to turn one single critic of the period 1939–1951 into the embodiment of the period's *Zeitgeist*, in the same way Salazar was for the Second Republic. What best captures the *Zeitgeist* of early Francoism, anyway? Is it the Falange, with its hegemony in the early days of the regime and its desire to transform Spain and bring about the *Nuevo Estado*? The Falange was certainly highly visible, especially in the context of European fascisms, but it was just one of several factions under the Francoist government, and it quickly started to lose influence to groups that shared the Falange's worship of the Spanish past, but perhaps not so much the wish to transform it into a source of renovation for the future. It would not be accurate to describe early Francoism simply as the practical implementation of Falange ideals, and by the same token it would not be accurate to portray Sopeña as the hegemonic critic of early Francoism, no matter how much he tried to mimic Salazar's career or how influential he is still nowadays in topics of Spanish contemporary music. In a way, Sopeña was an anomaly rather than the norm, with his interest in and curiosity for new music: even when he dismissed a particular composer or work, his criticism was based on reflection and built up to a comprehensive frame for understanding and writing about new music.

It is perhaps this lack of interest for the new that makes it equally difficult for any other critics to rise to the status of hegemonic; after all, there was supposed to be something *new* about the *Nuevo Estado*. Joaquín Turina, Nemesio Otaño, and Higinio Anglès all could have some claim to having a hegemonic role in music criticism, by simultaneously being critics and holding prominent administrative positions in music administration under the Franco regime. And yet their critical writings, individually considered, failed to capture particular aspects of the musical life and climate of the 1940s: Turina mostly wrote daily music reviews that were reactions to particular events rather than an attempt at building an overarching doctrine of what Spanish music should be, as Sopeña had done. Otaño and Anglès, through their engagement with Spanish early music, provided a crucial link between musicological research and public dissemination—but they both practically limited themselves to writing about early music and did not show an interest in writing daily concert reviews, let alone in systematically engaging with contemporary music.

What this demonstrates, however, is the protean nature of the Franco regime, and how it embraced conservatism and nationalism—also in music and music criticism—as broad labels that could accommodate a range of positions, even, in the case of Julio Gómez, a mild form of dissent with prevailing early music policies or, as with Joaquín Rodrigo, a continuation of ideas supposedly expelled from Spain during the Civil War. Indeed, the early Franco regime in a way catalyzed forms of musical nationalism that had been developing from the late nineteenth century onward. The generation born in the 1910s—including Sopeña and other critic-composers discussed in this book, such as Montsalvatge and Suriñach—was the last to come of age in an environment in which music nationalism was pretty much the hegemonic option. Not that nationalism and debates around it totally disappeared without a trace from Spanish music after 1951: Rodrigo, Rodolfo Halffter, Ernesto Halffter, and other composers who can be loosely described as nationalist lived until the late twentieth century, and in any case, the Generation of '51 and the Spanish avant-garde were not completely oblivious to the category of the national.[7] Nevertheless, after the 1950s—probably with some delay, with respect to the rest of Europe—the time of musical nationalism in Spain had certainly gone by, despite Sopeña's hopes for Spanish music. It is therefore the period 1939–1951 that last saw some of the main actors of Spanish music engaging with the questions of national identity and tradition that had preoccupied their predecessors for at least the preceding five decades, contributing to an ongoing debate under the pressures of press deadlines, censorship, and the need to adapt their opinions, and sometimes looking for spaces of dissent within the requirements of the new regime.

NOTES

1. Joaquín Rodrigo, "Lo que fue para nosotros," *Arriba*, Oct. 7, 1958, 29; Enrique Franco, "Crítica creadora," *Arriba*, Oct. 7, 1958, 29; Cristóbal Halffter, "Guía de la música española," *Arriba*, Oct. 7, 1958, 29; Ramón Barce, "Adolfo Salazar. La obra y el hombre," *Índice*, no. 20 (1958), 23.
2. Emilio Casares Rodicio, "Música y músicos de la Generación del 27," in *La música en la Generación del 27. Homenaje a Lorca 1915–1939*, ed. Emilio Casares Rodicio (Madrid: Ministerio de Cultura/INAEM, 1986), 22; Casares Rodicio, "La música española hasta 1939, o la restauración musical," in *España en la música de Occidente*, ed. Emilio Casares Rodicio, Ismael Fernández de la Cuesta, and José López Calo, vol. 2 (Madrid: Instituto Nacional de las Artes Escénicas y de la Música, 1987), 315; Consuelo Carredano, "Danzas de conquista: herencia y celebración de Adolfo Salazar," in *Música y cultura en la Edad de Plata 1915–1939*, ed. María Nagore, Leticia Sánchez de Andrés, and Elena Torres (Madrid: ICCMU, 2009), 195.

3. Julio Gómez, "Comentarios del presente y del pasado," *Harmonía*, October–December (1958), 5.

4. María Palacios, "El Grupo de los Ocho bajo el prisma de Adolfo Salazar," in *Música y cultura en la Edad de Plata 1915–1939*, ed. María Nagore, Leticia Sánchez de Andrés, and Elena Torres (Madrid: ICCMU, 2009), 282; Javier Suárez-Pajares, "Adolfo Salazar: luz y sombras," in *Música y cultura en la Edad de Plata 1915–1939*, ed. María Nagore, Leticia Sánchez de Andrés, and Elena Torres (Madrid: ICCMU, 2009), 201–208.

5. Teresa Cascudo and María Palacios, "Introducción," in *Los señores de la crítica. Periodismo musical e ideología del modernismo en Madrid (1900–1950)*, ed. Teresa Cascudo and María Palacios (Sevilla: Doble J, 2011), xii–xiii.

6. Consuelo Carredano (ed.), *Adolfo Salazar. Epistolario 1912–1958* (Madrid: Fundación Scherzo/Publicaciones de la Residencia de Estudiantes, 2008); Adolfo Salazar, *Textos de crítica musical en el periódico El Sol*, ed. José María García Laborda and Josefa Ruiz Vicente (Sevilla: Doble J, 2009).

7. José Luis García del Busto, "Manuel de Falla y los compositores de la Generación del 51: Ruptura/presencia," in *Manuel de Falla: Latinité et universalité*, ed. Louis Jambou (Paris: Presses de l'Université de Paris-Sorbonne, 1999), 509–513.

Publications, 1939–1951

NEWSPAPERS
ABC

Began: 1905

Ended: still published today. At the beginning of the Civil War, the Republican government confiscated its offices and nationalized the newspaper. In turn, the nationalist side started its own *ABC* (under the name *ABC Sevilla*) in Seville. At the end of the war, *ABC* and *ABC Sevilla* merged.

Print run: 16,000 subscribers according to *Anuario de la Prensa 1945–46* (subscriptions typically amounted to 10–30 percent of the total print run of a newspaper). It was mainly distributed in Madrid, Barcelona, Zaragoza, Valencia, Málaga, and Alicante.

Founder/publisher: initially founded by Torcuato Luca de Tena. The private company Prensa Española, owned by the Luca de Tena family, regained control of the newspaper after the Civil War.

Contents: from its foundation, *ABC* was well known for conservative, monarchist content, which it continued throughout the Franco regime. A music column was published almost daily, featuring reviews of recent concerts and musical events.

Staff: guitarist and composer Regino Sáinz de la Maza accepted the position of staff music critic in April 1939; he held the post until 1952. He was occasionally replaced—for example, in the case of conflict of interest—by other arts critics such as Jacinto Miquelarena.

El Alcázar

Began: 1936

Ended: 1988

Print run: 3,500 subscribers (*Anuario de la Prensa 1945–46*). It was circulated mainly in Madrid and Toledo.

Founder/publisher: initially founded in 1936 in Toledo during the siege of the Alcázar, it then became the "diary of the front of Madrid" under the control of the Falange. After the war, it was initially run by the Hermandad del Alcázar de Toledo (Veterans of the Battle of the Alcázar of Toledo); in 1945, after the newspaper incurred financial hardship, its staff created a co-op to prevent it from disappearing. In 1949, the Hermandad leased the newspaper out to Prensa y Ediciones, a private company with links to the Opus Dei.

Contents: *El Alcázar* was at the time mainly influenced by falangist ideology. A music column was published almost daily, focusing on concert life in Madrid.

Staff: the composer and conductor Conrado del Campo was the staff music critic at *El Alcázar* from 1939 until his death in 1953.

Arriba

Began: 1939

Ended: 1979

Print run: 90,880 (*Anuario de la Prensa 1943–44*). It was circulated mainly in Madrid, the capitals of the Spanish provinces, and other larger towns.

Founder/publisher: *Arriba* was founded by José Antonio Primo de Rivera in 1935, and suspended by the government of the Republic the following year. Just before the Civil War came to an end, the Falange refounded *Arriba* through the company Prensa del Movimiento.

Contents: as the flagship publication of the Falange, *Arriba* can be regarded as the official newspaper of the regime, in that other newspapers were encouraged by the censorship apparatus to follow its editorial line, sometimes even explicitly. In regard to music, it focused mainly on daily musical life of Madrid, but it also included more extended articles on historical or aesthetic matters than other newspapers.

Staff: Federico Sopeña, who was at the beginning of his career and served as secretary of the Comisaría de Música, was the staff music critic from 1939 to 1943; he then left his post to take up a place at the Vitoria seminary. He was replaced by Antonio Fernández-Cid but continued writing occasional pieces of criticism.

Hoja Oficial del Lunes (Madrid)

Began: 1930

Ended: 1982

Print run: unknown

Founder/publisher: as with other newspapers of the same name published in various Spanish cities, *Hoja Oficial del Lunes* was the only newspaper to be published on Mondays, since the others were not allowed to have their staff work on Sundays. All papers with the title *Hoja Oficial del Lunes* were published by professional societies of journalists (Asociación de la Prensa) of the relevant provinces.

Contents: it followed mostly the official line of the regime. Most issues included a section on concert reviews.

Staff: concert reviews were normally penned by Víctor Ruiz Albéniz (under the pseudonym Acorde), a former military soldier in Morocco and the president of the Asociación de la Prensa of Madrid from 1939 to 1944.

Informaciones

Began: 1922

Ended: 1983

Print run: no numbers are given by *Anuario de la Prensa*. It was mainly circulated in the cities of Madrid, Córdoba, Cáceres, Badajoz, Málaga, Sevilla, Salamanca, Jaén, Ciudad Real, Guadalajara, Valladolid, Zamora, Burgos, and Palencia (*Anuario de la prensa*, 1945–46).

Founder/publisher: founded by Leopoldo Romeo, from 1925 it fell under the control of the banker Juan March. In the pre–Civil War years it developed significant connections with German companies to overcome its financial problems.

Contents: during the Second World War, *Informaciones* was one of the main supporters of the Axis. Music information was mostly limited to reviews of concerts in Madrid.

Staff: Antonio de las Heras was in charge of musical criticism through the 1940s. Víctor Ruiz Albéniz, under the pseudonym Chispero, regularly wrote a short satirical column, which often featured comments about *zarzuela*.

Pueblo

Began: 1940

Ended: 1984

Print run: 86,880 (*Anuario de la Prensa 1943–44*)

Founder/publisher: *Pueblo* was the official organ of the falangist trade unions (Organización Sindical); as such, it was part of the line-up of newspapers and other media of Prensa del Movimiento.

Contents: *Pueblo* followed falangist ideals. It included a daily music section, focusing on concert reviews in Madrid.

Staff: the composer Joaquín Rodrigo was in charge of musical criticism until 1946; after that, he was replaced by Dolores Palá Berdejo.

La Vanguardia Española

Began: 1881 (as *La Vanguardia*)

Ended: still published today (again, under the name of *La Vanguardia*, which was reintroduced after the Franco era)

Founder/publisher: it was founded by the Godó family and was confiscated by the Catalonian government during the Civil War, after which it went back to the Godós. It is the only daily newspaper discussed in this book that is published in Barcelona.

Contents: although before the Civil War *La Vanguardia* had a liberal tradition, during the 1940s it was closely controlled by the regime; the Dirección General de Prensa appointed Luis de Galinsoaga (a self-proclaimed anti-Catalanist) as its editor.

Staff: Urbano F. Zanni was in charge of writing daily reviews of concerts and news of the musical life of Barcelona. However, the most noteworthy contributions of the newspaper to musical criticism were extended articles and series of articles by the composers Xavier Montsalvatge and José Forns.

Ya

Began: 1935 (interrupted during the Civil War)

Ended: 1998

Print run: no numbers from *Anuario de la Prensa*. It was circulated mainly in Madrid, Valencia, Sevilla, Bilbao, and Barcelona (*Anuario de la Prensa 1945–46*).

Founder/publisher: founded and managed by the private company Editorial Católica

Contents: *Ya* can be classified as a conservative-Catholic newspaper; in this regard, it took over from *El Debate*, also owned by Editorial Católica, which was never published again after the Civil War. It included a daily column on music focusing mostly on concert reviews in Madrid.

Staff: Joaquín Turina worked briefly as staff music critic during the summer of 1939; he was then replaced by the composer and conductor José María Franco, with rather frequent contributions by another composer, Ángel Martín Pompey.

MUSIC PERIODICALS

Anuario Musical

Began: 1946

Ended: still published today

Frequency: annual

Founder/publisher: it was published by the Instituto Español de Musicología; Higinio Anglès was founding editor.

Contents: *Anuario Musical* was the only academic periodical specializing in musicology published during the first decade of the Franco regime. Most of the submissions were consonant with the research trends that characterized the activity of the Instituto during these years: historical musicology focused on Spanish topics (mainly sixteenth and seventeenth centuries), with a specific interest in sources and a positivistic approach, and secondarily, folk music research.

Staff: pieces were written by the Instituto staff and collaborators. This includes, apart from Anglès, the German scholars Marius Schneider and Walter Spanke, and Spanish researchers such as José Antonio de Donostia, José Subirá, Miguel Querol, José María Madurell, and Nicolás A. Solar Quintes.

Boletín del Colegio de Directores de Bandas de Música Civiles

Began: first published in 1935; it ceased publication in 1936 owing to the Civil War. Publication was then resumed in 1945.

Ended: 1950

Frequency: monthly

Print run: 400 (*Anuario de la Prensa 1945–46*)

Founder/publisher: the Committee of the Colegio de Directores de Bandas de Música Civiles (association of civil wind band conductors)

Contents: *Boletín* acted as a newsletter for the members of the Colegio; it included information on the latest activities of the association and focused on problems specific to wind bands (working conditions of wind band conductors, legislation, etc.), with occasional articles on historical topics (mainly biographies of composers) or discussions of contemporary composition trends.

Staff: Victoriano Echevarría and Rodrigo A. de Santiago, both of them composers and wind band composers, were among the most prolific contributors to the *Boletín*; wind band conductors from all over Spain were also regularly invited to contribute articles and commentaries.

Harmonía

Began: 1916

Ended: 1959 (publication was interrupted from 1936 to 1939 because of the Civil War)

Frequency: quarterly

Print run: 350 (*Anuario de la Prensa 1943–44*) to 400 (*Anuario 1945–46*).

Founder/publisher: founded by composer and wind band conductor Mariano San Miguel

Contents: *Harmonía* was addressed to wind band conductors, and it came with the score of an arrangement or an original piece for wind band and a catalogue of recently published music for wind band. Extended articles focused mainly on Western art music (primarily biographies of composers) and on contemporary problems in the musical life of Spain, such as contemporary Spanish composition, music education, opportunities for young composers, problems specific to wind bands, etc.

Staff: in the years 1939–1951, its main contributors were Ángel Andrada, Julio Gómez, Ángel Arias Macein, Victoriano Echevarría, and José Subirá.

Música. Revista Quincenal Ilustrada

Began: 1944

Ended: 1946

Frequency: bimonthly

Print run: 5,000 (*Anuario de la prensa 1945–46*)

Founder/publisher: the journalist Rodrigo Royo Masiá was its founder and editor.

Contents: *Música* focused mostly on contemporary music, both Spanish and international, including concert reviews (Madrid, and from February 1946 also Barcelona) and informal interviews with some of the main Spanish performers and composers.

Staff: most of the collaborators of *Música* were music critics active elsewhere, such as Federico Sopeña, Antonio Fernández-Cid, and Regino Sáinz de la Maza. It also invited occasional contributions from other intellectuals interested in music, such as Gerardo Diego and Eugenio D'Ors. In February 1946, the periodical opened an office in Barcelona; its main contributors there were Federico Mompou, Xavier Montsalvatge, and Carlos Suriñach Wrokona.

Revista Literaria Musical

Began: 1945

Ended: 1967

Frequency: initially monthly, quarterly from August 1945, bimonthly from January 1950

Print run: 1,000 (*Anuario de la Prensa 1945–46*).

Founder/publisher: Unión de Compositores y Escritores (Union of Composers and Writers)

Contents: as the title indicates, *Revista Literaria Musical* focused on both musical and literary topics. It featured information on musical events in Spain and abroad, historical topics mainly for a nonspecialist readership, and interviews with Spanish composers and conductors.

Staff: most of the collaborators were members of the Unión de Compositores y Escritores and did not have significant writing careers elsewhere. It most prolific contributors were Manuel Chausa, Santiago Riopérez y Milá, and Javier del Valle. The section about musical life abroad was covered by a number of foreign correspondents.

Ritmo y Melodía

Began: 1944

Ended: 1950

Frequency: monthly

Print run: 7,000 (*Anuario de la Prensa 1945–46*). It was circulated mainly in Madrid, Barcelona, and Valencia.

Founder/publisher: its founding editor was Luis Araque, a medical doctor and amateur jazzman.

Contents: *Ritmo y Melodía* was the only Spanish periodical of the time focusing primarily on jazz. It included information about the jazz scene in Spain and abroad, reviews of recordings, and articles about the specific issues concerning jazz in Spain, alongside articles focusing on other forms of urban popular music and occasionally art music. In September 1949 it was redesigned to include other forms of entertainment such as theater and cinema.

Staff: most of the collaborators were part of at least one of the "Hot Clubs" active in some of the largest Spanish cities, such as Araque and Alfredo Papó.

Ritmo

Began: 1929; interrupted 1936–1940 because of the Civil War

Ended: still published today

Frequency: nine or ten issues per year

Print run: 6,000 (*Anuario de la Prensa 1943–44* and *1945–46*)

Founder/publisher: it was founded by Rogelio Villar, a composer and critic, in 1929. Contents: *Ritmo* focused on topics of both Spanish and non-Spanish music history, with a particular focus on Spanish early music, concert reviews in Madrid and other Spanish cities, and contemporary trends in music composition.

Staff: after Rogelio Villar died in 1937, Nemesio Otaño was appointed the editor of *Ritmo* in 1940; he was then replaced by Fernando Rodríguez del Río, who had collaborated in the foundation of the periodical back in 1929. *Ritmo* boasted a large number of collaborators, some of whom were active as performers, composers, or critics in other publications (Eduardo López-Chavarri, Julio Gómez, Federico Sopeña, Antonio Massana, Bonifacio Gil, Noberto Almandoz, José Subirá, etc.), whereas others left very few records of their activity outside this newspaper.

Tesoro sacro-musical

Began: 1917 (interrupted temporarily during the Civil War)

Ended: 1978

Frequency: monthly

Print run: 750 (*Anuario de la Prensa 1943–44*) to 1,000 (*Anuario 1945–46*)

Founder/publisher: Congregación de Misioneros del Corazón de María (Association of Missionaries of the Heart of Mary)

Contents: *Tesoro sacro-musical* focused almost exclusively on sacred music, including historical topics (mainly early music), information about music in cathedrals and monasteries of Spain, and translations of articles on sacred music published elsewhere.

Staff: most of its contributors were church musicians or members of the Catholic Church and were not active as composers, performers, or critics elsewhere.

OTHER PERIODICALS

Arbor

Began: 1944

Ended: still published today

Frequency: bimonthly

Founder/publisher: Consejo Superior de Investigaciones Científicas

Contents: the periodical was subtitled *Ciencia, pensamiento y cultura* (Science, thought, and culture) and aimed to present a panorama of the various scientific and humanistic disciplines under the umbrella of the Consejo Superior de Investigaciones Científicas. It usually consisted four to six academic articles, followed by a column (*Crónica*) providing information about recent events and developments in Spanish science and culture. Although music was initially underrepresented in *Arbor*, it became more prominent from 1947 onward, with about four extended articles per year; similarly, *Crónica* started to include more information about musical life in Spain and abroad. The articles focused on the history of Spanish music, contemporary trends in European music, and the philosophy of music.

Staff: two of the main contributors on musical topics were Higinio Anglès (who worked at the Consejo as head of the Instituto Español de Musicología) and Federico Sopeña.

Destino

Began: 1939

Ended: 1985

Frequency: weekly

Print run: 13,000 (*Anuario de la Prensa 1943–44* and *1945–46*), distributed mainly in Barcelona, Palma de Mallorca, and Valencia

Founder/publisher: founded by Ignacio Agustí Peypoch, who was then director of Publicaciones y Revistas

Contents: *Destino* focused on politics and culture, and during the Second World War it was more pro-Allies than most other publications under the regime. It usually included a small section (less than one full page) on music, mainly focusing on reviews of recent concerts in Barcelona.

Staff: the Catalan composer Xavier Montsalvatge was in charge of the music section through the 1940s.

Dígame

Began: 1940

Ended: 1971

Frequency: weekly

Print run: 53,000 (*Anuario de la Prensa 1943–44*); 40,500 (*Anuario 1945–46*); it was circulated mainly in Madrid, Barcelona, and Valencia.

Founder/publisher: Editorial Católica (see *Ya*)

Contents: *Dígame* included some lighthearted articles on political topics, but focused mostly on middle- and working-class leisure activities, such as cinema, bullfighting, football, etc., and included some political articles as well. Almost all issues included a short review of recent concerts in Madrid.

Staff: the composer Joaquín Turina was in charge of music criticism until his death in 1949. He was then replaced by José Forns.

El Español

Began: 1942

Ended: 1947 (but was published again from 1953 to 1962)

Frequency: weekly

Print run: 31,421 (*Anuario de la Prensa 1943–44*) to 45,000 (*Anuario 1945–46*)

Founder/publisher: it was published by the Delegación Nacional de Prensa (Press National Delegation), controlled by the Falange.

Contents: *El Español* focused mainly on political issues; during the Second World War, it was overtly pro-Axis. It did not have a specific music section, but occasionally included articles on music focusing on a range of topics: musical life (mainly the visits of German conductors or ensembles before the end of the war), music history both in Spain and abroad, and concert reviews.

Staff: *El Español* did not have a staff music critic. Some of its occasional contributors were critics and musicologists active elsewhere, such as Federico Sopeña, Ángel Sagardía, Joaquín Rodrigo, José Forns, and Tomás Andrade de Silva.

Escorial

Began: 1940

Ended: 1950

Frequency: monthly

Print run: 6,500 (*Anuario de la Prensa 1943–44*) down to 1,800 (*Anuario 1945–46*)

Founder/publisher: members of the Falange Liberal, including Pedro Laín Entralgo and Dionisio Ridruejo, founded *Escorial* in 1940. It was published by the Delegación Nacional de Prensa y Propaganda (Press and Propaganda National Delegation), then controlled by the Falange.

Contents: *Escorial* aimed to help shape the *Nuevo Estado* by promoting discussion and debate in the arts and humanities. In comparison with other humanities, music played a rather ancillary role, with about three or four articles per year, most of them addressing issues of contemporary music life.

Staff: some of the leading critics writing for other newspapers and periodicals, such as Federico Sopeña and Joaquín Rodrigo, also contributed to *Escorial*. During the Second World War years, the periodical invited contributions from German music critics, such as Karl Holl and Heinz Drewes.

La estafeta literaria

Began: 1944

Ended: 1946

Frequency: bimonthly

Print run: 20,000 (*Anuario de la Prensa 1943–44*) to 25,000 (*Anuario 1945–46*)

Founder/publisher: Delegación Nacional de Prensa

Contents: a publication about cultural life, targeted toward a general readership. It usually included one or two pages about music in each issue, mainly focusing on contemporary issues of Spanish musical life (concerts, new composition trends, etc.).

Staff: Antonio Fernández-Cid was usually responsible for the information about music.

Radio Nacional

Began: 1938

Ended: 1945

Frequency: weekly

Print run: 45,800 (*Anuario de la Prensa 1943–44*)

Founder/publisher: Delegación Nacional de Prensa

Contents: *Radio Nacional* was the newsletter of the Spanish state-funded radio station, Radio Nacional. It included several articles on current topics aimed at a nonspecialized readership. Music articles typically focused on the role of radio in dissemination of music, contemporary composition and music life (Spanish and international), and historical topics (mostly biographies of famous composers and performers).

Staff: *Radio Nacional* received contributions from a number of music critics active elsewhere, such as Otaño, Eduardo López-Chavarri, Rodrigo, and Forns.

Revista de ideas estéticas

Began: 1943

Ended: 1979

Frequency: quarterly

Founder/publisher: Instituto Diego Velázquez, which was a section of the Consejo Superior de Investigaciones Científicas

Contents: an academic publication about aesthetics. One or two articles per year dealt with music aesthetics issues.

Staff: contributors on musical aesthetics included Federico Sopeña, Carlos Bosch, and Juan José Mantecón.

Vértice

Began: 1937

Ended: 1944

Frequency: monthly

Print run: 14,630 (*Anuario de la Prensa 1943–44*)

Founder/publisher: Delegación Nacional de Prensa

Contents: *Vértice* was founded as a high-end illustrated magazine with propaganda aims. It included historical and cultural articles consonant with the main focuses of the Falange at the time (creation of national conscience, fostering friendship with Italy and Germany). Most of its issues (but not all) included an article on music, focusing mainly on historical topics (predominantly Spanish early music).

Staff: several well-known names can be found on articles contributed to *Vértice*, such as Federico Sopeña, Regino Sáinz de la Maza, Víctor Espinós, and Antonio de las Heras.

APPENDIX II
Music Critics

HIGINIO ANGLÈS
(Maspujols, Tarragona, 1888–Rome, 1969)

A priest and musicologist, Anglès had already established his reputation on the international musicological scene before the Franco regime; he became vice president of the International Musicological Society in 1933. A strong supporter of Catalan language and culture before the Civil War, he had to downplay his Catalan nationalist past during the war and first years of the Franco regime, and was eventually appointed first director of the Instituto Español de Musicología (IEM) on its foundation 1943. As such, he was the main editor of the *Monumentos de la música española* collection, focusing on Spanish medieval, Renaissance, and Baroque music. In 1947 he moved to Rome as director of the Pontificio Istituto di Musica Sacra, but he kept his appointment at the IEM. As a contributor to the music press, he wrote mainly for academic publications: he was the editor of *Anuario Musical* and contributed regularly to *Arbor*. Contributions to nonacademic periodicals include occasional articles for *Ritmo* or *Radio Nacional*, in which Anglès wrote mainly about Spanish early music.

LUIS ARAQUE
(Zaragoza, 1914–Madrid, 1971)

Jazz performer, composer, and medical doctor. As a music critic, he focused on defending and disseminating jazz. He was a founder and one of the main contributors to the periodical *Ritmo y Melodía*, specialized in jazz music, and from 1947 onward also wrote regularly for *Ritmo*.

CONRADO DEL CAMPO

(Madrid, 1878–Madrid, 1953)

Composer, conductor, and teacher. Throughout the 1940s, he was professor of composition at the Real Conservatorio of Madrid and conductor of the Radio Nacional orchestra, and his works were premiered and performed regularly. As a music critic, he was employed by *El Alcázar* to write daily reviews of concert life in Madrid.

VICTORIANO ECHEVARRÍA

(Palencia, 1898–Madrid, 1965)

Composer and conductor. He was one of the main contributors to the *Boletín del Colegio de Directores de Bandas de Música Civiles*, in which he analyzed a number of historical and contemporary issues affecting music, especially those related to wind bands.

VÍCTOR ESPINÓS

(Alcoy, Alicante, 1875–Madrid, 1948)

Medical doctor. Although during the 1940s his career as a music critic was largely limited to occasional lecture recitals in collaboration with well-known performers and composers and occasional articles for selected publications, he was still an influential and highly regarded figure in the domain of musical criticism.

ANTONIO FERNÁNDEZ-CID

(Ourense, 1916–Bilbao, 1995)

Fernández-Cid started his career in the early 1940s; he was one of the few to work primarily as a music critic and not be significantly involved in composition, performance, or music administration. He replaced Federico Sopeña as staff music critic at *Arriba* in 1943 and also wrote for *La estafeta literaria* from 1944 to 1946, besides contributing to other publications such as *Música. Revista quincenal, Ritmo*, and *Radio Nacional*. He focused on a variety of contemporary issues around musical and historical topics and had a particular interest in *zarzuela*, for which he advocated extremely protectionist measures.

JOSÉ FORNS
(Madrid, 1898–Geneva, 1952)

Composer, musicologist, and teacher. He was particularly influential in the domains of music history and aesthetics: his books *Estética aplicada a la música* and *Historia de la música*, originally published in the 1920s, were reprinted several times during the 1940s and widely used as texts in conservatories. As a staff music critic, he replaced Turina at the weekly newspaper *Dígame* in 1949. At the beginning of the decade, he also wrote regularly for *Radio Nacional*, dealing with contemporary composers, particularly those coming from Germany and Italy, and from the mid-1940s he also contributed to *La Vanguardia* with a series of articles on particular musical topics (German opera, British music, modernism, etc.).

JOSÉ MARÍA FRANCO
(Irún, Guipúzcoa, 1894–Madrid, 1971)

Composer, conductor, and teacher. During the 1940s, he was very active as a conductor in Madrid, performing frequently with the Orquesta Sinfónica de Madrid, Orquesta Clásica, Orquesta Nacional de España, Orquesta de Educación y Descanso, and others. He was also the staff music critic at the newspaper *Ya*, sharing this role with Ángel Martín Pompey and writing daily reviews of concerts taking place in Madrid.

JULIO GÓMEZ
(Madrid, 1886–Madrid, 1973)

Composer, musicologist, and, at the Real Conservatorio, music librarian and teacher. His main contribution to musical journalism was as an editor and writer at the periodical *Harmonía*, which specialized in wind band music; he also wrote occasionally for other periodicals such as *Ritmo*. He focused mainly on critical analysis of several aspects of musical life (music education, contemporary composition, public policies, etc.), as well as on nineteenth-century Spanish music.

ANTONIO DE LAS HERAS

(birth and death dates unknown)

During the 1940s, he was the staff music critic of the newspaper *Informaciones*, covering daily the musical life of Madrid. In 1943 he replaced Federico Sopeña as secretary of the Comisaría de Música. At the Comisaría, he was involved in several activities of musical propaganda, such as promotional trips and talks about Spanish music history.

EDUARDO LÓPEZ-CHAVARRI

(Valencia, 1881–Valencia, 1970)

Composer and teacher. The bulk of his critical work during the 1940s remains outside of the scope of this study: he wrote mainly for the Valencian newspaper *Las Provincias*, which he had been doing since 1898. However, he made occasional contributions to some of the main Madrid periodicals, such as *Ritmo*. Moreover, he continued being an influential and well-respected figure as a researcher of Spanish folklore (he collaborated with the Sección Femenina in composing and editing educational material) and as one of the most active supporters of Wagner in Spain.

ÁNGEL MARTÍN POMPEY

(Montejo de la Sierra, Madrid, 1902–Madrid, 2001)

Composer and teacher. During the 1940s, he was remarkably active as a composer in Madrid, with several premières of his works by some of the most relevant orchestras. In the field of musical journalism, during the 1940s he shared the position of staff music critic at the newspaper *Ya* with José María Franco, and in 1947 he started to write a column of concert reviews for *Ritmo*.

XAVIER MONTSALVATGE

(Girona, 1912–Barcelona, 2002)

Composer. As a music critic, during the 1940s he contributed weekly to the magazine *Destino* covering the main events in Barcelona; as such, he also devoted some attention to discussing and promoting the works of contemporary Catalan composers. In the late 1940s, he started to write extended articles on musical topics for *La Vanguardia*.

NEMESIO OTAÑO

(Azkoitia, Guipúzcoa, 1880–San Sebastián, 1956)

Priest, composer, teacher, and musicologist. During the Civil War, he contributed to the war effort on the Francoist side by giving public talks about music and organizing musical events, and also served as director of Radio Nacional; after the end of the conflict he enjoyed an influential position in musical life, first at the Comisaría de Música and then at the Conservatorio de Madrid. As a music journalist, he contributed to Falange publications such as *Radio Nacional* and *Vértice*; his most significant contribution, however, was as the editor of *Ritmo* from 1940 to 1943. In his writings, he dealt mainly with historical topics, particularly religious and military music.

DOLORES PALÁ BERDEJO

(Calanda, Teruel, 1922–Madrid 1981)

She replaced Joaquín Rodrigo as staff music critic of *Pueblo* in 1946 and held that post until 1952.

JOAQUÍN RODRIGO

(Sagunto, Valencia, 1901–Madrid, 1999)

Composer. During the 1940s, his career as a composer was especially fruitful, beginning with the premiere of the *Concierto de Aranjuez* in 1940. He taught at the ONCE (Spanish National Organization for the Blind) and the Conservatorio de Madrid and was also remarkably active as a critic: he wrote almost daily for the newspaper *Pueblo* from 1940 to 1946, after which he was replaced by Dolores Palá Berdejo. He then went on to write weekly music reviews for the sports newspaper *Marca*. He also contributed to a number of musical and cultural periodicals, notably *Escorial, Radio Nacional, El Español, Vértice, Ritmo,* and *Música. Revista quincenal.* In his writings, he addressed a number of musical topics, both historical (focusing on Spanish sixteenth- and seventeenth-century music) and contemporary. In this regard, he was particularly keen on discussing and suggesting policies that could improve promotion of Spanish contemporary music, and especially the working and living conditions of composers.

VÍCTOR RUIZ ALBÉNIZ

(Mayagüez, Puerto Rico, 1885–Madrid, 1954)

After having served as a military doctor and war journalist during the African wars of the earlier twentieth century, during the 1940s he worked mainly as a journalist and propagandist of the regime, serving as president of the Asociación de la Prensa. The nephew of composer Isaac Albéniz, he showed a keen interest in music and wrote occasional music criticism in the newspaper *Informaciones* under the pseudonyms Acorde and Chispero.

REGINO SÁINZ DE LA MAZA

(Burgos, 1896–Madrid, 1981)

Guitarist and professor of guitar at the Conservatorio de Madrid. He supported Franco's military uprising from the very beginning and was engaged in musical propaganda activities during the Civil War. In April 1939 he became staff music critic for *ABC* and held the post until 1952. He also occasionally wrote articles for *Música, Radio Nacional,* and *Vértice,* focusing mainly on Spanish early music.

RODRIGO ALFREDO DE SANTIAGO

(Barakaldo, Bizkaia, 1907–A Coruña, 1985)

Composer and wind band conductor. As a critic, he wrote mainly for *Harmonía* and *Boletín del Colegio de Directores de Banda de Música Civiles,* which both focused on wind band music. His contributions dealt predominantly with contemporary issues of musical life at large (education, composition, administration, public policies, etc.), and in particular the effects and implications of those issues for wind bands.

FEDERICO SOPEÑA

(Valladolid, 1917–Madrid, 1991)

He started his career in 1939 as staff music critic for *Arriba* and was appointed secretary of the Comisaría de Música in 1940. He also contributed to *Radio Nacional, Escorial,* and *Vértice.* A member of the Falange

Liberal, he left Madrid and music criticism in 1943 to take a place at the Vitoria seminary; after being ordained as a priest, he went back to Madrid and contributed to some of the most significant publications of the time, including *Arbor, El Español*, and *Música. Revista quincenal*. He maintained his influential position throughout the Franco regime and beyond, holding offices at the Conservatorio de Madrid and the Comisaría de Música.

JOAQUÍN TURINA

(Sevilla, 1882–Madrid, 1949)

Composer and teacher. During the 1940s, he was professor of composition at the Conservatorio de Madrid and director of the Comisaría de Música. Before the Civil War he was staff music critic for the newspaper *El Debate*; after the conflict, he wrote briefly for *Ya* in the summer of 1939, but his most noteworthy contribution as a critic was at the weekly newspaper *Dígame*, where he reviewed the musical life of Madrid.

REFERENCES

Anonymous. "Schönberg." *Ritmo*, no. 69 (1933), 7–9.

———. "Música." *Arriba España*, Jan. 19, 1937, 4.

———. "Música." *Heraldo de Aragón*, Jan. 30, 1937.

———. "Música." *Heraldo de Aragón*, Feb. 18, 1937.

———. "Peregrino de la Falange por los senderos de España." *Vértice*, no. 7–8 (1937–38), 22.

———. "Una conversación sobre Radio con el Excelentísimo Sr. Ministro del Interior." Interview with Ramón Serrano Suñer. *Radio Nacional*, no. 1 (1939), 3.

———. "Informaciones y noticias musicales." *ABC*, July 6, 1939, 19.

———. "Música militar española." *Radio Nacional*, no. 2 (1939), 7.

———. "La radio como factor de educación musical." *Radio Nacional*, no. 34 (1939), 3.

———. "El sexteto de Radio Nacional." *Radio Nacional*, no. 39 (1939), 5.

———. "Concierto de Aranjuez." *Radio Nacional*, no. 108 (1940), 5.

———. "Los nuevos académicos de Bellas Artes." *Ritmo*, no. 134 (1940), 3.

———. "Propósitos." *Ritmo*, no. 133 (1940), 3.

———. "Tres centenarios." *Ritmo*, no. 135 (1940), 3.

———. "El centenario de T. L. de Victoria." *Ritmo*, no. 135 (1940), 12.

———. "Nuestro número extraordinario." *Ritmo*, no. 141 (1940), 111–112.

———. "Conrado del Campo dirige en Berlín dos conciertos." *El Alcázar*, Jan. 10, 1942, 6.

———. "Ha regresado de Berlín el maestro Conrado del Campo." *El Alcázar*, Jan. 23, 1942, 7.

———. "Homenaje a Barbieri en la Asociación de Cultura Musical." *Pueblo*, May 5, 1942, 7.

———. "La semana musical hispano-alemana a través de la prensa del Reich." *Ritmo*, no. 159 (1942), 7.

———. "El sindicato nacional del espectáculo y sus recientes disposiciones." *Ritmo*, no. 159 (1942), 3.

———. "Bodas de oro del Orfeón Pamplonés." *Tesoro sacro-musical*, no. 12 (1942).

———. *Cancionero*. Madrid: Departamento de Publicaciones de la Delegación Nacional del Frente de Juventudes, 1943.

———. "La Orquesta Nacional, en Lisboa." *Arriba*, Apr. 3, 1943, 7.

———. "Federico Sopeña." *Arriba*, Oct. 6, 1943, 7.

———. "Nuevos institutos." *Arbor*, vol. 1, no. 1 (1944), 1.

———. "Editorial." *Boletín del Colegio de Directores de Bandas de Música Civiles*, no. 23 (1945), 3.

———. "Sobre la educación musical de la radio." *Música. Revista quincenal*, no. 8 (1945), 3.

———. "Editorial." *Revista Literaria Musical*, no. 27 (1945), 3.

———. "Editorial." *Revista Literaria Musical*, no. 28 (1945), 3.

———. "Conversación con Juan Manén sobre el jazz." *Ritmo y melodía*, no. 8 (1945), 5.

——— [as El predicador en el desierto]. "El jazz, tema de moda." *Ritmo y Melodía*, no. 9 (1945), 10.

———. "Entrevista con Carlos Suriñach Wrokona." *Ritmo y melodía*, no. 12 (1945), 6.

———. "Joaquín Rodrigo no cree en el hot." *Ritmo y melodía*, no. 13 (1945), 5.

———. "Editorial." *Música. Revista quincenal*, no. 22 (1946), 3.

———. "Doctrinales." *Revista Literaria Musical*, no. 36 (1947), 5.

——— [as El predicador en el desierto]. "La locura del swing." *Ritmo y Melodía*, no. 18 (1946), 7.

——— [as El predicador en el desierto]. "¿Existe un público español de jazz?" *Ritmo y Melodía*, 20 (1947), 9.

———. "Crónica cultural. La musicología en España." *Arbor*, vol. 7, no. 20 (1947), 209.

———. "Música 'capitalista y retrógrada' se estrenará en el Metropolitan." *Pueblo*, Feb. 14, 1948, 5.

———. "Reacciones anticomunistas de Hollywood." *La Vanguardia*, May 8, 1948, 7.

——— [as Bill el repórter]. "Aaron Copland el notable compositor norteamericano triunfa en Europa con su tercera sinfonía." *Revista Literaria Musical*, no. 40 (1948), 19–20.

———. "Dos farsantes: James y Cugat; y una decepción: 'Casa de locos'." *Ritmo y Melodía*, no. 20 (1948), 10.

———. "Éxito de los Coros y Danzas como productores de divisas." *El Alcázar*, Oct. 10, 1950, 5.

———. "Consternación en Bélgica." *ABC*, May 24, 1951, 16.

———. "Crónica." *Anuario Musical*, 6 (1951), 230.

———. "Crónica de la Academia." *Academia*, no. 7 (1958), 109.

———. *Miscelánea en homenaje a Monseñor Higinio Anglés*. Barcelona: Consejo Superior de Investigaciones Científicas, 1958–1961.

Acker, Yolanda. "Ernesto Halffter: A Study of the Years 1905–1946." *Revista de Musicología*, vol. 17, no. 1–2 (1994), 97–176.

Adelaida. "Orientación general de la enseñanza de la música en los distintos grados de la escuela primaria." *Radio Nacional*, 52 (1939), 13.

Ahmad, Qasim. *Britain, Franco Spain, and the Cold War, 1945–1950*. New York: Garland, 1992.

———. "Britain and the Isolation of Franco, 1945–1950." In *Spain in an International Context, 1936–1959*, ed. Christian Leitz and David J. Dunthorn, 219–243. New York: Berghahn Books, 1999.

Albert Torrellas, A. *Historia de la música*. Barcelona: Seix Barral, 1942.

de Alcaraz, Juan. "Nuevos juicios sobre la música pura y la música de programa." *Radio Nacional*, no. 237 (1943), 5.

Almandoz, Norberto. "Música." *Heraldo de Aragón*, Aug. 22, 1938.

———. "Leyendo libros." *Ritmo*, no. 136 (1940), 8.

Alonso Tomás, Diego. "Música nacional de categoría universal: catalanismo, modernidad y folclore en el ideario estético de Roberto Gerhard tras el magisterio Schönberguiano (1929–31)." In *Discursos y prácticas musicales nacionalistas (1900–1970)*, ed. Pilar Ramos López, 255–275. Logroño: Universidad de La Rioja, 2012.

Álvarez Pérez, Antonio. *Enciclopedia*. Miñón: Valladolid, 1971.

Amezúa, Ramón G. "El órgano, artísticamente." *Radio Nacional*, no. 133 (1941), 14–15.

Andrade de Silva, Tomás. "Labor musical de la Delegación Nacional de Propaganda." *Arriba*, Nov. 7, 1943, 2.

——. "El año musical." *Música. Revista quincenal*, no. 2 (1945), 3.

——. "La canción española fuera de España." *Revista Literaria Musical*, no. 34 (1947), 4.

Anglès, Higinio. Unpublished letter to José Subirá, Jan. 27, 1932.

——. Unpublished letter to Josep Maria Lamaña, Nov. 1, 1938.

——. Unpublished letter to Josep Maria Lamaña, Nov. 13, 1938.

——. "Las cantigas de Santa María del Rey don Alfonso el Sabio." *Radio Nacional*, no. 59 (1939), 4–5.

——. "Las cantigas de Santa María del Rey don Alfonso el Sabio." *Radio Nacional*, no. 87 (1940), 4–5.

——. "A propósito de las ediciones originales de Victoria." *Ritmo*, no. 141 (1940), 91–101.

——. Unpublished letter to Diego Angulo, Sep. 2, 1940.

——. *La música española desde la Edad Media hasta nuestros días: Catálogo de la exposición histórica celebrada en conmemoración del primer centenario del maestro Felipe Pedrell (18 mayo–25 junio 1941)*. Barcelona: Diputación Provincial de Barcelona, 1941.

——. "La música española en la España imperial." *Radio Nacional*, no. 140 (1941), 6–7.

——. Unpublished letter to José Subirá, Mar. 4, 1942.

—— (ed.), *La música de las cantigas de Santa María del Rey Alfonso el Sabio. Facsímil, transcripción y estudio crítico*, vol. 1. Barcelona: Diputación Provincial de Barcelona/Biblioteca Central, 1943.

——. Unpublished letter to José Subirá, Nov. 6, 1943.

——. Unpublished letter to José Subirá, Dec. 29, 1943.

—— (ed.), *La música en la corte de Carlos V*. Barcelona: Consejo Superior de Investigaciones Científicas, 1944.

——. Unpublished letter to José Subirá, Feb. 9, 1944.

——. "España en la historia de la música universal." *Arbor*, vol. 11, no. 30 (1948), 1–51.

Antequera, José Antonio. "La música clásica y la radiodifusión." *Radio Nacional*, no. 119 (1941), 5.

Antliff, Mark. "Fascism, Modernism, and Modernity." *Art Bulletin*, vol. 84, no. 1 (2002), 148–169.

Araque, Luis. "El jazz como filosofía musical." *Ritmo*, no. 205 (1947), 18.

——. "¡Dejemos en paz al folklore!" *Ritmo*, no. 213 (1948), 14.

Arozamena, José María. "Español: Recital de guitarra Sainz de la Maza." *ABC*, June 7, 1939, 20.

Artero, José. "La pobreza de Tomás Luis de Victoria." *Ritmo*, no. 136 (1940), 4–5.

——. "Dos problemas psicológicos de Victoria." *Ritmo*, no. 137 (1940), 4–5.

——. "Obras históricas de Victoria." *Ritmo*, no. 138 (1940), 6–7.

——. "Obras históricas de Victoria." *Ritmo*, no. 139 (1940), 4–5.

——. "Obras históricas de Victoria." *Ritmo*, no. 139 (1940), 7–8.

Ascunce Arenas, Aránzazu. *Barcelona and Madrid: Social Networks of the Avant-Garde*. Lewisburg, PA: Bucknell University Press, 2012.

Asensio Llamas, Susana. "Eduardo Martínez Torner y la Junta para Ampliación de Estudios en España." *Arbor*, vol. 187, no. 851 (2011), 857–874.

Barberá, F. "Tomás Luis de Victoria, músico español." *Ritmo*, no. 141 (1940), 73–77.

Barce, Ramón. "Adolfo Salazar. La obra y el hombre." *Índice*, no. 20 (1958), 23.

Bautista, Julián. "Lo típico y la producción sinfónica." *Música*, no. 3 (1938), 23–27.

Belmonte, Florence. "Los periodistas de la prensa del Movimiento (1937–1945): entre la ética y el realismo." In *Del gacetero al profesional del periodismo. Evolución histórica de los actores humanos del cuarto poder*, ed. Carlos Barrera, 145–154. Madrid: Fragua, 1999.

Ben-Ghiat, Ruth. "Italian Fascism and the Aesthetics of the 'Third Way'." *Journal of Contemporary History*, vol. 31, no. 2 (1996), 293–316.

Benedito, Rafael. *Historia de la música*. Madrid: Sección Femenina de FET y de las JONS, 1946.

Betts, Paul. "The New Fascination with Fascism: The Case of Nazi Modernism." *Journal of Contemporary History*, vol. 37, no. 4 (2002), 541–558.

Blanco Tobío, M. "Música antidemocrática." *Pueblo*, Feb. 12, 1948, 5.

Busto Miramontes, Beatriz. "El poder en el folklore: los cuerpos en NO-DO (1943–1948)." *Trans. Revista Transcultural de Música*, no. 16 (2012), 1–30.

Cadarso García de Jalón, Agustín. Unpublished letter to Nemesio Otaño, Feb. 22, 1937.

Cal, Rosa. "Apuntes sobre la actividad de la Dirección General de Propaganda del Franquismo (1945–1951)." *Historia y Comunicación Social*, no. 4 (1999), 15–34.

Calvo Serer, Rafael. *España, sin problema*. Madrid: Rialp, 1949.

del Campo, Conrado. "Primer festival hispano-alemán." *El Alcázar*, Jan. 27, 1942, 7.

———. "La música." *El Alcázar*, Oct. 31, 1941, 7.

———. "Música." *El Alcázar*, Mar. 13, 1946, 8.

Canés Garrido, Francisco. "Las misiones pedagógicas: educación y tiempo libre en la Segunda República." *Revista Complutense de Educación*, vol. 4 no. 1 (1993), 147–168.

Carré, Pedro. "Shostakovich, el compositor enigma." *Ritmo*, no. 208 (1948), 8.

Carredano, Consuelo (ed.). *Adolfo Salazar. Epistolario. 1912–1958*. Madrid: Fundación Scherzo/Publicaciones de la Residencia de Estudiantes, 2008.

———. "Danzas de conquista: herencia y celebración de Adolfo Salazar." In *Música y cultura en la Edad de Plata 1915–1939*, ed. María Nagore, Leticia Sánchez de Andrés, and Elena Torres, 175–197. Madrid: ICCMU, 2009.

Carreras, Juan José. "Hijos de Pedrell: la historiografía musical española y sus orígenes nacionalistas." *Il Saggiatore Musicale*, no. 8 (2001), 121–169.

Casals, Enrique. Unpublished letter to Nemesio Otaño, Aug. 19, 1940.

———. Unpublished letter to Nemesio Otaño, Dec. 2, 1940.

Casares, Francisco. "Música 'de diario'." *ABC*, Oct. 2, 1941, 16.

Casares Rodicio, Emilio. "Música y músicos de la Generación del 27." In *La música en la Generación del 27. Homenaje a Lorca 1915–1939*, ed. Emilio Casares Rodicio, 20–34. Madrid: Ministerio de Cultura/INAEM, 1986.

———. "La música española hasta 1939, o la restauración musical." In *España en la música de Occidente*, ed. Emilio Casares Rodicio, Ismael Fernández de la Cuesta, and José López Calo, vol. 2, 261–322. Madrid: Instituto Nacional de las Artes Escénicas y de la Música, 1987.

Cascudo, Teresa, and María Palacios. "Introducción." In *Los señores de la crítica. Periodismo musical e ideología del modernismo en Madrid (1900–1950)*, ed. Teresa Cascudo and María Palacios, i–xx. Sevilla: Doble J, 2011.

de Castro, Cristóbal. "Coros y Danzas de las regiones españolas." *Revista Literaria Musical*, no. 30 (1946), 7.

Chase, Gilbert. *The Music of Spain*. New York: Norton, 1941.

———. *La música de España*. Buenos Aires: Hachette, 1943.

Clark, Walter Aaron. *Isaac Albéniz: Portrait of a Romantic*. New York: Oxford University Press, 1999.

————. *Enrique Granados: Poet of the Piano*. New York: Oxford University Press, 2005.

————, and William Craig Krause. *Federico Moreno Torroba: A Musical Life in Three Acts*. New York: Oxford University Press, 2013.

Clastrier, Françoise, and Oscar Candendo. "Órganos franceses en el País Vasco y Navarra (1855–1925)." *Cuadernos de la sección de música*, no. 7 (1994), 145–212.

Contreras, Igor. "Un ejemplo del reajuste del ámbito musical bajo el Franquismo: la depuración de los profesores del Conservatorio Superior de Música de Madrid." *Revista de musicología*, vol. 32, no. 1 (2009), 569–583.

————. "El 'empeño apostólico-literario de Federico Sopeña." In *Los señores de la crítica. Periodismo musical e ideología del modernismo en Madrid (1900–1950)*, ed. Teresa Cascudo and María Palacios, 309–348. Sevilla: Doble J, 2011.

de Contreras y López de Ayala, Juan [as Marqués de Lozoya]. "Algunas noticias familiares de Tomás Luis de Victoria." *Ritmo*, no. 135 (1940), 4.

————. "Algunas noticias familiares de Tomás Luis de Victoria." *Ritmo*, no. 141 (1940), 17–25.

————. Unpublished letter to Joaquín Turina, Oct. 16, 1945.

Cortés i Mir, Francesc. "El nacionalisme en el context català entre 1875 i 1936." *Recerca musicològica*, no. 14–15, 27–45.

Daranos, Mariano. "Abolengo de nuestra música de cámara." *ABC*, Jan. 16, 1942, 3.

Davies, Peter, and Derek Lynch. *The Routledge Companion to Fascism and the Far Right*. London: Routledge, 2002.

Delgado Gómez-Escalonilla, Lorenzo. *Imperio de papel. Acción cultural y política exterior durante el primer Franquismo*. Madrid: Consejo Superior de Investigaciones Científicas, 1992, 123.

Delibes, Miguel. *La censura de prensa en los años 40 (y otros ensayos)*. Madrid: Ámbito, 1995.

Gerardo Diego. "Notas teatrales." *ABC*, Dec. 12, 1940, 10.

————, Joaquín Rodrigo, and Federico Sopeña. *Diez años de música en España*. Madrid: Espasa Calpe, 1949.

Echevarría, Victoriano. "Aspectos: tema con variaciones." *Boletín del Colegio de Directores de Bandas de Música Civiles*, no. 29 (1945), 8–11.

————. "Orígenes de la zarzuela." *Boletín del Colegio de Directores de Banda de Música Civiles*, no. 34 (1946), 3–5.

Echevarría Bravo, Pedro. "España canta a través de sus juventudes y sus bandas de música." *Boletín del Colegio de Directores de Bandas de Música Civiles*, no. 40 (1946), 13.

Edwards, Jill. *Anglo-American Relations and the Franco Question 1945–1955*. Oxford: Clarendon Press, 1999.

de Falla, Manuel. *Escritos sobre música y músicos*. Buenos Aires: Espasa Calpe, 1950.

————. *On Music and Musicians*, ed. by Federico Sopeña, trans. by David Urman and J. M. Thomson. London: Boyars, 1979.

di Febo, Giuliana. *Ritos de guerra y de victoria en la España Franquista*. Bilbao: Desclée de Brouwer, 2002.

Fernández-Cid, Antonio. "La orquesta nacional y sus problemas." *La estafeta literaria*, no. 17 (1944), 8.

————. "Entrevista con Regino Sáinz de la Maza." *El Español*, no. 20 (1945), 12.

————. "El teatro lírico en España. Al margen de una campaña de género chico." *Música. Revista quincenal*, 14 (1945), 22.

————. "Música." *Arriba*, Apr. 10, 1948, 7.

————. "Música." *Arriba*, Mar. 1, 1949, 7.

————. *Panorama de la música en España*. Madrid: Espasa-Calpe, 1949.

———. *La década musical de los cuarenta*. Madrid: Real Academia de Bellas Artes de San Fernando, 1980.

Fernández Eleizgaray, Ignacio. Unpublished letter to Nemesio Otaño, day and month unknown, 1937.

Ferreira, Manuel Pedro. "Andalusian Music and the *Cantigas de Santa Maria*." In *Cobras e Son. Papers on the text, music and manuscripts of the "Cantigas de Santa María,"* ed. Stephen Parkinson, 7–19. Oxford: Legenda, 2000.

Ferrer Senabre, Isabel. "Cant i quotidianitat: visibilitat i gènere durant el primer franquisme." *Trans. Revista Transcultural de Música*, no. 15 (2011), 1–27.

Figuerido, César. Unpublished letter to Nemesio Otaño, Apr. 18, 1940.

Foard, Douglas W. "The Forgotten Falangist: Ernesto Giménez Caballero." *Journal of Contemporary History*, vol. 10, no. 1 (1975), 3–18.

———. *The Revolt of the Aesthetes: Ernesto Giménez Caballero and the Origins of Spanish Fascism*. New York: Lang, 1989.

Fonollosa, José M. "Sobre el concierto de Willie Smith 'The Lion' en Barcelona." *Ritmo y Melodía*, no. 42 (1950), 4.

Forns, José. "Siluetas radiofónicas de grandes músicos. El moderno renacimiento italiano." *Radio Nacional*, 136 (1941), 14.

———. "Arnold Schoenberg." *La Vanguardia Española*, Sep. 6, 1944, 7.

———. "La sociedad internacional para la música contemporánea ha reanudado sus actividades." *Harmonía*, no. 32 (1947), 11.

Franco, Enrique. "Crítica creadora." *Arriba*, Oct. 7, 1958, 29.

Franco, José María. "Informaciones musicales." *Ya*, July 11, 1939, 7.

———. "Música." *Ya*, Dec. 12, 1940, 6.

———. "Música." *Ya*, Jan. 11, 1944, 7.

Gan Quesada, Germán. "A la altura de las circunstancias … Continuidad y pautas de renovación en la música española." In *Historia de la música en España e Hispanoamérica, vol. 7: La música en España en el siglo XX*, ed. Alberto González Lapuente, 169–231. Ciudad de México: Fondo de Cultura Económica, 2012.

———. "*Músicas para después de una guerra* … Compromisos, retiradas y resistencias." In *Discursos y prácticas musicales nacionalistas (1900–1970)*, ed. Pilar Ramos López, 277–300. Logroño: Universidad de La Rioja, 2012.

———. "*De musica in verbis*. Notas sobre la literatura musical de Xavier Montsalvatge en un momento de transición (1948–1953)." In *Música, Ciencia y Pensamiento en España e Iberoamérica durante el siglo XX*, 87–105. Madrid: Universidad Autónoma de Madrid, 2013.

———. "Three Decades of Messiaen's Music in Spain: A Brief Survey, 1945–1978." In *Messiaen Perspectives 2: Techniques, Influence and Reception,* ed. Christopher Dingle and Robert Fallon, 301–322. Farnham: Ashgate, 2013.

García Cabrera, María Isabel. *Tradición y vanguardia en el pensamiento artístico español (1939–1959)*. Granada: Universidad de Granada, 1998.

García del Busto, José Luis. "Manuel de Falla y los compositores de la Generación del 51: Ruptura/presencia." In *Manuel de Falla: Latinité et universalité*, ed. Louis Jambou, 509–513. Paris: Presses de l'Université de Paris-Sorbonne, 1999.

García Gallardo, Cristóbal L. "La imposible inocencia del musicólogo: el proceso de construcción histórica de la Generación musical del 27 o de la República." In *Música y cultura en la Edad de Plata 1915–1939,* ed. María Nagore, Leticia Sánchez de Andrés and Elena Torres, 39–48. Madrid: ICCMU, 2009.

García Laborda, José María. "Compositores de la Segunda Escuela de Viena en Barcelona." *Revista de Musicología*, vol. 23, no. 1 (2000), 187–220.

García Leoz, Jesús. Unpublished letter to Joaquín Turina, May 2, 1940.

García Matos, Manuel. Unpublished letter to Nemesio Otaño, July 17, 1940.

García Morente, Manuel. *Idea de la Hispanidad*. Buenos Aires: Espasa Calpe,1938.

García Ruiz, Víctor, and Gregorio Torres Nebra. *Historia y antología del teatro español de posguerra*, vol. 1. Madrid: Fundamentos, 2003.

García Sánchez, Federico. "Por los siglos de los siglos. Navarra en el centenario de Sarasate y Gayarre." *ABC*, June 30, 1944, 17.

Gásser, Luis. "El "círculo Manuel de Falla" de Barcelona (1947–c. 1956)." In *Manuel de Falla: Latinité et universalité*, ed. Louis Jambou, 496–507. Paris: Presses de l'université de Paris-Sorbonne, 1999.

Gaztambide, Luis A. "El mundo musical invertido." *Ritmo*, no. 218 (1949), 4.

Giménez Caballero, Ernesto. *Genio de España*. Madrid: Ediciones de La Gaceta Literaria, 1932.

———. *La nueva Catolicidad. Teoría general del Fascismo en Europa, en España*. Madrid: Ediciones de La Gaceta Literaria, 1933.

———. *Arte y estado*. Madrid: Ediciones de La Gaceta Literaria, 1935.

———. "Por la radio se va derecho al cielo." *Radio Nacional*, no. 17 (1939), 5.

Goehr, Lydia. "In the Shadow of the Canon." *Musical Quarterly*, vol. 86, no. 2 (2002), 307–328.

Gómez, Julio. "Sociedad Filarmónica Cuarteto Rafael." *El liberal*, Mar. 28, 1933.

———. "Los vihuelistas españoles del siglo XVI." *Ritmo*, no. 134 (1940), 4–9.

———. "Un autógrafo de Bizet en la Biblioteca del Conservatorio." *Ritmo*, no. 138 (1940), 4–6.

———. Unpublished letter to José Subirá, Apr. 9, 1940.

———. Unpublished letter to José Subirá, June 23, 1940.

———. Unpublished letter to José Subirá, Dec. 26, 1940.

———. "Comentarios del presente y del pasado." *Harmonía*, April–June (1941), 1–5.

———. "Comentarios del presente y del pasado." *Harmonía*, July–September (1941), 1–5.

———. "Comentarios del presente y del pasado." *Harmonía*, October–December (1941), 1–5.

———. Unpublished letter to José Subirá, Mar. 24, 1941.

———. "Un concierto sinfónico español en 1875." *Ritmo*, no. 155 (1942), 4–5.

———. "La biblioteca del conservatorio." *Ritmo*, no. 160 (1942), 30–32.

———. "Comentarios del presente y del pasado." *Harmonía*, April–June (1943), 1–5.

———. "Comentarios del presente y del pasado." *Harmonía*, October–December (1943), 1–5.

———. "Comentarios del presente y del pasado." *Harmonía*, April–June (1944), 1–5.

———. "Comentarios del presente y del pasado." *Harmonía*, July–September (1944), 1–5.

———. "Pedagogía y autoanálisis." *Ritmo*, no. 176 (1944), 4–6.

———. "Comentarios del presente y del pasado." *Harmonía*, April–June (1945), 1–5.

———. "Comentarios del presente y del pasado." *Harmonía*, July–September (1945), 1–3.

———. "Comentarios del presente y del pasado." *Harmonía*, January–March (1946), 1–5.

———. "Comentarios del presente y del pasado." *Harmonía*, April–June (1946), 1–5.

———. "Comentarios del presente y del pasado." *Harmonía*, July–September (1946), 1–5.

———. "Comentarios del presente y del pasado." *Harmonía*, January–March (1947), 1–5.

———. "Cultura literaria aplicada a la música. Concepto y plan de la asignatura." *Harmonía*, April–June (1947), 1–9.

———. "Comentarios del presente y del pasado." *Harmonía*, October–December (1947), 1–5.

———. "Comentarios del presente y del pasado." *Harmonía*, October–December (1958), 1–5.

Griffin, Roger. "Fascism." In *The Blackwell Dictionary of Twentieth-Century Social Thought*, ed. William Outhwaite and T. B. Bottomore, 223–224. Oxford: Blackwell, 1993.

———. "Staging the Nation's Rebirth: The Politics and Aesthetics of Performance in the Context of Fascist Studies." In *Fascism and Theatre: Comparative Studies on the Aesthetics and Politics of Performance in Europe, 1925–45*, ed. Gunter Berghaus, 11–29. Providence; Oxford: Berghahn, 1996.

Gutiérrez, José Antonio. "La labor crítica de Joaquín Rodrigo en el diario *Pueblo* (1940–1946)." In *Joaquín Rodrigo y la música española de los años cuarenta*, ed. Javier Suárez-Pajares, 403–430. Valladolid: Glares, 1995.

Halffter, Cristóbal. "Guía de la música española." *Arriba*, Oct. 7, 1958, 29.

Halffter, Rodolfo. "Tres movimientos concertantes para violín, violonchelo y orquesta, op. 18, de Salvador Bacarisse." *La Voz*, May 15, 1935.

———. "Julián Bautista." *Música*, no. 1 (1938), 9–23.

———. "Manuel de Falla y los compositores del Grupo de Madrid de la Generación del 27." In *Rodolfo Halffter. Tema, nueve décadas y final*, ed. Antonio Iglesias, 409–422. Madrid: Fundación Banco Exterior, 1991.

Heine, Christiane. "El cuarteto de cuerda en el Concurso Nacional de Música de 1949." In *Joaquín Rodrigo y la música española de los añs cuarenta*, ed. Javier Suárez-Pajares, 149–172. Valladolid: Universidad de Valladolid, 2005.

Henares Cuéllar, Ignacio, and María Isabel Cabrera García. "El conflicto modernidad-tradición. La fundamentación crítica en la preguerra y su culminación en el Franquismo." In *Dos décadas de cultura artística en el Franquismo*, ed. Ignacio Henares Cuéllar, María Isabel Cabrera García, Gemma Pérez Zalduondo, and José Castillo Ruiz, 31–57. Granada: Universidad de Granada, 1991.

Hennessy, Alistair. "Ramiro de Maeztu: *Hispanidad* and the Search for a Surrogate Imperialism." In *Spain's 1898 Crisis: Regenerationism, Modernism, Postcolonialism*, ed. Joseph Harrison and Alan Hoyle, 105–120. Manchester: Manchester University Press, 2000.

de las Heras, Antonio. "Música." *Informaciones*, June 8, 1939, 7.

———. "Música." *Informaciones*, Nov. 16, 1939, 7.

———. "Mística y música de un imperio." *Vértice*, no. 29 (1939), 5.

———. "Música." *Informaciones*, Dec. 12, 1940, 6.

———. "La música en el año que termina." *Informaciones*, Dec. 31, 1940, 7.

———. "Música." *Arriba*, Apr. 15, 1942, 7.

———. "Música." *Informaciones*, June 12, 1942, 6.

———. "El primer problema que plantea la música española." *Arriba*, Nov. 7, 1943, 7.

———. "Éxito de Sáinz de la Maza en el Español." *Informaciones*, Nov. 28, 1944, 1 and 3.

———. "Regino Sainz de la Maza en el María Guerrero." *Informaciones*, Feb. 25, 1949, 5.

Hernández, Ferreol. "La cuna y la escuela de Tomás L. de Victoria." *Ritmo*, no. 141 (1940), 28–34.

Hernández, P. C. "El jazz, música popular." *Ritmo*, no. 204 (1947), 7–8.

Carol A. Hess. *Manuel de Falla and Modernism in Spain, 1898–1936*. Chicago: Chicago University Press, 2001.

———. *Sacred Passions: The Life and Music of Manuel de Falla*. Oxford: Oxford University Press, 2005.

Hewitt, Andrew. "Fascist Modernism, Futurism, and Post-modernity." In *Fascism, Aesthetics, and Culture*, ed. Richard J. Golsan, 38–55. Hanover and London: University Press of New England, 1992.

Hoyle, Alan. "Introduction: The Intellectual Debate." In *Spain's 1898 Crisis: Regenerationism, Modernism, Postcolonialism*, ed. Joseph Harrison and Alan Hoyle. Manchester: Manchester University Press, 2000, 9–54.

Huerta, Alberto. "Sarasate." *Arriba España*, Sep. 21, 1937, 4.

Iáñez, Eduardo. *No parar hasta conquistar: propaganda y política cultural falangista: el grupo de "Escorial," de la ocupación del Nuevo Estado a la posteridad (1936–1986)*. Gijón: Trea, 2011.

Iglesias, Antonio. *Escritos de Joaquín Rodrigo*. Madrid: Alpuerto, 1999.

Iglesias, Iván. "(Re)construyendo la identidad musical española: el jazz y el discurso cultural del Franquismo durante la Segunda Guerra Mundial." *Historia Actual Online*, no. 23 (2010), 119–135.

———. "Hechicero de las pasiones del alma: El jazz y la subversión de la biopolítica franquista (1939–1959)." *Trans. Revista Transcultural de Música*, no. 17 (2013), 1–23.

Irigaz, Fernando. "Cómo transformar la Marcha Granadera en himno nacional." *Heraldo de Aragón*, Jan. 6, 1937.

Jensen, Geoffrey. *Irrational Triumph: Cultural Despair, Military Nationalism, and the Ideological Origins of Franco's Spain*. Reno: University of Nevada Press, 2002.

Juliá, Santos. "¿Falange liberal o intelectuales fascistas?" *Claves de razón práctica*, no. 121 (2002), 1–18.

———. "La Falange liberal o de cómo la memoria inventa el pasado." In *Autobiografía en España: un balance*, ed. María Ángeles Hermosilla Álvarez and Celia Fernández Prieto, 127–144. Madrid: Visor Libros, 2004.

Kamhi de Rodrigo, Victoria. *Hand in Hand with Joaquín Rodrigo: My Life at the Maestro's Side*, transl. Ellen Wilkerson. Pittsburgh: Latin American Literary Review Press, 1992.

Kamper, Dietrich. "Nationale und international Aspekte in der Italienischen Musik des Frühen 20. Jahrhunderts." *Revista de Musicología*, no. 16 (1993), 631–639.

Kater, Michael H. "Forbidden Fruit? Jazz in the Third Reich." *American Historical Review*, no. 94 (1994), 11–43.

Labajo Valdés, Joaquina. "Política y usos del folklore en el siglo XX español." *Revista de Musicología,* vol. 16, no. 4 (1993), 1995–96.

Laín Entralgo, Pedro. *España como problema*. Madrid: Seminario de Problemas Hispanoamericanos, 1948.

Langa Nuño, Concha. "El periodista-combatiente. La imagen de la prensa desde la prensa 'nacional' (1936–1939)." In *Del gacetero al profesional del periodismo. Evolución histórica de los actores humanos del cuarto poder*, ed. Carlos Barrera, 127–138. Madrid: Fragua, 1999.

Lázaro, Domingo. Letter to Eduardo López-Chavarri, May 12, 1941. Reprinted in *Eduardo López-Chavarri. Correspondencia*, ed. Rafael Díaz Gómez and Vicente Galbis López. Valencia: Generalitat Valenciana, 1996, 323.

Levi, Erik. *Music in the Third Reich*. London: Palgrave Macmillan, 1994.

Linz, Juan J. "An Authoritarian Regime: The Case of Spain." In *Mass Politics: Studies in Political Sociology*, ed. Erik Allardt and Stein Rokkan, 251–283. New York: Free Press, 1970.

Lizarazu de Mesa, María Asunción. "En torno al folklore musical y su utilización. El caso de las Misiones Pedagógicas y la Sección Femenina." *Anuario Musical*, no. 51 (1996), 233–246.

Llano, Samuel. *Whose Spain? Negotiating Spanish Music in Paris, 1908–1929*. New York: Oxford University Press, 2012.

López-Chavarri, Eduardo. "Nuestros músicos." *Radio Nacional*, no. 48 (1939), 10–11.

————. "Sigue la matanza de los grandes maestros." *Ritmo*, no. 153 (1942), 4.

————. "Orientaciones." *Ritmo*, no. 182 (1944), 23.

————. *Eduardo López-Chavarri. Correspondencia*, ed. Rafael Díaz Gómez and Vicente Galbis López. Valencia: Generalitat Valenciana, 1996.

L. V. "La Coral de Madrid celebra hoy su XXV aniversario." *Arriba*, Jan. 21, 1945, 6.

McClary, Susan. "Terminal Prestige: The Case of Avant-Garde Music Composition." *Cultural Critique*, no. 12 (1989), 57–81.

de Maeztu, Ramiro. *Defensa de la Hispanidad*. Madrid: Acción Española, 1934.

Carlos Mainer, José. *Falange y literatura*. Barcelona: Labor, 1971.

————. *La Edad de Plata (1902–1931): ensayo de interpretación de un proceso cultural*. Barcelona: Asenet, 1975.

Marco, Tomás. *Música española de vanguardia*. Madrid: Guadarrama, 1970.

————. *La música de la España contemporánea*. Madrid: Publicaciones Españolas, 1970.

————. "Los años cuarenta." In *España en la música de Occidente*, ed. Emilio Casares Rodicio, Ismael Fernández de la Cuesta, and José López Calo, vol. 2, 399–412. Madrid: Instituto Nacional de las Artes Escénicas y de la Música, 1987.

————. *Spanish Music in the Twentieth Century*. Cambridge and London: Harvard University Press, 1993.

Martí i Pérez, Josep. "Felip Pedrell i l'etnomusicologia." *Recerca musicològica*, no. 11–12 (1991), 211–229.

————. "Folk Music Studies and Ethnomusicology in Spain." *Yearbook for Traditional Music*, no. 29 (1997), 107–140.

Martínez del Fresno, Beatriz. *Julio Gómez. Una época de la música española*. Madrid: ICCMU, 1999.

————. "Mujeres, tierra y nación. Las danzas de la Sección Femenina en el mapa político de la España franquista (1939–1952)." In *Discursos y prácticas musicales nacionalistas (1900–1970)*, ed. Pilar Ramos López, 229–254. Logroño: Universidad de La Rioja, 2012.

Martínez Torner, Eduardo. Letter to Adolfo Salazar, Feb. 12, 1924, reprinted in *La música en la Generación del 27. Homenaje a Lorca 1915–1939*, ed. Emilio Casares Rodicio, 164. Madrid: Ministerio de Cultura/INAEM, 1986.

Mateo Box, Julieta. "España por el arte." *Revista Literaria Musical*, no. 53 (1951), 11–12.

Medina, Ángel. "Primeras oleadas vanguardistas en el área de Madrid." In *España en la música de Occidente*, ed. José López-Calo, Ismael Fernández de la Cuesta, and Emilio Casares Rodicio, vol. 2, 369–398. Madrid: Instituto Nacional de las Artes Escénicas y de la Música, 1987.

Méndez, Sebastián. "Música negroide o extranjera." *Boletín del Colegio de Directores de Bandas de Música Civiles*, 31 (1945), 7.

Mendo, Eugenio S. "Unificación del jazz." *Ritmo y Melodía*, no. 47 (1950), 5.

Menéndez Aleyxandre, Arturo. "Cultura Musical." *Ritmo*, no. 223 (1949), 4.

Meyer, Michael. "The Nazi Musicologist as Myth Maker in the Third Reich." *Journal of Contemporary History*, vol. 10, no. 4 (1975), 649–665.

de Miguel, Armando. *Sociología del franquismo. Análisis ideológico de los ministros del Régimen*. Barcelona: Euros, 1975.

Millet, Luis. "Recuerdos sobre Victoria." *Ritmo*, no. 141 (1940), 87–90.

Mompeón, Antonio. Unpublished letter to Nemesio Otaño, Feb. 21, 1937.

Montsalvatge, Xavier. "Strawinsky y Shostakovich, polos opuestos." *La Vanguardia Española*, Aug. 7, 1948, 8.

————. "Schoenberg o la música atomizada." *La Vanguardia Española*, July 25, 1951, 5.

Morcillo, Aurora. *True Catholic Womanhood: Gender Ideology in Franco's Spain.* DeKalb: Northern Illinois University Press, 2000.

Moreda Rodríguez, Eva. "Italian Musicians in Francoist Spain, 1939–1945: The Perspective of Music Critics." *Music and Politics,* 2 (2008), http://quod.lib. umich.edu/m/mp/9460447.0002.105/--italian-musicians-in-francoist-spain-1939–1945?rgn=main;view=fulltext (accessed June 2016).

———. "'La mujer que no canta no es . . ¡ni mujer española!': Folklore and Gender in the Earlier Franco Regime." *Bulletin of Hispanic Studies,* vol. 89, no. 6 (2012), 627–644.

———. "Musical Commemorations in Post-Civil War Spain: Joaquín Rodrigo's *Concierto Heroico.*" In *Twentieth-Century Music and Politics: Essays in Memory of Neil Edmunds,* ed. Pauline Fairclough, 177–190. Farnham: Ashgate, 2012.

———. "A Catholic, a Patriot, a Good Modernist: Manuel de Falla and the Francoist Musical Press." *Hispanic Research Journal,* vol. 14, no. 3 (2013), 212–226.

———. "Hispanic-German Music Festivals During the Second World War." In *The Impact of Nazism on Twentieth-Century Music,* ed. Erik Levi, 309–322. Vienna: Böhlau Verlag, 2014.

Morell, Eduardo S. "La cultura musical en algunos pueblos." *Boletín del Colegio de Directores de Bandas de Música Civiles,* no. 34 (1946), 14–15.

Múgica, José. Unpublished letter to Nemesio Otaño, Feb. 2, 1937.

Neila Hernández, José Luis. "The Foreign Policy Administration in Franco's Spain: From Isolation to International Realignment." In *Spain in an International Context, 1936–1959,* ed. Christian Leitz and David J. Dunthorn, 277–299. New York: Berghahn, 1999.

Neri de Caso, Leopoldo. "Regino Sainz de la Maza: crítico musical en ABC (1939–1952)." In *Joaquín Rodrigo y la música española de los años cuarenta,* ed. Javier Suárez-Pajares, 371–401. Valladolid: Glares, 2005.

———. "La guitarra como símbolo nacional: de la música a la ideología en la España franquista" (2006), http://secc.es/media/docs/22_3_NERI_DE_CASO.pdf (accessed April 2014).

Nicolodi, Fiamma. "Nationalistische Aspekte im Mythos von der 'alten Musik' in Italien und Frankreich." In *Nationale Stil und Europäische Dimension von der Musik der Jahrhundertwende,* ed. Helga de la Motte-Haber, 102–121. Darmstadt: Wissenschaftliche Buchgesellschaft, 1991.

"Organería Española S.A." *Ritmo,* no. 146 (1941), 11.

D'Ors, Eugenio. "Glosas para abrir una revista nueva." *Música. Revista quincenal,* no. 1 (1944), 3.

Ortega León, R. "El primero de abril, Día de la Canción." *Pueblo,* Mar. 24, 1943, 3.

Ortega y Gasset, José. "Musicalia." *El Espectador,* no. 25 (1921).

———. *The Dehumanization of Art,* trans. by Helene Weyl. Princeton: Princeton University Press, 1968.

Otaño, Nemesio. Unpublished letter to Valentín Ruiz Aznar, Jan. 20, 1937.

———. Unpublished letter to Higinio Anglès, July 29, 1937.

———. Unpublished letter to Higinio Anglès, Jan. 25, 1938.

———. Unpublished letter to Higinio Anglès, Mar. 14, 1938.

———. Unpublished letter to Higinio Anglès, May 19, 1938.

———. Unpublished letter to Higinio Anglès, May 22, 1938.

———. Unpublished letter to Manuel de Falla, Nov. 17, 1938.

———. "Los solemnísimos funerales de José Antonio en El Escorial." *Radio Nacional,* no. 57 (1939), 12–13.

————. Unpublished letter to Higinio Anglès, Jan. 8, 1939.

————. Unpublished letter to Manuel de Falla, Mar. 1, 1939.

————. Unpublished letter to Manuel de Falla, July 20, 1939.

————. "El eminente director de orquesta alemán Herbert von Karajan, en Madrid." *ABC*, May 21, 1940, 16.

————. "El himno nacional español." *Ritmo*, no. 133 (1940), 4–5.

————. "El himno nacional y la música militar." *Ritmo*, no. 138 (1940), 3

————. "La temporada musical en Madrid." *Ritmo*, no. 139 (1940), 3.

————. "Fundamentos de las tendencias espirituales y artísticas de Victoria." *Ritmo*, no. 141 (1940), 39–60.

————. "Los últimos años de Victoria en Madrid." *Ritmo*, no. 141 (1940), 103–110.

————. Unpublished letter to Higinio Anglès, Apr. 21, 1940.

————. Unpublished letter to Higinio Anglès, Apr. 29, 1940.

————. Unpublished letter to Manuel de Falla, July 1, 1940.

————. Unpublished letter to Manuel de Falla, July 20, 1940.

————. "La música en las emisoras de radio." *Ritmo*, no. 145 (1941), 3.

————. Unpublished letter to Manuel de Falla, Aug. 20, 1941.

Padín, Francisco. "A propósito de una campaña a favor de la música española." *Ritmo*, no. 147 (1941), 15.

————. "Nuevamente en favor de la buena música." *Ritmo*, no. 157 (1942), 8.

————. "La música de jazz y sus estragos" *Ritmo*, no. 170 (1943), 7–8.

Painter, Karen. *Symphonic Aspirations: German Music and Politics 1900–1945*. Cambridge, MA: Harvard University Press, 2009.

Palacios, María. *La renovación musical en Madrid durante la dictadura de Primo de Rivera. El Grupo de los Ocho (1923–1931)*. Madrid: Sociedad Española de Musicología, 2008.

————. "El Grupo de los Ocho bajo el prisma de Adolfo Salazar." In *Música y cultura en la Edad de Plata 1915–1939*, ed. María Nagore, Leticia Sánchez de Andrés, and Elena Torres, 287–295. Madrid: ICCMU, 2009.

Papó, Alfredo. "Notas sueltas." *Ritmo y Melodía*, no. 23 (1947), 7.

————. "Wenceslao Fernández Flórez y la música demente." *Ritmo y Melodía*, no. 30 (1948), 5.

Parralejo, Francisco. "Crítica musical y radicalización política durante la II República: el caso de *ABC*." *Revista de musicología*, vol. 20, no. 1 (2009), 537–552.

————. "Jóvenes y selectos: Salazar y Ortega en el entorno europeo de su generación." In *Los señores de la crítica. Periodismo musical e ideología del modernismo en Madrid (1900–1950)*, ed. Teresa Cascudo and María Palacios, 55–94. Sevilla: Doble J, 2011.

Payne, Stanley G. *The Franco Regime. 1936–1975*. Madison: University of Wisconsin Press, 1987.

————. *Fascism in Spain, 1923–1977*. Madison: University of Wisconsin Press, 1999.

Pedrell, Felipe. *Por nuestra música*. Barcelona: Heinrich, 1891.

————. *Cancionero musical popular español*. Valls: E. Castells, 1922.

Pérez Camarero, María Dolores. "Una escuela de instructoras de música en la Ciudad Lineal." *Arriba*, Mar. 10, 1946, 7.

Pérez Zalduondo, Gemma. "La utilización de la figura y la obra de Felip Pedrell en el marco de la exaltación nacionalista de posguerra (1939–1945)." *Recerca Musicològica*, no. 11–12 (1991), 467–487.

————. "La música en la revista *Vértice* (1937–1946)." *Nassarre*, no. 11 (1995), 407–426.

————. "La música en el contexto del pensamiento artístico durante el franquismo." In *Dos décadas de cultura artística en el Franquismo (1936–1956)*, ed. Ignacio

Henares Cuéllar, Cabrera García, María Isabel, Gemma Pérez Zalduondo, and José Castillo Ruiz, 83–104. Granada: Universidad de Granada, 2001.

———. *La música en España durante el franquismo a través de la legislación (1936–1951).* Granada: Universidad de Granada, 2002.

———. "Continuidades y rupturas en la música española durante el primer franquismo." In *Joaquín Rodrigo y la música española de los años cuarenta*, ed Javier Suárez-Pajares, 55–78. Valladolid: Glares, 2005.

———. "Racial Discourses in Spanish Musical Literature, 1915–1939." In *Western Music and Race*, ed. Julie Brown, 216–229. Cambridge: Cambridge University Press, 2007.

———. "El imperio de la propaganda: la música en los fastos conmemorativos del primer Franquismo." In *Discursos y prácticas musicales nacionalistas (1900–1970),* ed. Pilar Ramos López, 339–361. Logroño: Universidad de La Rioja, 2012.

———. "De la tradición a la vanguardia: música, discursos e instituciones desde la Guerra Civil hasta 1956." In *Historia de la música en España e Hispanoamérica, vol. 7: La música en España en el siglo XX,* ed. Alberto González Lapuente, 101–167. Ciudad de México: Fondo de Cultura Económica, 2012.

Pinillas, José Luis. "Crónica cultural." *Arbor,* vol. 12, no. 40 (1949), 611–612.

Piñeiro Álvarez, María del Rocío. "Los convenios hispano-norteamericanos de 1953." *Historia Actual Online,* no. 11 (2006), 175–181.

Piquer Sanclemente, Ruch. "Clasicismo, Nuevo clasicismo y neoclasicismo. Aproximación al concepto estético de neoclasicismo musical en España." *Revista de Musicología,* vol. 28, no. 2 (2005), 977–998.

Pollack, Benny, and Graham Hunter. *The Paradox of Spanish Foreign Policy: Spain's International Relations from Franco to Democracy.* London: Pinter, 1987.

Potter, Pamela. "Did Himmler Really Like Gregorian Chant? The SS and Musicology." *Modernism/Modernity,* vol. 2, no. 3 (1995), 45–68.

———. *Most German of the Arts.* New Haven: Yale University Press, 1998.

Prados y López, Manuel. *Ética y estética del periodismo español.* Madrid: Espasa Calpe, 1943.

Primo de Rivera, José Antonio. *Discurso fundacional de Falange Española.* Madrid: Consejo Nacional del Movimiento, 1970.

Puiggrós, Juan. Unpublished letter to Nemesio Otaño, Apr. 11, 1940.

Pujol, David. "Ideas estéticas de T. L. de Victoria." *Ritmo,* no. 141 (1940), 79–86;

Pujol, Francesco. "La estética en la obra de Tomás Luis de Victoria." *Ritmo,* no. 141 (1940), 61–72.

Quesada, Manuel. "La música y su influencia en la cultura nacional." *Ideal de Granada,* Dec. 27, 1936, 2.

Ramos López, Pilar. "Mysticism as a Key Concept of Spanish Early Music Historiography." In *Early Music—Context and Ideas II. International Conference in Musicology.* Cracow: University of Cracow, 2008, campusvirtual.unirioja.es/titulaciones/musica/fotos/13_ramos.pdf.

Rein, Raanan. "La lucha por los restos de Manuel de Falla." *Journal of Iberian and Latin American Studies,* no. 2 (1996), 22–39.

Rey García, Emilio. "La etnomusicología en España. Pasado, presente y futuro." *Revista de musicología,* no. 20, 877–886.

Richards, Michael. *A Time of Silence: Civil War and the Culture of Repression in Franco's Spain, 1936–1945.* Cambridge: Cambridge University Press, 1998.

Richmond, Kathleen. *Women and Spanish Fascism: The Women's Section of the Falange 1934–1959.* London and New York: Routledge, 2003.

Ridruejo, Dionisio. "Excluyentes y comprensivos." *El Ateneo*, no. 8 (1952).

Riopérez y Milá, Santiago. Untitled article. *Revista Literaria Musical*, no. 41 (1949), 5–6.

———. "Empresas nobles de nuestra España." *Revista Literaria Musical*, 49 (1950), 21–23.

Rivera Centeno, José. "Triste paradoja. Dos facetas de nuestro Folklore." *Ritmo*, no. 229 (1950), 8.

Rodrigo, Joaquín. "La música en la radiodifusión." *Radio Nacional*, no. 52 (1939), 12.

———. "La música en 1940." *Pueblo*, Dec. 31, 1940, 8.

———. "Reaparición de la revista *Ritmo*." *Radio Nacional*, no. 88 (1940), 15.

———. "Concierto homenaje a Manuel de Falla." *Pueblo*, Oct., 1941, 3.

———. "Rosa Mas en la A.D.C.M. Interpretación de *El poema de una sanluqueña*." *Pueblo*, Nov. 1, 1941, 7.

———. "Orquesta Sinfónica con Enrique Jordá, estreno de 10 canciones populares vascas de Jesús Guridi. La pianista Ginette Doyen." *Pueblo*, Dec. 24, 1941, 7.

———. "Necesidad de una estrecha colaboración musical." *Radio Nacional*, no. 117 (1941), 10.

———. "En torno al homenaje a Falla." *Escorial*, no. 12 (1941), 120–124.

———. "Gran semana de música hispanoalemana." *Pueblo*, Jan. 27, 1942, 7.

———. "El Día de la Canción ha de ser el preludio alegre de una gran labor anual." *Pueblo*, Mar. 21, 1942, 7.

———. "El dinero de los músicos sinfónicos." *Pueblo*, May 14, 1942, 7.

———. "Conferencia de Sáinz de la Maza." *Pueblo*, Dec. 30, 1942, 7.

———. "Los festivales de música hispano-alemanes." *Radio Nacional*, no. 170 (1942), 12.

———. "Al margen del festival de música hispanoalemán." *Escorial*, no. 17 (1942), 423.

———. "Clausura del ciclo de conferencias." *Pueblo*, Jan. 5, 1943, 7.

———. "Concurso de música de cámara." *Pueblo*, Jan. 26, 1943, 7.

———. "Música." *Pueblo*, Mar. 25, 1943, 7.

———. "Música." *Pueblo*, Apr. 22, 1943, 7.

———. "Segundo concurso nacional de folklore." *Pueblo*, Oct. 18, 1943, 7.

———. "Cuarto concierto de la Orquesta Nacional." *Pueblo*, Nov. 13, 1943, 7.

———. "Conrado del Campo y la Orquesta Clásica, Orquesta Sinfónica con Jordá." *Pueblo*, Dec. 20, 1943, 6.

———. "Música negra y música blanca." *El Español*, Jan. 29, 1944, 6.

———. "Estreno de *En una aldea extremeña*." *Pueblo*, Sep. 25, 1944, 7.

———. "Concierto de música española de la Vicesecretaría de Educación Popular." *Pueblo*, Oct. 13, 1944, 7.

———. "Estadísticas y comentarios." *Pueblo*, Nov. 1, 1944, 7.

———. "José Cubiles en el Español. Música española en el programa: 23 por 100." *Pueblo*, Nov. 14, 1944, 7.

———. "Orquesta Sinfónica en el Monumental; director, Enrique Jordá. Música española en el programa: cero." *Pueblo*, Nov. 20, 1944, 6.

———. "Música." *Pueblo*, Nov. 25, 1944, 7.

———. "Agrupación Nacional de Música de Cámara." *Pueblo*, Jan. 19, 1945, 7.

———. "La Orquesta Sinfónica, en el Monumental." *Pueblo*, Mar. 19, 1945, 7.

———. Unpublished letter to Rafael Rodríguez Albert, June 10, 1946.

———. "Lo que fue para nosotros." *Arriba*, Oct. 7, 1958, 29.

Rodríguez del Río, Fernando. Unpublished letter to Nemesio Otaño, July 22, 1940.

———. Unpublished letter to Nemesio Otaño, Oct. 18, 1940.

———. "El Frente de Juventudes y sus competiciones artísticas." *Ritmo*, no. 166 (1943), 9.

Rodríguez Jiménez, José Luis. "El antisemitismo en el Franquismo y en la Transición." In *El antisemitismo en España*, ed. Gonzalo Álvarez Chillida and Ricardo Izquierdo Benito, 245–266. Cuenca: Ediciones de la Universidad de Castilla-La Mancha, 2007.

Rubio, Jesús. "Discurso del Ilmo. Sr. Subsecretario de Educación Nacional D. Jesús Rubio en el día de la inauguración del Centenario en Ávila (7 de mayo de 1940)." *Ritmo*, no. 141 (1940), 9–15.

Ruiz Aguirre, Manuel. "La guitarra." *El Español*, Nov. 11, 1944, 8.

Ruiz Albéniz, Víctor [as Chispero]. "Canta la guitarra." *Informaciones*, Dec. 12, 1940, 6.

———— [as Acorde]. "Zarzuela española." *Arriba*, Nov. 7, 1943, 11.

Sagardía, Ángel. "El españolismo de Pablo Sarasate a través de sus actos, frases y labor de compositor." *El Español*, Aug. 5, 1944, 6.

Sáinz de la Maza, Regino. "Artistas imperiales. Antonio de Cabezón, músico y organista." *Vértice*, no. 14 (1938), 8.

————. "Si no escucháis la música, amigos . . ." *ABC*, Aug. 6, 1939, 3.

————. "Revuelo y júbilo en la grey musical." *ABC*, Oct. 7, 1939, 3.

————. "Acorde en la ausencia del maestro Arbós." *Vértice*, no. 23 (1939), 7.

————. "Informaciones teatrales. Orquesta Sinfónica." *ABC*, Feb. 27, 1940, 14.

————. "Don Luis Millán y la música cifrada para vihuela." *Vértice*, no. 30–31 (1940), 8.

————. "El director Franz Kowitschny y el tenor Alf Rauch, en el círculo de Bellas Artes." *ABC*, Feb. 12, 1941, 12.

————. "Acción educadora de la música." *Radio Nacional*, no. 135 (1941), 16.

————. "Don Luis Millán y la música cifrada para vihuela." *Radio Nacional*, no. 151 (1941), 4.

————. "Informaciones musicales." *ABC*, June 12, 1942, 13.

————. "La masa coral de Educación y Descanso de Lugo inicia el primer concurso folklórico." *ABC*, Mar. 2, 1943, 17.

————. "Informaciones musicales." *ABC*, Mar. 25, 1943, 16.

————. "Canción de Castilla." *Vértice*, no. 67 (1943), 39.

————. "Variaciones sobre la guitarra." *Música. Revista quincenal*, no. 4 (1945).

————. "Noticias musicales." *ABC*, Feb. 28, 1947, 17.

————. "Informaciones musicales." *ABC*, Nov. 11, 1947, 16.

————. "Informaciones musicales." *ABC*, Apr. 1, 1948, 17.

Salazar, Adolfo. *La música contemporánea en España*. Madrid: Ediciones La Nave, 1930.

————. "El estado de la música española al terminar el primer año de la República." *El Sol*, Jan. 1, 1932, 6.

————. "La República y el Cancionero de Barbieri." *El Sol*, Apr. 14, 1933, 35.

————. "Musicología." *El Sol*, Feb. 20, 1934, 5.

————. *Textos de crítica musical en el periódico El Sol*, ed. José María García Laborda and Josefa Ruiz Vicente. Sevilla: Doble J, 2009.

Salazar, Rafael. "Miguel Fleta." *Radio Nacional*, no. 73 (1941), 5.

Sánchez Aranda, José Javier, and Carlos Barrera del Barrio. *Historia del periodismo español desde sus orígenes hasta 1975*. Pamplona: Eunsa, 1992.

Sánchez Mazas, Rafael. "Ha muerto en la Argentina el maestro Falla." *Arriba*, Nov. 15, 1946, 3.

Sánchez Recio, Glicerio. "Familias políticas, estructuras de poder, instituciones del régimen." In *Las culturas políticas del fascismo en la España de Franco (1936–1975)*, ed. Miguel Ángel Ruiz Carnicer, 217–229. Zaragoza: Institución Fernando el Católico, 2013.

de Santiago, Rodrigo A. "Los concursos nacionales de música." *Boletín del Colegio de Directores de Bandas de Música Civiles*, no. 36 (1946), 12.

———. "Tomás Bretón." *Boletín del Colegio de Directores de Bandas de Música Civiles*, no. 80 (1950), 6.

———. "El nacionalismo como antecedente de lo universal." *Boletín del Colegio de Directores de Bandas de Música Civiles*, no. 83 (1951), 5–8.

Sanz de Madrid, Enrique. "Verdadero valor del jazz." *Ritmo y Melodía*, no. 32 (1949), 9.

Schmitt, Thomas. "*Con las guitarras abiertas*. El neopopularismo como reacción y progreso en las canciones españolas de los años 30 del siglo XX." *Anuario Musical*, no. 66 (2011), 263–282.

Schoenberg, Arnold. "Mi evolución." *Nuestra música*, no. 16 (1949).

Sopeña, Federico. "Sobre el Conservatorio Nacional." *Arriba*, Oct. 26, 1939, 7.

———. "Otra vez sobre el Conservatorio Nacional." *Arriba*, Nov. 2, 1939, 7.

———. "Prólogo a la quincena musical." *Arriba*, Sep. 8, 1940, 7.

———. "Un estreno de Ramón Usandizaga." *Arriba*, Sep. 15, 1940, 7.

———. "Homenaje a Falla." *Arriba*, Oct. 16, 1941, 3.

———. "Música, ausencias y homenaje." *Arriba*, Oct. 30, 1941.

———. "El 150 aniversario de la muerte de Mozart." *Arriba*, Dec. 9, 1941, 6.

———. "El 150 aniversario de la muerte de Mozart." *Arriba*, Dec. 16, 1941, 7.

———. "Notas sobre la música contemporánea." *Escorial*, no. 3 (1941), 101–122.

———. "Joaquín Turina." *Escorial*, no. 7 (1941), 244–288.

———. "Igor Strawinsky." *Radio Nacional*, no. 161 (1941), 7.

———. "Igor Strawinsky." *Radio Nacional*, no. 162 (1941), 6.

———. "Igor Strawinsky." *Radio Nacional*, no. 163 (1941), 5.

———. *Dos años de música en Europa*. Madrid: Espasa Calpe, 1942.

———. "Cuatro estados de la crítica musical madrileña. En torno a Peña y Goñi." *El Español*, Mar. 27, 1943, 9.

———. "La música de estos años." *Arriba*, Oct. 1 1943, 3.

———. "Informaciones musicales." *ABC*, Nov. 11, 1943, 19.

———. "Madrigalistas." *Arriba*, Apr. 10, 1945, 7.

———. "Joaquín Rodrigo, crítico musical." *Música. Revista quincenal*, no. 16 (1945), 6.

———. *Joaquín Rodrigo*. Madrid: Ediciones y Publicaciones Españolas, 1946.

———. *Joaquín Turina*. Madrid: Ediciones y Publicaciones Españolas, 1946.

———. "Una sinfonía rusa." *Alférez*, no. 1 (1947).

———. "La música europea de estos años." *Arbor*, vol. 8, no. 23 (1947) 165–177.

———. "El nacionalismo en la música de estos años." *Arbor*, vol. 9, no. 27 (1948), 401–476.

———. "La música en la Generación del 98." *Arbor*, vol. 11, no. 36 (1948), 459–464.

———. "Música." *Arriba*, Mar. 1, 1949, 6.

———. "*Strawinsky*, de Alexandre Tansman." *Arbor*, vol. 12, no. 37 (1949), 152–153.

———. "Schönberg-Bartok." *Arriba*, Oct. 26, 1950, 7.

———. "El problema de la música contemporánea." *Arbor*, vol. 19, no. 67–68 (1951), 449–456.

———. *Historia de la música española contemporánea*. Madrid: Rialp, 1958.

———. "Vicente Salas Viu." *Cuadernos Hispanoamericanos*, no. 216 (1967), 650–652.

———. *Defensa de una generación*. Madrid: Ediciones Taurus, 1970.

———. *Escrito de noche*. Madrid: Espasa Calpe, 1985.

———. *Vida y obra de Manuel de Falla*. Madrid: Turner Música, 1988.

Stevenson, Robert M. *Spanish Cathedral Music in the Golden Age*. Berkeley and Los Angeles: University of California Press, 1961.

———. "Tributo a Higinio Anglès." *Revista musical chilena*, vol. 24, no. 112 (1970), 7.

Suárez-Pajares, Javier. "Joaquín Rodrigo en la vida musical y la cultura española de los años cuarenta. Ficciones, realidades, verdades y mentiras de un tiempo extraño." In *Joaquín Rodrigo y la música española de los años cuarenta*, ed. Javier Suárez-Pajares, 15–64. Valladolid: Glares, 2005.

———. "Adolfo Salazar: luz y sombras." In *Música y cultura en la Edad de Plata 1915–1939*, ed. María Nagore, Leticia Sánchez de Andrés, and Elena Torres, 199–219. Madrid: ICCMU, 2009.

———. "Festivals and Orchestras: Nazi Musical Propaganda in Spain During the Early 1940s." In *Music and Francoism*, ed. Gemma Pérez Zalduondo and Germán Gan Quesada, 59–98. Turnhout, Belgium: Brepols, 2013.

Subirá, José [as Jesús A. Ribó]. *Historia universal de la música*. Madrid: Plus Ultra, 1945.

Suriñach, Carlos. "Estados que intervienen en las creaciones musicales." *Música. Revista quincenal*, no. 27 (1946), 14.

Taruskin, Richard. "Revising Revision." *Journal of the American Musicological Society*, no. 46 (1993), 114–138.

———. "A Myth of the Twentieth Century: The Rite of Spring, the Tradition of the New, and 'The Music Itself'." *Modernism/Modernity*, vol. 2, no. 1 (1995), 1–26.

Terrón, Javier. *La prensa de España durante el regimen de Franco. Un intento de análisis politico*. Madrid: Centro de Investigaciones, 1991.

Testoni, Giancarlo. "El riff." *Ritmo y Melodía*, no. 26 (1948), 9.

Torres, Dámaso. "El gusto y su fabricación." *Boletín del Colegio de Directores de Bandas de Música Civiles*, no. 90 (1951), 8.

Torres Clemente, Elena. "El 'nacionalismo de las esencias': ¿una categoría estética o ética?" In *Discursos y prácticas musicales nacionalistas (1900–1970)*, ed. Pilar Ramos López, 27–52. Logroño: Universidad de La Rioja, 2012.

Torres Climent, Antonio. "La música de esta posguerra." *Música. Revista quincenal*, no. 19 (1945), 9.

Treitler, Leo. "What Kind of Story Is History?" *19th-Century Music*, vol. 7, no. 3 (1984), 363–373.

Turina, Joaquín. "Musique espagnole moderne." *Le Courier Musical*, no. 4 (1926).

———. "El año musical." Jan. 1, 1932, 6.

———. "Música." Jan. 18, 1933, 7.

———. Unpublished diary, Jan. 1–Dec. 31, 1937.

———. "La Orquesta Sinfónica 1939." *Ya*, July 19, 1939, 7.

———. "Recital de Sainz de la Maza." *Ya*, Nov. 18, 1939, 6.

———. "La nueva España musical." *Radio Nacional*, no. 50 (1939), 13.

———. Unpublished letter to Eduardo López-Chavarri, Oct. 7, 1939.

———. Unpublished diary, Jan. 1–Dec. 31, 1939.

———. "Disonancias musicales." *Dígame*, Feb. 27, 1940, 7.

———. "Ya somos tres." *Dígame*, Apr. 23, 1940, 7.

———. "En el yunque." *Dígame*, Apr. 30, 1940, 6.

———. "El pollo de la mano al pecho." *Dígame*, May 14, 1940, 7.

———. "Rodrigo de Vivar." *Dígame*, Dec. 17, 1940, 7.

———. Unpublished diary, Jan. 1–Dec. 31, 1940.

———. "Homenaje a Falla." *Dígame*, Oct. 21, 1941, 9.

———. Unpublished diary, Jan. 1–Dec. 31, 1941.

———. Unpublished letter to Paquita Velerda, Apr. 12, 1941.

———. "Los muñecos de Petruchka." *Dígame*, Apr. 10, 1942, 7.

———. "¡Bien por ese sindicato!" *Dígame*, Nov. 29, 1942, 6.

———. "Crónica pianística'." *Dígame*, Jan. 15, 1944, 7.

———. "In memoriam." *Dígame*, Feb. 1, 1944, 7.

———. "Y va de cuento." *Dígame*, Feb. 15, 1944, 6.

———. Unpublished letter to Marquis of Lozoya, Oct. 2, 1945.

———. Unpublished letter to Eduardo López-Chavarri, Oct. 25, 1945.

———. "Música, clarines y voces." *Dígame*, Apr. 2, 1946, 7.

———. "Las divagaciones de un oyente." *Dígame*, Oct. 15, 1946, 6.

———. Unpublished letter to Pilar Mendicuti, Mar. 2, 1946.

———. *Escritos de Joaquín Turina*, ed. Antonio Iglesias. Madrid: Alpuerto, 1982.

Valbuena Esgueva, Sergio. "Orientaciones." *Boletín del Colegio de Directores de Bandas de Música Civiles*, no. 38 (1946), 4–5.

del Valle, Javier. "Páginas folklóricas." *Revista literaria musical*, no 31 (1946), 4.

del Valle Lersundi, Fernando. "La supuesta pobreza de Victoria." *Ritmo*, no. 141 (1940), 35–37.

Valls, Manuel. *La música española después de Manuel de Falla*. Madrid: Revista de Occidente, 1962.

Villaseca, Rafael. "De 'Guzmán el Bueno' a la 'Verbena de la Paloma'." *ABC*, Mar. 10, 1951, 15.

Wahnón, Sultana. "The Theatre Aesthetics of the Falange." In *Fascism and Theatre: Comparative Studies on the Aesthetics and Politics of Performance in Europe, 1925–45*, ed. Gunter Berghaus, 191–209. Providence, RI, and Oxford: Berghahn, 1996.

Walter, Michael. "Music of Seriousness and Commitment: The 1930s and Beyond." In *The Cambridge History of Twentieth-Century Music*, ed. Nicholas Cook and Anthony Pople, 286–305. Cambridge: Cambridge University Press, 2004.

White, Julian. "Promoting and Diffusing Catalan Musical Heritage: Roberto Gerhard and Catalan Folk Music." In *The Roberto Gerhard Research Companion*, ed. Monty Adkins and Michael Russ, 49–77. Farnham: Ashgate, 2013.

Yáñez, P. "César Frank." *Radio Nacional*, no. 42 (1939), 13.

de Ybarra, Gabriel. "Gayarre y su Roncal. Memorias en la tierra que le oía cantar." *El Español*, Aug. 5, 1944, 7.

INDEX